Murder 101

Murder 101
Homicide and Its Investigation

Robert L. Snow

Westport, Connecticut
London

Library of Congress Cataloging-in-Publication Data

Snow, Robert L.
  Murder 101 : homicide and its investigation / Robert L. Snow.
    p. cm.
  Includes bibliographical references and index.
  ISBN 0–275–98432–X (alk. paper)
  1. Murder—Investigation—United States. 2. Murder—United States. 3. Trials (Murder)—United States. I. Title: Murder one hundred one. II. Title: Murder one hundred and one. III. Title.
HV8079.H6S58 2005
363.25'9523—dc22   2004028758

British Library Cataloguing in Publication Data is available.

Library of Congress Catalog Card Number: 2004028758
ISBN: 0–275–98432–X

First published in 2005

Praeger Publishers, 88 Post Road West, Westport, CT 06881
An imprint of Greenwood Publishing Group, Inc.
www.praeger.com

Printed in the United States of America

The paper used in this book complies with the Permanent Paper Standard issued by the National Information Standards Organization (Z39.48–1984).

10 9 8 7 6 5 4 3 2 1

For Kay and Phyllis,
sisters nonpareil

Contents

CHAPTER 1

Murder in America

On the morning of February 8, 2000, Indianapolis Police Department homicide detectives responded to a call from an apartment complex on the West Side of Indianapolis. At 8:30 a.m., a tenant of the apartments had gone out to the Dumpster with a bag of trash and discovered a woman's body inside.

As the captain in charge of the Indianapolis Police Department's Homicide Branch, I responded to the scene with my detectives, and indeed we found the body of a young black female, wearing only slacks and a bra, bound with duct tape and tossed into the Dumpster. As a part of his investigation, the lead detective assigned to the case, Ken Martinez, first began attempting to ascertain the identity of the victim, since the body had no identification on it. Within a few hours of the news media announcing the discovery of the body, the anxious parents of twenty-year-old Tahnesia Towner called the homicide office. Their daughter had been missing since the previous day, and they feared the woman in the Dumpster might be her. Unfortunately for them, the body did turn out to be their daughter's.

Once the family had positively identified the body as that of Towner, Detective Martinez began a check of Towner's background. While we often find that homicide victims have lifestyles that make them more susceptible to murder than non-homicide victims, that wasn't the case here.

What we found was simply a law-abiding, twenty-year-old college student from a good family, for whose murder we could see no apparent reason. Although partially clad, Towner's body, the autopsy revealed, showed no evidence of sexual molestation.

"This was a difficult case to deal with," Detective Martinez said. "I'm much better with cases of guys killing each other over dope. This woman was a totally innocent victim."[1]

Detective Martinez then began what turned out to be a non-stop investigation. (I noticed for several days following his assignment to this case that he wore the same clothing, and I later found out that he hadn't gone home for almost three days.) The detective's hard work, however, soon began to pay off. He quickly discovered that whoever the murderer was, he or she was well acquainted with the area around the apartment complex where the body was found. (Towner didn't live in the apartment complex where the tenant discovered her body, but several miles west.) The coroner fixed Towner's time of death, caused by strangulation, at between 4:00 and 6:00 p.m. the day before the tenant found her. Upon canvassing the neighborhood, homicide detectives assisting Martinez talked to several people who reported seeing a suspicious car around the Dumpster at about 9:30 p.m. the night before Towner's body was discovered. The Dumpsters at the apartment complex, we found, were routinely emptied between 2:00 and 4:00 a.m. each day, which meant that, if the suspicious car had dropped the body there, then by the time the resident carried her trash bag out at 8:30 a.m., the body should have been picked up with the trash and likely compacted with the Dumpster contents. However, we also discovered something that the murderer hadn't planned on. The man who ran the trash pickup route had called in sick that night, and so consequently no pickup was made.

Through her employment records, Detective Martinez found that Towner had clocked out at her job at 4:07 p.m.; and, through interviews and obtaining the victim's phone records, he confirmed that at 4:30 p.m. she had called the manager of her apartment complex and asked that her locks be changed because this was the second time she had come home to find her apartment door unlocked. However, when maintenance personnel arrived at her apartment fifteen minutes later, they discovered the door unlocked but no one home. They also found several pieces of furniture apparently overturned. Although her family tried several times to reach her that evening, no one knew where Towner was until the tenant found her in the Dumpster the next morning. Consequently, we fixed Towner's time of death at between 4:30 and 4:45 p.m.

The day after the tenant reported finding Towner's body, Detective Martinez received a call in the homicide office from a district uniformed police officer. She told the detective that she had been called to take a burglary report at the apartment across the hall from Towner's, where the door had been kicked in, and that she had found Towner's door also kicked in. This incident had obviously occurred after Towner's murder because Detective Martinez knew that, in response to her call, maintenance personnel had installed new locks on her door.

As is common with unsolved murders, we sat around the office and discussed the case. We knew there had likely been at least a five-hour period between the murder and the placing of Towner's body in the Dumpster. "If you're the murderer," we mused, "what do you do with the body until you can take it to the Dumpster?" We reasoned that the murderer probably couldn't have carried Towner out to his or her car immediately after the murder without being seen, because this is an extremely busy time in the area, with many people coming and going from work. The murderer, we decided, likely hid the body somewhere until dark. This meant that the killer probably hid Towner's body somewhere in the apartment building and that the killer was possibly one of the other tenants. We also reasoned that hiding Towner's body in her own apartment until an opportune time to take it to the Dumpster would have been risky since the maintenance personnel could have found her, or a family member with a key could have stopped by to check on her. Just as risky would have been trying to hide Towner's body in one of the utility areas. It seemed more likely, our working hypothesis concluded, that she had been hidden in one of the other apartments until dark.

Consequently, Detective Martinez went to work checking on the other tenants of the apartment building. The tenants across the hall from the murder victim, a Mr. and Mrs. Desmond Loftus, the ones who had claimed that their apartment had been broken into about the same time as the murder victim's, reported that several items from their apartment had been taken in the burglary. Detective Martinez obtained a list of the items the couple claimed had been stolen and, as is routinely done, compared the list against recent pawn tickets. He immediately perked up when he found that the items, rather than being stolen, had actually been pawned several weeks earlier by Desmond. Although the couple across the hall also both claimed not to have been home at the time of the murder, Desmond, who was unemployed, could not account for where he was. A background check showed that Desmond had a history of violence.

Detective Martinez served a search warrant on the Loftus apartment and found a roll of duct tape that the crime lab said matched exactly the tape used to bind the victim. Also in the couple's apartment, Detective Martinez discovered a shipping box addressed to Towner that contained Desmond's fingerprints, while a similar box, also containing his finger-prints, had been recovered from the Dumpster in which Towner was found. In addition, evidence technicians lifted one of Desmond's finger-prints from under the lip of a dresser drawer in Towner's apartment. Detective Martinez brought Desmond in for questioning, and he failed a voice stress test (a device, discussed in detail later, used to detect deception) when asked about the murder.

"He came close a couple of times to breaking down," Detective Martinez said. "He was close to tears."[2] Interestingly, Detective Martinez added, while Desmond wouldn't admit to the crime, he never denied it either.

Based on Detective Martinez' information, a court issued a murder warrant for Desmond Loftus. His wife, we discovered, had been at work during the time of the murder and the later dumping of the body and didn't, we believe, have any knowledge of the crime.

In his case summary, Detective Martinez theorizes that Desmond was likely in the process of burglarizing Towner's apartment when she came home unexpectedly. He apparently hid as best he could in the small apartment while she talked on the telephone about needing new locks on her door. When she was changing her clothing after the phone call (which explains her partially undressed state when we found her), she either stumbled onto Desmond or he panicked and confronted her. A struggle probably ensued, which explains the over-turned furniture the maintenance personnel found.

Detective Martinez also believes that, after strangling Towner to death, Desmond likely carried her body back over to his own apartment, where he kept her hidden until taking her to the Dumpster later that night. Although Desmond didn't have to kick in Towner's door when he burglarized her apartment just before the murder—possibly meaning he had a key—maintenance personnel changed the locks soon afterward. Detective Martinez theorizes that Desmond for some reason needed to get back into her apartment after the murder, possibly to recover some evidence left behind, so he kicked in her door. He then kicked in his own door in an attempt to throw off suspicion. Tying up the last loose end in the investigation, Detective Martinez also discovered that Desmond Loftus had previously worked at a location within view of the Dumpster where the tenant found Towner's body and consequently would have known the schedule for emptying it.

"This was an exhausting case," Detective Martinez said. "But I really felt good about solving it."[3]

On August 15, 2001, a jury returned guilty verdicts against Desmond Loftus for murder, burglary, and theft. On October 9, 2001, a judge sentenced Desmond to eighty-five years in prison.

As sad and horrible as the case above is for the family of Tahnesia Towner, this is by no means an isolated incident. In every area of America, it seems, incidents such as this have become commonplace today. What just a few decades ago would have been seen as an act of incomprehensible violence is today seen as simply just another horrible, but inevitable, crime. Increasingly, violent acts perpetrated against innocent victims have become commonplace in our country.

As an example of how common murder is in our country, during 2002 police agencies across the United States responded to reports of 16,204 homicides (defined as the willful killing of one human being by another), or one every thirty-two minutes during the year.[4] Murder is so prevalent in the United States that on December 31, 2002, 3,557 prisoners sat on the various death rows across the nation for the crime of murder. Interestingly, 8 percent of these 3,557 death row inmates have a prior conviction for murder.[5] And while the number of homicides in the United States dropped each year from 1992 to 1999, in 2000 the number of murders nationwide began climbing again. In 2002, cities with populations of 50,000 to 99,999 reported a murder increase of 7.2 percent over the previous year, while suburban counties showed an even higher increase of 11.7 percent.[6]

"That's crazy in a city like this to reach that number in a year," said Detective Tom D'Aguanno of the Phoenix Police Department. "It's amazing."[7] The number Detective D'Aguanno was talking about was the 247 murders that had been reported in Phoenix by December 15 for the year 2003, a number that had already eclipsed the previous record of 245 murders in all of 2001. By comparison, Indianapolis, approximately two-thirds the size of Phoenix, recorded seventy-five murders as of December 15, 2003.

"I think for anybody, it makes them sad that there are children who can't feel safe riding a bike or going to the store," said Shikha Hamilton, president of the Detroit chapter of the Million-Mom March.[8] Ms. Hamilton is referring to the fact that in 2003 the number of children murdered in Detroit doubled from the number in 2002 and likely would be higher than in any other large city in the United States.

"It's safe to say that we have a crisis," said Cincinnati Councilman David Pepper, commenting on Cincinnati's fifth year in a row of seeing an increase in the murder rate. "We're now in the company of cities that have reputations of being very dangerous."[9]

An article in the *Los Angeles Times* on April 2, 2004, reported that, even though Chief of Police William J. Bratton had set a goal of reducing murders in Los Angeles by 20 percent during 2004, murders during the first three months instead rose 5 percent over the previous year. Some individual police districts in Los Angeles saw increases of more than 500 percent over the numbers for the first three months of 2003.[10]

These increases in the murder rate in areas all across our country have confounded many elected and appointed officials. In the 1990s, many police chiefs and mayors were touting programs and claiming responsibility for the murder rate going down. Now they are hiding and dodging questions about the upswing in the murder rate. What these officials didn't tell the public during the 1990s was that the murder rate in the United States had more than doubled between 1960 and 1980; hence, any drop in the rate, such as the one that occurred in the 1990s, could be seen as miraculous.[11]

So, given that murder is becoming an increasing concern almost everywhere in the United States, who commits all of these murders, and who are the most likely victims? According to murder statistics from 1976 to 2000, compiled by the U.S. Department of Justice, the largest number of murderers in our country comes from the age group eighteen to twenty-four (34.7 percent). The largest number of murder victims during this same time period, however, belonged to the age group twenty-five to thirty-four (29.2 percent). These same statistics, however, also show that 49,334 of this period's murder victims were aged seventeen or younger.[12] Consequently, according to statistics from the Centers for

Disease Control, homicide is the fourth leading cause of death for those aged one to nine, fifth for those aged ten to fourteen, and second for those aged fifteen to nineteen.[13]

Adding to these already disturbing statistics, records show that it's not strangers but family members who kill 71 percent of the very young children murdered every year in the United States.[14] And in contrast to statistics for adult murders, which show women perpetrators accounting for only 10 percent of all the murders nationally, women account for 43 percent of the murders of children under age twelve, with 75 percent of these victims being under age six. Additionally, it has been found that women who commit murder kill members of their families 79 percent of the time.[15] In addition to the above statistics, many experts believe that the number of children up to four years old who are murdered every year in our country is vastly underreported. A study of three years of murder records in Missouri found that only 39 percent of the fatalities of children in this age group that definitely had resulted from maltreatment, and only 18 percent of the fatalities that had possibly resulted from maltreatment, were reported as murders.[16]

However, when one looks at long-term national murder statistics, males, as may be expected, are much more often both the murderers (ten times as likely as females) and the murder victims (three times as likely), and more than three times as many males kill females as the reverse.[17] Interestingly though, while many elderly people feel anxious about crime and worry about becoming the victims of murder, those in the fifty and above age group actually have a very low victimization rate. This doesn't mean that murder doesn't happen to those fifty and older, only that their chances are smaller than for most other age groups.[18] And while many people may want to believe otherwise, overwhelmingly the races of both the murderer and murder victim are the same. From 1976 to 2000, 86 percent of whites were killed by whites, and 94 percent of blacks were killed by blacks.[19] Finally, statistics show that being killed by a lone murderer is much more likely than being murdered by a gang or a group of offenders, the chances being about four to one.[20]

When I first became a police officer more than thirty-six years ago, a large percentage of the murders we saw then were intimate partner murders. This type of murder, naturally, is relatively easy to solve. Unfortunately for the homicide clearance rate, though, this type of murder is no longer as prevalent. According to figures from the U.S. Department of

Justice, the number of intimate partner murders has dropped dramatically since the mid-1970s. From 1976 to 2000, for example, the number of men murdered by intimates dropped 68 percent, while the number of women killed by intimates stayed level for nearly two decades during this period, then finally declined 22 percent.[21] As commander of the Indianapolis Police Department Homicide Branch, I find that today a large number of our murders are drug-related, which means that the murderer and murder victim often don't have an intimately close relationship. Unfortunately, this makes solving these murders much more difficult.

However, regardless of this decrease in intimate partner homicide, murder is still a very personal crime. In the large majority of cases, murderers kill someone they know. Statistics compiled by the Federal Bureau of Investigation show that in 2002, only 14 percent of the murders in the United States where there was an arrest were committed by strangers.[22]

Finally, a major misconception many people in the United States have about murder, police officers find, is that it is mostly the province of urban areas. The truth is that no area in our country is exempt from the threat of murder. While the nation's cities had a murder rate of seven per 100,000 population in 2002, the suburbs still suffered a rate of four murders per 100,000 population, followed by rural areas, which experienced a rate of 3.8 murders per 100,000 population.[23]

Given all these statistics, many readers undoubtedly wonder, what causes all of these murders? While there may be many contributing factors, the police find that, overall, arguments are the most common reason given for murder (26.5 percent in 2002), followed closely (16.5 percent in 2002) by murder during the commission of another felony (rape, robbery, and so on).[24] Although the 2001 statistics cited drugs as the reason for fewer than 5 percent of the murders nationally, I've found during my time as homicide commander that this motive is vastly underreported.[25] A large percentage of the arguments that result in a murder, I've found, are arguments over drugs, and many of the robbery murders are robberies to buy drugs.

"If a person is not involved with narcotics, gangs, or an abusive relationship, their chances of being a homicide victim in Phoenix are pretty darn slim," Lieutenant Mike Hobel of the Phoenix Police Department told me. "Our most experienced investigators estimate that 60–70 percent of the murders in Phoenix are drug-related."[26] I and many other homicide commanders across the nation can echo Lieutenant Hobel's words.

As I mentioned earlier, the most likely murder victim in the United States is a person between the ages of twenty-five and thirty-four. However, this in no way means that anyone, young or old, is immune to becoming a murder victim. And while, as I also stated earlier, many of those who commit murder in our country are in their teens and early twenties, this too, as I show below, does not exclude anyone, young or old, from becoming a murderer.

On February 29, 2000, a six-year-old boy who reportedly lived in a crack house with his uncle found a loaded .32 caliber semi-automatic pistol under a blanket in his uncle's house. Stuffing the pistol down his pants, the youngster took it with him to Buell Elementary School in Flint, Michigan, where he attended the first grade. The six-year-old boy walked up to a classmate, six-year-old Kayla Rolland, with whom he had fought the previous day, and shot her in the chest. Doctors pronounced Kayla dead a short time later.

While ordinarily a six-year-old child cannot be held accountable for committing a crime, even murder, since someone so young usually doesn't understand the ramifications of such an act (the boy reportedly sat down and began drawing pictures after being questioned by the police), this certainly doesn't lessen the apprehension of parents everywhere about the safety of their children. It certainly doesn't lessen the grief of Kayla's parents.

As the head of a major city homicide unit, I naturally see many murder victims every year, and I deal with many grieving relatives. Even when the murder victims are far from ideal citizens, their relatives still grieve. We had a case recently here in Indianapolis in which we found a drug enforcer, whom we suspected of committing at least a half-dozen killings, murdered in his van. When his family came to the scene, the grief they displayed was obviously very genuine, despite the victim's lengthy criminal record and his constant association with extremely violence-prone individuals.

Yet, as the Tahnesia Towner and Kayla Rolland murders clearly demonstrate, it is not just criminals and those who associate with criminals, but often truly innocent people who can become the victims of murder. These cases are the hardest for the family, the community, and the police to deal with. While police officers can harden themselves when dealing with the murders of drug dealers and holdup men, this isn't as easy to do when dealing with murders like the ones below.

On the evening of December 15, 1996, when firefighters forced their way into a burning two-story house in suburban Marion County, Indiana, they stumbled onto a horrifying scene. Just inside the smoke-filled living room they found the body of sixty-four-year-old Cleta Mathias, her hands bound behind her, her head split open. Nearby, under a Christmas tree, they discovered the body of Cleta's husband, sixty-four-year-old Frederick Mathias, pastor of the nearby Northminster Presbyterian Church, an ax still sticking out of his head. The firefighters immediately called for the Marion County Sheriff's Department.

Although large in physical stature, Reverend Mathias had been well known around the community as a gentle and compassionate man, loved by almost everyone who knew him. Mrs. Mathias, a registered nurse who had worked in a geriatric clinic, also didn't seem to know anyone who didn't love her.

Because of the popularity of the couple, the 1,700 members of Reverend Mathias' upscale church were naturally stunned and aghast at the gruesomeness of the crime. Why would anyone, they asked themselves, want to so brutally murder such a harmless couple?

"This is a tough jolt for us in the holiday season," said P. E. MacAllister, a longtime member of the church.[27]

Early in the investigation of this crime, homicide detectives from the sheriff's department conferred with members of the arson squad and quickly determined that the fire had been intentionally set. While the police then knew that the fire had been started in an unsuccessful attempt to cover up the murders, they didn't know whether murder had been the original plan or if perhaps the murdered couple had simply arrived home unexpectedly while someone was in their home, possibly in the process of burglarizing it.

As is standard practice in homicide investigations where no suspect is readily apparent, and operating on the assumption that, because of its viciousness, this wasn't just a random crime, investigators began looking into the couple's background in an attempt to find someone who harbored enough hatred of either victim to warrant splitting their heads open with an ax. Detectives also began looking into the activities of Reverend and Mrs. Mathias in the days and hours preceding the crime, again searching for interaction with someone who might have had a reason to commit such a vicious crime.

Reverend Mathias, the homicide detectives learned through their background investigation, had served as the pastor of Northminster Presbyterian Church for the previous thirteen years and for a number of years had also served as a pastor during the summer at the Big Moose Community Chapel in upstate New York. Every person the detectives talked to only confirmed over and over that everyone who knew Reverend Mathias loved and respected him.

"Fred's approach was to preach love," said a member of the congregation.[28]

Mrs. Mathias, known both in Indianapolis and Big Moose as a gracious hostess and a caring wife, mother, and grandmother, also seemed to be universally loved and respected. During their initial look at the couple, detectives could find no apparent enemies or any reason for such a gruesome murder.

"We just cannot believe that this can happen to such a fine couple," said Ida Winter, a member of the Big Moose congregation. "They were such wonderful people."[29]

However, digging deeper, the police finally uncovered a possible lead. When checking on the couple's activities preceding the crime, they discovered that the day before the murder a fifteen-year-old member of the church, Sean Rich, had been in the Mathias house helping to carry out a rug. In addition, witnesses placed a young man fitting this teenager's description in the neighborhood of the Mathias home the night the crime occurred. Further investigation revealed that Rich's mother had previously been convicted of arson and that Reverend Mathias had interceded in the case and persuaded the judge to sentence her to home detention rather than jail. But what really sparked the detectives' interest in this young man was his history of violence. In court documents recovered by homicide investigators, Rich's mother described him as "physically violent." Also, they found, in a fit of anger a year or so before, he reportedly broke his sister's nose. But why, detectives asked, would he want to murder Reverend and Mrs. Mathias so brutally?

Digging even deeper, homicide detectives finally found a possible motive for the murder. The investigators discovered that Reverend Mathias had recently fired fifteen-year-old Sean Rich from his job as an usher at the church when a congregation member reportedly caught Rich stealing money from the offering plate. For a teenage boy, detectives knew, this type of humiliation could be enough to cause intense hatred. Also, several students told the detectives that Rich had flashed a large amount of cash around school the day after the double murder.

"The best suspect we have," was how Marion County Sheriff Jack Cottey described the teen when asked by the news media about the Mathias case.[30]

All experienced homicide detectives know, however, that having a suspect and having enough actual evidence to warrant the arrest of that suspect are often far from being synonymous. Rich's mother claimed that her son had an alibi for the time of the murder, and consequently refused to allow officers to speak with him, insisting that her son, though at times untrustworthy and violent, could never commit such a horrible crime. So, the case stalled for over a year.

"We've by no means given up," said the lead homicide detective on the case, John Gray, when asked many months after the murders what progress the police were making.[31] These murders had struck a raw nerve not just with the community but also with the police officers investigating them.

Yet, despite this detective's perseverance, it still took over a year of sifting through information and talking to more than 200 witnesses before the police could amass enough evidence to finally arrest the now sixteen-year-old Sean Rich and another youth, eighteen-year-old Paul Brightman, charging them both with the Mathias murders. Surprised homicide detectives found that after they turned up information that led them to Brightman, he almost immediately, upon being brought in for questioning, broke down crying and admitted to being present at the crime scene, implicating Rich as the murderer.

"We didn't have any direct evidence at first to connect Sean Rich to the crime," said Detective John Gray, explaining why it took the questioning and subsequent arrest of Paul Brightman before they could finally also arrest Sean Rich for the murders. "But we highly suspected him."[32]

Brightman, a reputed drug dealer who had a quantity of illegal drugs in his apartment when arrested, told homicide investigators that Rich had convinced him the Mathias home would be an easy burglary target since he had been there and cased the house the previous day. However, during the break-in, the elderly couple returned home unexpectedly and surprised the two young burglars. Brightman told the police that Rich held the couple at bay with a handgun he had brought along. While their hands were being bound, Reverend and Mrs. Mathias reportedly begged the youths to just take whatever they wanted and leave without hurting them. Rich, however, allegedly told Brightman to bring him an ax from the Mathias garage, and then he murdered the elderly couple with savage blows to the head.

"He wanted me to do it," Brightman said. "I'm not a murderer. I'm a very sensitive person."[33] Brightman claimed that before the murders he had pled with Rich to just leave, but he said Rich told him, "No, because they know me."[34]

As he split Reverend Mathias' head open with the ax, Rich, according to Brightman, reportedly screamed, "I didn't steal your fucking money!"[35] The detectives, of course, believed Rich was referring to the recent accusation that he had stolen money from the offering plate. Following this, also according to Brightman, Rich then started a fire in the hope that it would cover up the crime.

Despite Brightman's confession, however, Sean Rich steadfastly denied any involvement in the murders. He and several members of his family claimed that he had been at home on the evening of December 15. They said they remembered this because Rich had gotten into trouble for being on the telephone all evening talking to friends. Investigators discovered, however, that the records they subpoenaed from the telephone company didn't support this alibi. In addition, a girlfriend of Rich's told the police that he had confided to her that he was upstairs at the Mathias home on the night of the murders, and that it was Brightman who had killed the couple.

Not just Rich's family, though, but even church members didn't want to believe that another member could commit such a crime. "It would be easier," Marianne Hedges said, "to believe such an atrocity was the work of outsiders such as a cult. That's the stuff of tabloids. You can separate yourself from that."[36]

In March 1999, however, a jury found Sean Rich guilty of burglary, theft, and criminal confinement, but couldn't reach a decision as to whether Rich or Brightman actually swung the ax that killed the Reverend and Mrs. Mathias. Consequently, the jury didn't render a verdict on the murder charges (a frustrating but fairly common occurrence we will discuss in a later chapter). While Rich faces the likely possibility of another trial on the murder charges, a judge sentenced him to ninety-three years in prison for the crimes the jury did convict him of. In Indiana, this means that, with good behavior, Rich will have his first parole hearing in 2045, when he is sixty-three years old. In June 2000, because of his cooperation with the police, Paul Brightman, who pled guilty to his part in the crime, received a shorter sentence of sixty-five years.

"There was a lot of relief in the office when this case was solved," said Detective John Gray. "We never gave up on it."[37]

What the preceding incidents involving Tahnesia Towner, Kayla Rolland, and the Reverend and Mrs. Mathias clearly demonstrate is that anyone, no matter how innocent, can become the victim of murder. A person doesn't have to be in a violent domestic relationship or involved in crime in order to become a murder victim.

The police, of course, are tasked with the job of solving these murders, with arresting and jailing the perpetrators, and then with assisting in the prosecution. Doing this can occasionally be easy, but more often is extremely difficult. Solving most murders is a complex task that involves using both deductive reasoning and the ability to see what on the surface may not appear to be, but actually are, relationships of cause and effect. Solving murders also requires the assistance of many other professionals, such as forensic anthropologists, entomologists, pathologists, crime lab technicians, fingerprint analysts, criminal profilers, psychologists, and others.

However, before we get into how murders are solved, it's important to explain the different types of murders and other incidents of death, such as suicide, that homicide detectives investigate. I will begin with murder; as the following anecdotes demonstrate, murder can come in many forms.

On March 18, 2001, according to reports in the *St. Petersburg Times*, Phillip Walker, a convicted felon and drug addict, carried a gun with him when he walked into the Tampa Metro Treatment Center in Temple Terrace, Florida, a suburb of Tampa. The Tampa Metro Treatment Center distributes methadone to heroin users in order to wean them off their addiction to heroin. The management of the treatment center obviously realized that their organization dealt with unstable and dangerous individuals, and so consequently they kept the methadone, and the cash that addicts paid for it, inside a locked room in the treatment center offices.

On this day, Sergio Guedes, a treatment center employee, worked in the locked room with another treatment center employee, Shasta Lucey. Guedes left the room for a moment and almost immediately encountered Walker, who pointed the gun he carried at him.

"It's all about the money," Walker reportedly told Guedes. "Just give up the money."[38]

Walker then forced Guedes to walk with him back over to the locked door that led to the room containing the drugs and money. He told Guedes to knock on the door.

"If you don't open the door, I'll kill him!" Walker shouted to Lucey, who, despite the knocking, remained behind the locked door of the room.[39]

Finally though, after a few moments, Lucey cracked open the door, saw Walker and the gun, and immediately slammed the door back shut and re-locked it. According to court testimony, she afterward heard footsteps running toward the front door and then a single gunshot. Arriving police officers found Guedes lying half out of the front door, shot in the back of the head.

On April 2, 2001, acting on a tip, the police arrested Walker in Ybor City, Florida. Reportedly, he told the arresting officers over and over, "I am not going to resist. I am not going to resist."[40] Along with the murder charges, Walker also had outstanding warrants for heroin possession.

"[Walker] has a lengthy criminal record in Chicago and in this state," said Temple Terrace police chief Tony Velong. "He's a violent individual, and I have no reason to believe he's changed."[41]

On September 24, 2001, a court convicted Walker of attempted robbery and first-degree murder. He received a mandatory life sentence in prison.

In Wichita, Kansas, on April 24, 2003, Nathaniel Bell and Jose Felix-Martínez used beer to wash down between eight and sixteen Coricidin cold tablets, and then snorted a quantity of cocaine. Later that evening an argument erupted between Bell and Felix-Martínez, apparently because Felix-Martínez had flirted with someone Bell had shown interest in and because Bell didn't feel that Felix-Martínez appreciated the money that he regularly gave him.

For several hours, the argument continued and finally escalated to the point where Bell grabbed a knife and stabbed Felix-Martínez three times.

Shortly afterward, Felix-Martínez died from the stab wounds. On September 26, 2003, it took a jury only four hours to convict Bell of murder.

"Nathaniel killed Jose because he was ungrateful," said prosecutor Jennifer Hudson. "Those are his words."[42]

On February 14, 2003, a court in Houston, Texas, sentenced Clara Harris to twenty years in prison after a jury convicted her of the murder of her husband. She could have received a life sentence, but the jury felt that she should receive a lesser sentence because she had acted with "sudden passion."

Clara and David Harris, both dentists, were married on Valentine's Day 1992. Although she had tried to please her husband, Clara told the court, by undergoing liposuction, breast augmentation, and hiring a personal trainer to get her into shape, David apparently had a wandering eye and began an affair with his receptionist, Gail Bridges, a former beauty queen. A week before his death, David reportedly confessed to Clara about the affair and also told his wife that while she was overweight, a workaholic, and tried to dominate every conversation, Bridges was "petite and the perfect fit to sleep with, holding her all night."

"I couldn't believe he could sleep holding her all night," Clara testified at her trial, "because we had never slept like that—never!"[43]

A week after David's confession to her about the affair, Clara caught her husband and Bridges in a tryst at the same hotel where she and David had been married. After a brief physical altercation in the lobby, Clara followed her husband and his lover out to the parking lot. Fuming over the fact that not only was her husband having an affair but that he was doing it in the very hotel they had been married in, Clara climbed into her Mercedes-Benz. Apparently overcome with rage, even though she had her stepdaughter in the car with her, Clara suddenly floored the accelerator and sped toward her husband. A prosecution witness told the court that the on-scene investigation by the police showed that Clara had struck her husband with the Mercedes-Benz, then circled around the parking lot and ran over him at least two additional times.

Clara told the court that as she sped toward her husband and his lover, Bridges leaped to the right, but her husband leaped to the left. His attempted defensive movement sent him directly into the path of the speeding car.

"I saw some surprised eyes," Clara told the jury.[44]

The three incidents above are what homicide detectives most often have to deal with: murders during the commission of other crimes; murders over some perceived slight or insult, usually while the murderer is under the influence of some intoxicant; and murders between intimates where one party feels that he or she has been betrayed by the other. And even though, as stated earlier, this last type of murder has been decreasing in recent years, still, over 1,330 intimates murdered other intimates in 2002. As the statistics I gave earlier pointed out, and as shown in two of the three incidents above, arguments are most often the cause behind homicides, followed closely by murder during the commission of another felony (robbery in the incident above involving the drug treatment center).

Also demonstrated in the three incidents above and typical of most murders investigated by homicide detectives, the majority of murders in the United States are committed by a single perpetrator and have a single victim. In 2000, only 18 percent of the murders in the United States involved multiple offenders. This is up just a few percentage points since 1976. However, more disturbing is the slightly larger rise since 1976 in the number of murders involving not multiple offenders but multiple victims, disturbing because these murders usually have a large emotional impact on the community, both alarming and frightening its members.[45] While many single-victim murders appear on the surface to have a reason for the violence, most multiple-victim murders seem senselessly savage and make everyone feel vulnerable. Homicide detectives find that there are two basic types of multiple-victim murders: the single-incident, rampage murder (demonstrated below), and the serial murder.

Tim Thayer had been divorced from his wife Teresa for over a year. Twice in 2002 Teresa had taken out domestic violence protective orders against Tim, but had since let them lapse. On December 14, 2003, after a weekend visitation, Tim returned his nine-year-old son Paul and his seven-year-old daughter Kristy to Teresa's home in Thomasville, North Carolina. However, when he pulled into his ex-wife's driveway with his two children and new wife, Cindy, Tim noticed a strange vehicle parked there. As Teresa walked out of the house to meet the children, Tim asked her who the car belonged to. Teresa told him that she had a visitor, but Tim knew it was Teresa's new boyfriend, William Merritt.

Tim walked around to the rear of his vehicle and opened the trunk, ostensibly to retrieve the children's luggage. Instead, however, he snatched out a handgun and shot Teresa, who would die on the way to the hospital. He then raced up onto the porch and shot and killed his nine-year-old son Paul. Following this, Tim dashed into the house and killed Teresa's new boyfriend William Merritt. While Tim's new wife Cindy remained outside unharmed, seven-year-old Kristy, during the barrage of fire, fled next door to the safety of her grandparents' house. Meanwhile, inside Teresa's house, Tim finally turned the gun on himself and committed suicide.

"He cracked," said neighbor Peggy Grubb. "He wanted her for himself. He had another wife, but he just couldn't stand for her to have someone for herself."[46]

The above type of multiple-victim murder, unfortunately seen many times in the last few decades, is called a "rampage killing." Whether it's from increased reporting or the actual increase in the occurrence of multiple-victim murders, it seems that far too often these days, newspapers and television newscasts tell of a person who, in a sudden rage, kills a half-dozen family members or fellow employees.

In April 2000, the *New York Times* reported on a study it had conducted of 100 of these rampage killings that had occurred from 1949 to 1999. Through their research, investigators from the newspaper found a number of similarities among these killings. For example, at least half of the killers had previously experienced serious mental health problems, and 63 percent had made threats of violence before the rampage, half of them even specifying whom they planned to kill. The study also found that there was usually a precipitating event that sparked the rampage, and that almost 90 percent of the killers didn't leave the crime scene once they had finished their murder spree, with almost a third committing suicide.[47]

Another report on rampage murders, this one from the FBI Academy in Quantico, Virginia, and of rampage murders occurring between 1975 to 1999, showed that the murderers used firearms in 88 percent of the incidents studied, and that these type of murders were most likely to occur, in their order of magnitude, at restaurants, retail stores, government offices/facilities, schools/universities, and factories. Interestingly, the study also found that Mondays were the most likely day, and mornings the most likely time, for rampage murders.[48]

As the preceding incident involving the Thayers demonstrated, many multiple-victim murders are similar in motive and means to single-victim murders, with the victims quite often being family members or individuals known to the murderer. However, there is another type of multiple-victim murder that is much different from the rampage murder and, unfortunately, much more difficult for the police to solve. This is the serial murder, in which the multiple victims, rather than being murdered in one rampage incident, are killed in separate incidents over a long period of time, with the murderer often not knowing his or her victims.

At 10:10 a.m. on April 26, 2002, at Lucasville's Southern Ohio Correctional Facility, the state of Ohio injected forty-six-year-old Alton Coleman with a solution of sodium thiopental, then with a solution of pancuronium bromide, and finally with a solution of potassium chloride. The first injection put Coleman into a deep sleep, the second paralyzed his diaphragm and lungs, and the third stopped his heart, killing him. While Coleman had been convicted of four murders and sentenced to death in Ohio, which the state carried out on April 26, he had also been sentenced to death in two other states, Illinois and Indiana, a feat unequaled in American criminal justice history. What brought this about?

Coleman, who reportedly had been nicknamed "pissy" by his schoolmates because he regularly wet his pants, had become well known as a sex offender during his youth. Long before the 1984 murder spree that ended in his execution, Coleman had come to the attention of the police. He was accused of at least a half-dozen rapes between 1973 and 1984.

On May 29, 1984, his final crime spree began when Coleman, after making friends with her mother, left to go to the store with nine-year-old Venita Wheat of Kenosha, Wisconsin. Coleman strangled the little girl to death with a strand of cable television wire. On June 18, 1984, after teaming up with girlfriend Debra Brown, Coleman kidnapped seven-year-old Tamika Turks and her nine-year-old aunt in Gary, Indiana. After Coleman raped Turks, Brown allegedly held the seven-year-old girl down on the ground while Coleman stomped her to death. Following this, both Coleman and Brown reportedly raped the nine-year-old aunt, who was eventually able to escape and flee with her life.

The next day, Coleman and Brown allegedly kidnapped twenty-one-year-old Donna Williams of Gary, Indiana, whose body the police discovered in Detroit on July 11, 1984. On July 7, 1984, the duo reportedly killed thirty-year-old Virginia Temple and her ten-year-old daughter in Toledo. Four days later, Coleman and Brown strangled fifteen-year-old

Toney Storey in Cincinnati. (Both Coleman and Brown were convicted of this crime and sentenced to death. Governor Richard Celeste eventually commuted Brown's sentence to life imprisonment.) On July 13, 1984, Coleman and Brown befriended and then beat to death forty-four-year-old Marlene Walters in Cincinnati (the actual crime Coleman was executed for). Finally, on July 19, 1984, the police in Indianapolis linked Coleman and Brown to the shooting death of seventy-seven-year-old Eugene Scott. During their crime spree, Coleman and Brown did little to hide their involvement, leaving multiple fingerprints and other clues for the police.

As might be imagined, this murder spree put the police on high alert, and the authorities in every state in the Midwest began looking for Coleman and Brown. Coleman was even named on a "special edition" of the FBI's 10 Most Wanted list. Finally, on July 20, 1984, acting on a tip from a family friend, the police in Evanston, Illinois, arrested Coleman and Brown as they watched a pick-up basketball game. Although both armed, they surrendered without resistance.

During the fifty-three-day crime spree, Coleman and Brown reportedly killed eight people, raped more than a dozen women and children, and kidnapped three individuals. They also committed at least fourteen robberies.

"This was a real-life serial killer who callously picked his victims at random," said Lake County (Indiana) Prosecutor Jack Crawford of Coleman.[49]

"I think this guy is the poster boy for capital punishment," said Hamilton County (Ohio) Prosecutor Mike Allen. "If anybody deserves it, it's him."[50]

Debra Brown, while presently serving a life sentence in Ohio, is still under a sentence of death in Indiana. Her fate is yet to be decided.

The above incident is an example of a serial murderer. FBI agent Robert Ressler, who reportedly coined the term *serial murder*, defines it as "three or more murders (with) a cooling off period between the crimes.... It's very much based on a fantasy that builds and builds during this cooling-off period that leads to premeditation and planning for the next murder."[51] Agent Ressler devised this description in order to separate serial murders from rampage murders, which, as talked about earlier, involve multiple murders that occur during a rage that lasts only a short time.

Alton Coleman was what is known as a "disorganized serial murderer," in that he picked his victims at random and his murders lacked any ceremony or ritual. The disorganized serial murderer, police find, uses little planning, often does little to hide the bodies, and, like Coleman, generally leaves many clues for the police. The organized serial murderer, on the other hand, can be much more difficult to catch. Many organized serial murderers specifically pick their targets because of certain traits and then kill them in very special, ritualized ceremonies. Serial murderer Ted Bundy, for example, always selected college-age women with long brown hair. Some experts believe that he was killing women who resembled his former fiancée, who broke her engagement to him. The organized serial murderer often plans the crime in detail, including how to capture and restrain the victim and where to hide the body. He or she also often uses the same ritualized method to kill the victim, and generally leaves few clues for the police.

Researchers studying serial murderers have found a number of differences in the intellectual and emotional makeup of organized versus unorganized serial murderers. Organized serial murderers, for example, are often above average in intelligence, appear very socially competent, are usually in a consensual sexual relationship, and will almost always follow the story of their murders closely in the news media. Disorganized serial murderers, on the other hand, are usually below average in intelligence, socially inept, have sporadic relationships with the opposite sex, and often show no interest in the news media coverage of their crimes.

Besides the broad classifications of organized and disorganized, there are also several specific types of serial murderers within these classifications that are designated by their purpose for killing. There are, for example, the visionary serial murderers, who kill because they hear voices or because they believe they receive visits from God or spirits, who tell them to commit the killings. While visionary serial murderers are obviously psychotic, another type of serial murderer, the "serial murderer with a mission," may seem very normal to the people who meet him or her. These individuals, however, believe that they are on a mission to rid the world of a certain group of people whom they deem unworthy of life, such as prostitutes, homosexuals, drug addicts, or street people. The "thrill serial murderer," on the other hand, is different from the first two types and kills simply because he or she finds it exciting. Last and closely related to the thrill serial murderer is the serial murderer who kills for lust. This type of killer becomes very sexually aroused by the act of killing and will often prolong the death of the victim in order to prolong the sexual gratification.

Regardless, however, of the type of serial murderer, it has been found that these individuals can rarely empathize with their victims. To them, victims are simply objects that the serial murderer can use to live out a fantasy or satisfy a need to kill.

"He was as cold as a snake on a stone," said Homicide Detective Pete Piccini when describing serial murderer Charles T. Sinclair, who reportedly murdered at least a half-dozen people.[52]

Serial murderers also usually feel very little remorse over what they have done, no matter how heinous. The only regrets they often have are over mistakes they made that got them caught. Joseph Kondro, a serial murderer who was interviewed by a reporter for the *Seattle Post-Intelligencer*, said that if he could change just one thing, he would've been more careful in hiding the body of his last victim, the one the police arrested him for. "When a police officer can't find a body," Kondro said, "what can he do?"[53]

As stated above, serial murderers usually don't see their victims as real people, but simply as objects. Most often, a serial murderer's only real concern is his or her own satisfaction or benefit. As an example, serial murderer Keith Jesperson, who pled guilty to killing four people but was suspected of many more, was asked about other victims. He responded, "Is there more? Yeah. But do I want to expose them? No. Why should I? There's no benefit in it for me."[54]

Interestingly, many serial murderers will select prostitutes as their victims, later claiming that, because they were prostitutes, they deserved to die. Yet, these same serial murderers will often engage in sex with their victims before and after the murders. For example, Robert Lee Yates Jr. of Spokane, Washington, who was convicted of fifteen murders, would pick up prostitutes, shoot them, and then engage in post-mortem sex.

Keith Jesperson of Portland, Oregon (mentioned above), would first rape and then strangle his victims. Jesperson became known as the "Happy Face Killer" because of taunting letters he sent to the authorities that he signed with a happy face. Of course, readers might naturally wonder why anyone who had killed many people would want to increase the risk of apprehension by sending letters to the police, letters that eventually find their way into the news media. The reason is that most serial murderers are losers in their personal lives, and through the killings they are striving for a type of stardom, which they feel letters like this will bring them.

"The reason they are doing this is for their moment of glory," Marvin Hier, a researcher for the Simon Wiesenthal Center, said of serial murderers, "when they feel the whole world is stopping to take notice of them."[55]

This need for notoriety is so great that some individuals have claimed to be serial murderers when they really weren't. For example, a court in August 2000 convicted Joe Brown of killing his girlfriend. Soon afterward, Joe began claiming that he had killed at least thirteen other women. However, investigators found that Joe didn't have any of the information the real killer would have had about any of the murders he tried to confess to.

"Joe was full of it," said Detective Tony Mayhew, who investigated his claims.[56]

Along with this desperate need for notoriety, however, experts also find that many serial murderers do it for the exhilarating feeling it gives them. This exhilaration comes from having the power of deciding whether it will be life or death for a helpless victim, and this exhilaration becomes like a narcotic to them.

"If there is any one common motive among serial killers, it's playing God, having the power over life and death of another individual," says Gregg O. McCrary, a retired FBI agent who now works as a private criminal profiler.[57]

Ray Hazelwood, another former FBI profiler, extensively studied Harvey Glatman, known as the Lonely Hearts Killer. Initially, he was puzzled because even though Glatman would first incapacitate his victims in their homes, he would then take the tremendous risk of transporting them out into the desert before raping and killing them. "He could have raped and killed these women in their apartments," says Hazelwood. "But Glatman kept them alive at increased risk to himself. I realized that the enjoyment he took made the risk worth it to him. I later understood that enjoyment, that sense of possession, is power to the ritualistic offender, and total possession is absolute power."[58]

Ted Bundy told FBI agent Bill Hagmaier, "Murder isn't just a crime of lust or violence. It becomes possession. They are part of you.... You feel the last bit of breath leaving their bodies.... You're looking into their eyes.... A person in that situation is God!"[59]

An article in the *FBI Law Enforcement Bulletin* described the power desperately longed for by sexual serial murderers: "They tend to carry out their crimes in a ritualistic manner, to include a strong sexual component in their acts, and to rape or torture their victims.... Some leave their victims' bodies in poses that express and symbolize the feelings of power and pleasure they have achieved in the act of killing."[60]

While investigating the types of murder discussed so far keep homicide detectives busy enough, they are also tasked with the investigation of other types of death. For example, the police must investigate any time a private citizen kills someone in self-defense or in defense of another. They must also investigate whenever a police officer kills a violent felon in the line of duty.

The acts of police officers who kill violent felons, and of private citizens who kill in self-defense, are usually termed "justifiable homicides." They are routinely presented to local grand juries that usually (but not always) return a "no bill," which means that, although the person committed a homicide, it was justifiable and not a criminal act. However, homicide detectives must still investigate these incidents for the few cases they discover each year that, while originally appearing to be justifiable, are found upon investigation instead to be criminal.

In addition, homicide detectives also generally investigate reports of suicide. Suicide is the eleventh leading cause of death in the United States. In 2000, for example, 29,350 Americans committed suicide,[61] while in 2001 the amount rose to 30,622, numbers that far exceed the murder rate.[62] According to an article in the *Annals of Emergency Medicine*, eighty-five people commit suicide every day in the United States, and 2,000 attempt it.[63] What homicide detectives are looking for, though, are those very rare cases in which the event was actually a murder that was only staged to look like a suicide.

Yet, while the number of these staged suicides is actually quite small, interestingly enough, as a homicide commander I find that I receive many more complaints each year about my detectives' handling of suicide cases than I do about their handling of murder cases. Family members of suicide victims often call or come into my office complaining that while their loved one's death may have looked like a suicide, as one of my detectives determined, it was actually a murder. Often in these cases the victim has left behind a signed suicide note, has attempted or threatened to commit suicide before, and every bit of evidence at the scene points to suicide.

The problem rests in the fact that if the death is ruled a suicide, then family members and friends feel a sense of guilt for not stopping the individual or for adding to the stress that led to the suicide. However, if the incident is ruled a murder, then the family members or friends share no guilt in the death.

I recall a case we had several years ago in which a man, depressed because his family refused to accept his Vietnamese-born wife into their family, hung himself in his basement. He had both threatened and attempted suicide several times before, and in the final incident had left a note behind. He was a large person, well over two hundred and fifty pounds, and it took three men to get him down. The coroner agreed with my detectives and ruled it a suicide. The man's family, however, stormed into my office and demanded that the case be investigated as a murder, and that we definitely look at his new wife as the suspect. They told me that they believed she had somehow knocked him out and then hung him. When I pointed out to them that he weighed nearly three times as much as his wife did, and that toxicology showed only alcohol in his system, they brushed this objection aside with the comment that everyone knows Oriental people have secret methods for being able to do things like this.

Occasionally, police officers also run into incidents that at first appear to be suicides but that actually turn out to be accidental deaths. These are autoerotic deaths. These deaths come about because somehow it was discovered that there is an increase in sexual pleasure if an orgasm occurs during a compression of the neck (which reduces the blood flow to the brain). To accomplish this, individuals will fasten ligatures to a rafter or some other overhead structure and then around their necks, letting the ligature tighten as they masturbate. Unfortunately, sometimes during their excitement individuals go too far and lose consciousness. The slumping of the body then continues the shutoff of blood to the brain and eventually causes death.

This type of death is usually readily apparent because the people practicing this behavior, besides doing it in a securely locked or faraway location, often have an assortment of pornography lying open and nearby, and will usually have placed some soft object, such as a towel, between the ligature and the skin in order to prevent bruising or ligature marks on the neck. Also, the police, upon inspection of the scene, will often discover groves in the rafters showing repeated instances of this behavior, and will sometimes find mirrors carefully positioned so that the individuals can see themselves from several directions. In addition, the police will also often find some type of failed safety measure meant to prevent death in case of unconsciousness, such as a slipknot in the noose. These clues are important because few people who would attempt to stage such an event would go to the trouble to plant these clues. They are also important because families, almost always totally unaware of this behavior in their loved ones, seldom want to accept this type of death for what it is, and will instead usually insist that it is a staged murder. In a training class at a homicide seminar I attended, I watched the recording of a man interviewed about his father's autoerotic death. Even though the death had all of the clues above, the man insisted he wouldn't believe it even if the police had the act on videotape.

Closely related to the type of death above, I recall a case we had here in Indianapolis in which a man insisted to us that a girl he had met at a bar had insisted he choke her with his hands while they were having sex. She allegedly told him that she had done it many times before and loved it. He did and she died. Naturally, it was difficult for the jury to believe this, since the only one who could confirm it was dead.

The incidents above aside, while investigating apparent actual suicides, homicide detectives naturally look into the victim's history. Has the person talked about or attempted suicide before? Has the person recently suffered a significant personal stressor such as the death of a spouse or other close loved one, recently been divorced, been in trouble with the law, or been fired or laid off at work? Also, of course, the detectives search the suicide scene for evidence, such as notes or prescription medicine containers. While it is certainly not unheard of, few suicides are anything but what they appear to be. Yet still, for those rare cases that actually are murders, all suicides must be looked at closely.

There is a special type of suicide, however, that occurs far too often every year and which all police officers dread. This is what is known as "suicide-by-cop." These are acts perpetrated by individuals who are bent on suicide but who don't have the courage to do it themselves, or who don't want to tag themselves with the negative connotations that come with suicide. So consequently, they hope to be able to force the police to kill them. According to an article in *Police* magazine, "For those with suicidal tendencies, being killed by police can be more appealing than committing suicide, which comes with a 'loser' stigma.... It's a big media event. It's a positive thing for that person, but not the police."[64] Various studies have indicated that between 10 and 25 percent of all the fatal police shootings each year are actually suicide-by-cop incidents.[65]

However, readers should keep in mind that, even though prone to self-destruction, individuals attempting suicide-by-cop can be extremely dangerous because they will often do things such as shoot at police officers or innocent bystanders in order to force the police to kill them. In Rochester, New York, for example, William Griffin, after killing several people at his home, drove to the Security Trust Bank in Rochester, where he took a number of people hostage. When the police arrived, he demanded that they kill him. When they wouldn't, he ordered one of the female hostages to leave the bank, and then shot and killed her as she stepped outside. Following this, Griffin walked over and stood in front of a window, where the police killed him.

Very similar to the investigation of suicides, homicide detectives also investigate incidents that appear to be natural deaths but whose victims have no history to indicate that a death would occur. While there is little need to investigate the death of a long-term cancer patient, often in people with heart problems the first symptom is sudden death. What homicide detectives must do, as in suicides, is to be certain that the death was indeed natural and not actually a murder only made to look natural. Detectives must tread the fine line between being appropriately sympathetic to family members who have lost a loved one and suspicious enough to look into any events or circumstances that don't fit the picture of a natural death.

Whenever homicide detectives are called to hospitals to investigate what appears at first to be the natural death of a child that the hospital staff finds inexplicable, they must always suspect Munchausen Syndrome by Proxy. This is a psychiatric ailment that causes individuals to make others, usually children in their care, extremely ill in order to attract attention to themselves as caring and loving individuals who are genuinely concerned about the health of the person they are intentionally making sick.

Authorities find that the majority of people with Munchausen Syndrome by Proxy are women, who are often seen by friends, families, neighbors, and even medical personnel as extraordinarily loving parents who are vitally concerned about the health of one of their children. People with Munchausen Syndrome by Proxy, before being arrested, have even won awards for their seemingly selfless devotion. This kind of attention, however, is exactly why these individuals do what they do, and receiving this kind of attention will usually only bring on more of their dangerous and destructive behavior.

Individuals with Munchausen Syndrome by Proxy, in order to make their children sick, have been known to suffocate them and then call for help resuscitating them; or, if their children are in the hospital, they will turn off the life support equipment until their children stop breathing and then turn it back on and call for help. They have also been known to poison their children with various compounds that mimic certain illnesses, or to introduce blood or other contaminants into their children's urine before it is tested.

Since the children of individuals with Munchausen Syndrome by Proxy usually suffer attacks or relapses only when the parent is present, many hospitals have taken to planting hidden video cameras in the rooms of children whose parents are suspected of having Munchausen Syndrome by Proxy. We had just such a case here in Indianapolis several years ago, in which the videotape showed a mother introducing feces into a tube hooked into her child's arm.

In addition to all of the above, homicide detectives are also often called to accidental deaths caused by other than automobiles (which are usually handled by another branch of the police department). Like investigating suicides and natural deaths, homicide detectives are only there to be certain that the death was indeed simply an unfortunate accident, because often what looks suspicious can be explained without a crime. For example, exposure deaths in cold weather can often look like sexual homicides. During the final stages of hypothermia, the body feels very hot from the blood the brain sends out to the skin, and consequently hypothermia victims will often take all of their clothes off. Like investigating suicides and natural deaths, while investigating accidents homicide detectives must walk the fine line between being sympathetic to, and at the same time suspicious of, individuals who were at the accident scene.

"Our detectives spend quite a bit of time dealing with non-homicide deaths," Lieutenant Mike Hobel of the Phoenix Police Department told me. "We took 447 of those in 2002."[66] Likewise, in Indianapolis and most other large cities, homicide detectives spend a considerable amount of time dealing with non-homicide deaths.

Regardless of all these other duties, and despite what some may claim, homicide detectives give every murder case they're assigned, no matter whom the victim, their utmost effort. Professor Richard Lundman of Ohio State University conducted an in-depth study of homicide investigations and found, "Our results suggest homicide detectives work aggressively to clear all homicides, regardless of the race, sex, or social class of the victims involved."[67]

Still, despite the success of homicide detectives across the country, during my time as a homicide commander I've found that few books, television programs, or movies accurately depict the crime of murder or how it is solved. In the following chapters, I am going to take you step by step through how real-life homicide detectives solve these crimes and bring murderers to justice.

Almost universally when investigating murders, homicide detectives make their first stop at the crime scene. As we shall see in the next chapter, properly processing a crime scene is usually the most important step in any murder investigation. A proper and thorough investigation of the crime scene can often spell the difference between a solved and an unsolved murder.

CHAPTER 2

The Crime Scene

Ron Rudin, a sixty-four-year-old Las Vegas millionaire who had made his fortune in real estate, disappeared on December 18, 1994. Two days later, Margaret, his fifth wife, to whom he had been married seven years, reported his disappearance to the police. Several days following this, Ron's muddy 1993 Cadillac turned up parked behind the Crazy Horse Too topless club on Industrial Road in Las Vegas. The police found blood inside the vehicle, but no sign of Ron.

On January 21, 1995, several fishermen stumbled onto Ron's skull lying in a remote ravine near Nelson's Landing in the Lake Mead Recreational Area, southeast of Las Vegas. Police called to the scene discovered several items of Ron's jewelry next to his skull, while nearby in a firepit they found the charred remains of an old humpback trunk containing the rest of Ron's body. An autopsy showed that Ron had been shot four times in the head with a .22-caliber weapon.

Once Ron's disappearance became a murder, homicide detectives stepped in and took over the investigation.

The detectives discovered that for several years before his death, Ron had apparently been worrying that something violent might happen to him. In April 1991, he added the following amendment to his will: "I request that in the event my death is caused by violent means (for example, gunshot, knife or a violent automobile accident), extraordinary steps be taken in investigating the true cause of the death. Should said death be caused, directly or indirectly, by a beneficiary of my estate, said beneficiary shall be totally excluded from my estate and/or any trusts I may have in existence."[1]

Within a short time of the news media reporting the discovery of Ron's remains, homicide detectives spoke with an Augustine Lobato, who had contacted them and told the detectives that, soon after Ron's disappearance, Margaret had hired him to remove a mattress and box springs from Ron's and her bedroom. He also said that she had him pull up the bedroom carpeting, instructing him to get rid of all of it. Lobato told the police that the mattress and carpeting had brownish-red stains on them and smelled of mildew. Adding to their suspicion of Margaret, the police found that although a funeral was held for Ron, Margaret chose not to attend it.

The homicide detectives immediately obtained a search warrant for Ron's home and for an antique store run by Margaret. In the couple's bedroom the police found blood spatters on the walls and ceiling. They also located and recovered the box springs and part of the carpeting Lobato had carried out of the house. Though the coroner's office informed the police that Ron's charred remains couldn't supply any blood to compare with what they had found during their crime scene searches, homicide detectives discovered a handkerchief in the bathroom of his home that a maid said Ron had used for a nosebleed shortly before his disappearance.

The police also discovered evidence that Margaret had apparently wiretapped her husband's office so that she could overhear any calls he made or received there. According to witnesses, Margaret suspected Ron of being unfaithful to her, which he apparently was. Detectives found that on the day Ron disappeared, he had telephoned his lover and told her that he was considering confronting his wife about letters she had sent to his lover's children, telling them that their mother was a tramp.

Because of the evidence the police recovered during their searches, the trustees of Ron's estate filed a petition in court to exclude Margaret from any share in Ron's estate. Rather than testifying at a hearing held on the petition, Margaret instead entered into an agreement with the trustees to accept $600,000 from the estate rather than the $6–7 million Ron's will had left her.

The police, however, while recovering valuable and incriminating evidence during their crime scene searches, couldn't come up with the murder weapon, even though thoroughly searching the house and antique shop. Interestingly, the police found that soon after his marriage to Margaret, Ron had reported that a .22-caliber Ruger pistol fitted with a silencer had been stolen from his large gun collection. The police also discovered that he had commented to several people that he believed since he had his home and gun collection tightly alarmed and guarded, the only person who could have stolen the gun was Margaret. In July 1996, a diver finally found the gun in about fifteen feet of water in Lake Mead. The gun and silencer had been wrapped in a plastic bag. Ballistic tests showed that, along with it being Ron's stolen gun, it was also the weapon that had killed him.

This was the last piece of evidence the prosecutor felt he needed. On April 18, 1997, he obtained an indictment against Margaret for the murder of Ron. However, when the police attempted to arrest Margaret, they found that she had disappeared. For the next two years, the Las Vegas police searched unsuccessfully for Margaret, even featuring her story twice on the television program *America's Most Wanted*. In September 1998, a viewer of the television show called and said that an employee of a Phoenix hotel gift shop named Anne Boatwright looked like the picture shown on the show. Although the Phoenix police brought Boatwright in for questioning, they didn't have a picture of Margaret Rudin available, and so they released her. The Las Vegas police later confirmed that Boatwright had indeed been Margaret Rudin, who again disappeared.

Finally, in November 1999, police officers acted on a tip and, using the ruse of delivering a pizza Margaret had ordered, arrested her in Revere, Massachusetts, where she lived in a rundown apartment with a retired fireman. While her neighbors in Revere had liked Margaret, they thought it odd that she always wore a black wig, even though they could see her blond hair beneath. Residents called her "the wig lady," and the rumor spread that she was a cancer patient.

"I just figured she was a chemotherapy patient because you could see right underneath her wig," said a Revere resident.[2]

Eventually extradited to Nevada, Margaret asked for a public defender, telling the court that legal fees and living expenses had eaten up the $600,000 she had received from Ron's estate. After investigating her financial status, the court agreed she was indigent and appointed her a public defender.

Before Margaret's murder trial began, however, the police announced that they had recovered seven sealed cardboard boxes Margaret had mailed to the same friend who gave police the tip that she was in Revere, Massachusetts. Margaret reportedly told the friend she was mailing the boxes because she wasn't sure she could trust the man she was living with and that she planned to move soon.

In the boxes the police found a wallet belonging to Ron and a log of telephone calls to and from Ron's office. The final log entry concerned a call during which Ron made plans to meet his lover. The police also discovered in the boxes a number of audiotapes from Margaret's wiretap and six volumes of Margaret's diary, in which she discussed confronting Ron about his infidelity.

Margaret's murder trial finally began in February 2001. The prosecution presented evidence to the court that showed that the blood on the box springs, the carpeting, and on the bedroom walls and ceiling belonged to Ron. The man Margaret had hired to remove the items from Ron's and her bedroom also testified that she had had him clean up a reddish-brown spot near the washer and dryer. A firearms expert testified that the blood spatter pattern on the bedroom walls matched the pattern of a man shot in the head while lying in bed.

The prosecution also produced testimony from Margaret's sister, who told the court she had seen a humpback trunk that appeared identical to the charred one that had contained part of Ron's remains. She had seen it in Margaret's antique shop just days before Ron's disappearance. The sister also said that Margaret had made a detailed listing of Ron's estate even before his body was found, but had destroyed it and an audiotape just before the police served a search warrant on her house. The prosecution also produced an antiques dealer who testified that he had sold Margaret a humpback trunk with a pattern matching the floral pattern found on the charred one containing part of Ron's remains.

Although the defense presented its own testimony and evidence in an attempt to counter the prosecution's case, on May 2, 2001, the jury found Margaret guilty of murdering her husband Ron and of illegally wiretapping his office. The foreman of the jury said that no single piece of evidence carried the day. Rather, he said that the cumulative effect of dozens of witnesses and exhibits led the jurors to an inescapable conclusion.

"We couldn't get away from the evidence," the jury foreman said. "It was overwhelming. No matter how we cut this thing, it kept coming back to Margaret."[3]

On August 31, 2001, the judge in the case sentenced Margaret to life imprisonment with the possibility of parole. Under Nevada law, this means that fifty-eight-year-old Margaret Rudin can apply for parole after serving twenty years of her sentence.

The above quote from the jury foreman stresses the extreme importance of properly searching and preserving evidence from a crime scene (or multiple crime scenes as in the Rudin case). Doing so can make the difference of whether or not the prosecution's case is convincing to a jury. No matter how small, the police find, every piece of evidence must be collected from a crime scene and preserved, because when presented as a whole, all of this evidence, along with witness testimony, can demonstrate overwhelming proof of guilt. For example, in the case above, blood samples collected from Ron and Margaret's bedroom; the recognition, recording, and interpretation of the blood spatters found on the walls and ceiling; and the discovery of a handkerchief with Ron's blood on it all added immensely to the prosecution's case. Along with this, also bolstering the prosecution's case were the recovery and preservation of the humpback trunk at the secondary crime scene where the fishermen found Ron's body, and the discovery of the murder weapon that had been thrown into Lake Mead. While all of these pieces of evidence established for jurors the who, how, where, what, and when of the murder, the additional recovery of the wiretapping evidence answered the question of why.

Special Agent Kimberly A. Crawford of the FBI says, "With recent advances in evidence detection technology and forensic analysis, crime scene searches have become possibly the most important component in many criminal investigations."[4]

David W. Rivers, a retired homicide detective sergeant from Miami, says of crime scene investigation, "The three most important aspects of any death investigation are: crime scene, crime scene, crime scene."[5]

Yet, while the investigation conducted at the scene of a murder can be paramount to successfully prosecuting the murderer, there is no set procedure that can be used for every murder scene. Since each murder scene is unique, homicide detectives must adapt the procedures I will talk about in this chapter to fit the scene's specific characteristics. A research report published by the U.S. Department of Justice titled *Death Investigation: A Guide for the Scene Investigator*, states, "There is no 'system' of death investigation that covers the more than 3,000 jurisdictions in this country. No nationally accepted guidelines or standards of practice exist for individuals responsible for performing death-scene investigations."[6] Still, experienced homicide detectives have been able, as demonstrated by the fact that a larger percentage of murder cases are solved each year than any other crime, to use the methods outlined in this chapter to effectively evaluate, inspect, and process murder scenes.

For most murder investigations, as Detective Rivers points out above, the crime scene becomes not only the crucial starting point for homicide detectives, but often provides more clues about the crime than any other source. If properly protected and processed by the police, a crime scene can answer the who, where, when, what, how, and why of a murder case. Incidentally, evidence at a crime scene can also determine whether a crime was actually even committed or not (occasionally, scenes that at first appear to be a murder turn out to be a suicide or an accident).

Just as important, however, a carefully processed crime scene can also assist homicide detectives in establishing the key elements needed to prove the crime in court, can link a suspect to the crime, can corroborate or refute suspect and witness statements, and can possibly prove that a person believed guilty is actually not the perpetrator after all. For all of these reasons, police departments teach their uniformed officers, who are usually the first officers to respond to a murder scene, the value of throwing up barriers around the crime scene as quickly as possible to protect the evidence there.

"One of the most critical elements of a successful investigation is the crime scene," Detective John Wright of the Washington State Patrol told me. "To that end, a properly contained scene will yield a wealth of viable evidence and clues."[7]

However, even before this crucial act of protecting the crime scene can be done, several other even more important things must be attended to. When uniformed police officers are dispatched to a crime scene, for safety's sake they must presume that the crime is still going on. Therefore, when officers arrive at a murder scene their first concern is the safety of the others at the scene, to say nothing of their own safety. Their immediate priority becomes, is the murderer still in the vicinity with the weapon? If so, arrest and detention become the next immediate concern. Following this, any suspects detained must be quickly removed from the murder scene in order to prevent them from contaminating any of the evidence. In addition, all suspects detained must be immediately examined for any evidence of the murder, such as blood or hair from the victim, dust or dirt specific to the crime scene, and so on.

The initially responding officers must also consider this question: are there conditions at the scene that it make it dangerous for individuals nearby, for example, a car on fire, explosives lying around, a building about to collapse? If so, the uniformed officers are trained to immediately call for backup or for the assistance of a specialized unit to handle the specific type of threat. In addition, first-responding officers must be aware of the various subtle clues of danger, such as the odor of natural gas or a meth lab (street-level methamphetamines are usually clandestinely manufactured under very crude and extremely hazardous conditions).

Uniformed police officers are also taught to never pick up or handle any evidence at a murder scene, or to allow anyone else, including other police officers, witnesses, and family members, to touch or pick up evidence, but rather to leave the evidence where found. The only time evidence might be picked up and/or handled is in extreme situations involving officer and bystander safety or when leaving evidence where it is will cause more harm than picking it up, such as a bloody knife left in the rain, an important piece of paper lying on the ground when it is windy, and so on.

Police officers are additionally taught to never do anything that will change the crime scene from the way they found it. The U.S. Department of Justice document *Crime Scene Investigation: A Guide for Law Enforcement* states, "Persons should not smoke, chew tobacco, use the telephone or bathroom, eat or drink, move any items, including weapons (unless necessary for the safety and well-being of persons at the scene), adjust the thermometer or open windows or doors (maintain scene as found), touch anything unnecessarily (note and document any items moved), reposition moved item, litter, or spit within the established boundaries of the scene."[8]

While the above advice would seem to most readers to be common sense, every police department has stories of a detective who thought he or she had found a key piece of evidence, only to discover later that it came from a police officer at the scene, or to discover later that a true key piece of evidence had been fatally contaminated by a police officer. In the O. J. Simpson case, for example, first-responding police officers used Nicole Simpson's telephone to report her murder, thereby making the telephone useless as evidence.

One might argue, after reading all of the above, that the absolute first thing a police officer should do when arriving at a murder scene is to check on the condition of the victim to be certain that he or she actually is dead (people can often suffer horrendous wounds yet still survive). However, taking this type of action can be a deadly mistake. In Indianapolis a number of years ago we had a case in which an officer responding to the scene of a shooting saw the victim lying on the living room floor. Rather than first checking the area for safety, the officer rushed to the victim to see if he could help him. The murderer was standing behind a curtain in the living room, and while the officer was bent over checking on the victim the murderer shot the officer in the back of the head and killed him.

However, once uniformed officers have ascertained whether or not the suspect is still in the vicinity and have assured the safety of the crime scene, they then immediately check on the condition of the victim, calling for medical assistance if there appears to be any spark of life or possibility of survival. In the cases where it does appear that the victim is not yet dead, but soon will be, officers will often attempt to take a "dying declaration." Under certain circumstances, these can be used as evidence in court and often make for compelling testimony. If medical personnel are summoned, the initially responding officers must guide them through the crime scene so that they will disrupt as little evidence as possible. The officers note the names and unit numbers of the medical personnel for the case file. However, often medical personnel are called to the scene before the police are, and so it is important that police departments train all emergency responders in the importance of preserving a crime scene.

"Police and emergency personnel are the most crucial elements in the proper preservation of crime scenes," Detective David Hatch of the Las Vegas Police Department told me. "I cannot stress enough the need to train these personnel in the proper preservation of crime scenes. We can re-interview and re-investigate all phases of a violent crime, but we cannot undo a scene that has been compromised and evidence destroyed."[9]

Following checking on the condition of the victim, the uniformed officers then begin blocking off, usually using yellow crime scene tape—and occasionally police cars, wooden barricades, and other items—an area larger than the actual crime scene. It has been found that it is much easier to later decrease the size of a crime scene than it is to attempt to enlarge it once it has been established. If a crime scene is made too small, individuals moving around outside the crime scene can trample crucial evidence. Human nature being what it is, flashing lights and sirens have the tendency to attract large crowds of people who want to see what is going on, and moving them back without destroying what evidence might be where they are standing can be challenging at best. In addition, the news media have a vested interest in being at a murder scene and reporting to the public what is happening. Consequently, they attempt to get as close to the crime scene as possible. While the public and the press have a right to be there, they don't have the right to impede a criminal investigation. Hence, the larger-than-necessary crime scene. Also, it is important when deciding on the size of the crime scene to attempt to determine the possible entry and exit points of the suspects. These must be included within the crime scene because they often contain valuable evidence, such as tire tracks, cigarette butts, or discarded weapons.

For murders that are extraordinarily newsworthy, there will often be a blocked-off inner crime scene where the actual murder victim and all of the evidence are, and a blocked-off outer crime scene around that. The outer crime scene is for high-ranking police officers, politicians, and others who will inevitably show up at crime scenes that have strong newsworthiness. This gives these individuals proximity to the actual crime scene without the worry that they might step on or disturb the evidence. A uniformed officer usually mans the entry point to the inner crime scene to prevent unauthorized entry and to record the names of everyone who does enter the inner crime scene. Every police department has horror stories of some high-ranking officer coming to a crime scene and picking up or handling a crucial piece of evidence.

"A crime scene is in perfect condition until the arrival of the first police officer," says retired Detective Sergeant David W. Rivers. "It goes to hell in direct geometric proportion to the number and rank of the supervisors that show up."[10]

For large murder scenes, or those murder scenes of intense interest to the press, a command post may be set up close to, but away from, the murder scene. Along with most major cities, Indianapolis has a large motor home for this purpose. This vehicle is equipped with a meeting area, communications equipment, computers, a restroom, and so on. The high-ranking officers and others who come to a crime scene are directed to the command post, where they can receive a briefing of the situation. Many jurisdictions at large, newsworthy crime scenes, also rope off a special news media area, where reporters can set up their cameras and other equipment close to the crime scene, but not close enough to interfere in it. At these large, newsworthy crime scenes, the police department's public information officer usually handles releases of information to the news media, while at small murder scenes one of the detectives will often talk to them.

Dealing with the news media is a crucial part of any murder investigation. The news media can be extremely helpful or extremely damaging to a murder investigation depending on how the homicide detectives deal with them. The most important aspect of dealing with the news media is that detectives must be open and honest with them. However, this doesn't mean telling them everything. Some circumstances of a murder cannot or should not be released for a number of reasons. Some information may be very personal to the victim or the victim's family, and detectives may want to withhold some information so that suspects will not know how much the police know. In addition, homicide detectives may also withhold some information about a murder so that they can be certain that a person confessing to the crime really is the murderer (on high-profile cases with lots of news media interest, many times emotionally disturbed people will try to falsely confess to being the murderer). Still, the news media must be informed of the major facts of a murder investigation or otherwise they will obtain and then print or broadcast information gotten from much-less-reliable sources, which can occasionally be damaging to the case. A friendly, open relationship with the news media, with the understanding that some information cannot be released, works to the advantage of both sides.

Once the responding uniformed officers have secured the murder scene, their next responsibility is to locate, detain, and separate any witnesses to the crime. It is important to do this as soon as possible because witnesses, for a number of reasons, often don't want to stay around. They may not want to become involved, they may know who the murderer is and not want to have to tell the police, or the police may want them for other crimes. In addition, occasionally a person who actually had a hand in the murder may appear to the first-arriving police officers to be just a witness, and he or she certainly does not want to stay around. It is also important not just to detain but also separate the witnesses so that each person's story is just that: his or her version of what happened without the contamination of hearing what other people say they saw happen. Many people who aren't certain of what they saw will become certain if they hear it from another person, and especially if they hear it from several people. In addition, individuals can change their minds about what they saw if they hear a different version from several other people. Separating witnesses can also stop collusion between witnesses who may want to help the murderer by telling the police the exact same story.

It is also important for police officers to identify any family members of the victim who happen to be on the scene. While they may often be suspects or have information about the crime, they will also often be distraught and perhaps even hysterical. These individuals must be identified because they have been known to charge into the murder scene and grab and hug the body. While understandable, doing this can destroy vital evidence. Most police departments use chaplains, who have been trained in assisting both the family members and homicide detectives, to take charge of any family members at the scene who are not suspects.

When he or she arrives at the murder scene, the lead homicide detective (the detective who has the overall responsibility for the murder investigation, though he or she will be assisted by other detectives who may handle other parts of the investigation, such as witness interviews, neighborhood canvass, or obtaining information at the hospital) will usually first talk with the initial responding uniformed police officer to find out what the police know so far. With this information, the lead detective can then decide what other resources, such as additional lighting, crime lab specialists, more uniformed officers for crowd control, aerial photography of the area, and so on, will be needed in order to properly process the crime scene. Occasionally, part or the entire crime scene may be under water, and the lead detective will need to request the assistance of a scuba team and perhaps sidescan sonar or underwater cameras.

The initial responding uniformed police officer will have been taking notes since his or her arrival at the murder scene, documenting such vital information as the condition of the crime scene upon arrival, any alterations of the crime scene (such as the intrusion of medical personnel attempting to treat the victim, family members who found the body, etc.), and any transient evidence (such as smells, smoke, etc.). The initial responding officer will also have made a list of the suspects and witnesses being detained. The officer, of course, shares these notes with the lead detective.

As stated above, it is vital that the lead detective be made aware of any alterations to the crime scene. Along with the intrusion of medical personnel or family members, was any piece of evidence picked up and/or moved for any reason? Were any lights turned on during the security search of the scene? Did the person who found the body touch or move it in any way? All of these things can possibly change the interpretation of evidence. This is why it is important to have a crime scene photographed as soon as possible, and preferably before any more people, other than those who are absolutely necessary, have entered it.

Just as important as getting all of this information, though, the lead detective must also decide whether a search warrant is needed to properly process the crime scene. Although search warrants aren't needed for murders that take place on public streets, anytime detectives must enter a vehicle or building where people have an expectation of privacy, obtaining a search warrant is a good idea. While the courts have ruled that police officers can make warrantless entries into buildings under exigent circumstances, such as to rescue crime victims, to search for armed criminals, while in hot pursuit, and to prevent evidence from being destroyed, the U.S. Supreme Court in *Mincey v. Arizona* stated that a homicide crime scene in and of itself did not constitute an exigent circumstance.[11] The Supreme Court has also held that all searches without a warrant are presumed to be unreasonable; and therefore, when making warrantless searches, the burden falls onto the state to show that exigent circumstances did exist and that the search was reasonable.[12] Obtaining a search warrant is not that complicated or difficult, and most homicide detectives will usually obtain one if there is any question at all about their right to enter and search a building or vehicle.

Once this has been taken care of, the lead homicide detective then takes a preliminary tour of the crime scene, being careful not to disturb anything, but also noting important pieces of evidence. Usually, small brightly colored and numbered cones are placed by each important piece of evidence. This makes locating the evidence easier and prevents inadvertently kicking or stepping on it. Because of the possibility of pathogens, everyone inside the crime scene usually wears, at a minimum, latex gloves. Other crime scenes, depending on their nature, can demand more stringent health protection.

The lead homicide detective, during the initial walkthrough, looks for possible entry and exit points of the suspect, including any forced entries, as well as evidence of the suspect's mode of travel to and from the crime scene. During the initial walkthrough, the lead detective additionally tries to reconstruct mentally what has happened, and notes any evidence that is fragile or likely to disappear if not processed immediately, such as fingerprints on objects that may be touched or brushed against, footprints in light dust, or certain recognizable smells. The detective also assesses the size of the crime scene and expands it if necessary and possible. In addition, the detective notes and corrects any threats to crime scene integrity, such as areas without crime scene tape or streets that need to be blocked by cars or barricades. In the event there are two or more crime scenes, the lead homicide detective assigns detectives to handle the other crime scenes and then remains in contact with them.

During the initial walkthrough, the lead homicide detective develops theories about what happened and who likely did it, but never comes to any conclusions at this point because new evidence can often radically change a case. With each additional piece of evidence found at a crime scene, old theories can quickly be eliminated and replaced by new theories. It has been discovered that detectives who draw conclusions rather than develop theories are much more likely to overlook or ignore evidence that doesn't fit the conclusions. Good homicide detectives doubt and question even what appears to be definitive and damning evidence until the investigation is complete.

In addition to not reaching conclusions, however, good homicide detectives also never assume anything at a crime scene, because things are not always as they appear. For example, while at a homicide seminar recently I saw a security videotape of the abduction of a young female employee from a convenience store. The police later found the woman raped and murdered. Because the counter and the area behind it appeared untouched, the lead homicide detective at first theorized that for some reason the woman had come out from behind the counter and been abducted from the middle of the store, where a considerable number of things had been knocked over. This, however, wasn't what happened. The security videotape showed the abductor reaching across the counter and grabbing the woman, pulling her over and across the counter. However, because the woman was so small and slim, she didn't disturb anything at all on the counter, including numerous small cardboard displays sitting there. Apparently, the act of grabbing and pulling her over the counter had caught her by surprise and the woman didn't begin violently struggling until dragged to the middle of the store, where the overturned items were found.

During the initial walkthrough, while the detective is developing theories, he or she can also make a mental "shopping list" of the evidence that needs to be looked for. As more facts surface, and theories change, items can be added to or deleted from this list.

However, during the initial walkthrough, the lead detective must also be alert to signs that the scene has been staged to appear to be something it really isn't. For example, occasionally murderers will try to make it appear as though the victim committed suicide or died accidentally. In these cases, though, the body condition or position, the appearance of the wounds, and the location of various pieces of evidence will often not be consistent with a suicide or accident. For example, a body that is staged to look like a suicide will often not have wounds consistent with a suicide. As we will talk about in the next chapter, close contact wounds, the type of most suicides, are readily identifiable and usually not present in staged crime scenes.

In a recent case involving the accidental death of a limousine driver at the home of former NBA star Jayson Williams, for example, witnesses claimed that Williams attempted to stage the scene to make the incident appear to be a suicide, including wiping fingerprints off of the weapon and attempting to put the victim's fingerprints on it. Apparently, the gun had gone off accidentally when Williams was showing it to some friends at his house, striking and killing the limousine driver. But the staging didn't fool the police.

New Jersey State Trooper Thomas Muehleisen testified at Williams' trial that when he examined the body he knew it really wasn't a suicide. "It's obvious it wasn't a contact wound," the trooper told the court.[13]

On April 30, 2004, a jury convicted Williams on four counts involving his attempt to cover up his involvement in the shooting. The jury, however, could not reach a verdict on the charge of reckless manslaughter, and the prosecutor has decided to retry Williams on that charge.

Because of the possibility of this staging, in most jurisdictions all suicides and accidental deaths are investigated as homicides until proven otherwise. Usually, though, genuine accidents and suicides are readily apparent and easily distinguished from homicides.

Once the initial walkthrough is completed, providing the victim hasn't been taken to the hospital, the detective then examines the body, but without touching or moving it. If the victim has been transported to a hospital, the lead homicide detective will usually send another detective to the hospital to gather all of the evidence there, including any statements from family members or witnesses who accompanied the victim, bullets recovered, the victim's clothing, and so on. While I will discuss in the next chapter all of the clues that can come from a murder victim's body, a homicide detective can learn much about the crime just from what is visible on or near the body. An experienced homicide detective knows that the more contact the suspect and victim had during the murder, the more evidence there will be.

The homicide detective will first note the body's position. For example, bodies facedown with their heels up and elbows raised usually suggest being dragged to the final location. Body position will also often tell what happened just before the murder: were the victims fleeing, fighting, or defending themselves, or were they apparently unaware that a murder was about to occur?

According to Dr. Jay Dix, a medical examiner in Missouri, "As a rule, the more twisted the position, the more sudden the death."[14]

The investigator will also check the body for any defensive wounds on the hands, arms, and feet. These are wounds the victim sustained while attempting to ward off the attack. Often, the crime scene around the body will also show evidence of a struggle if there was one, such as overturned furniture, broken items, or moved throw rugs.

The detective additionally looks at the victim's clothing. Has someone possibly re-dressed the victim? Is the victim's clothing torn or bloody? Are there rolls, folds, or marks that show the victim has been dragged? If the victim is wearing socks but no shoes, are they clean or dirty on the soles? Also, are the victim's glasses on and straight when the violence of the murder shows they shouldn't be? This would indicate that someone has altered the original condition of the body.

Naturally, the detective will look for any obvious wounds that may have caused the death. Many times it is apparent (though never certain) what killed a murder victim, and using this information, homicide detectives then know what kind of weapon and evidence to look for. Also, is the victim missing hair or teeth? These should be looked for at the crime scene or perhaps on a suspect.

While I will discuss the importance of blood and blood spatter patterns in the chapter on evidence of murder, the homicide detective notes the presence of any blood, how much, which way it has spattered, and whether any of it could be someone's other than the victim's. Often, particularly in stabbing and slashing murders, the attacker will be cut by the wild swings of the murder weapon and consequently leave some of his or her own blood behind in addition to the victim's.

But just as important as where there is blood is where there isn't any, but should be. This can mean that something stopped the blood spatter, such as a suspect, and this also means that the homicide detectives should check all suspects for the victim's blood. Additionally, the presence of any items that should have interrupted a blood spatter pattern, but don't have any blood on them, means that they were likely moved there after the murder. Finally, finding blood on the bottoms of a victim's feet usually means that he or she ran or walked for a bit after being attacked.

However, large amounts of blood do not necessarily mean murder. People often fall when they are dying naturally and will hit their heads and bleed profusely. In addition, people can die a number of ways naturally that bring about large-scale bleeding. Chronic alcoholics, for example, often bleed excessively from cirrhosis of the liver, which backs up the blood. We had a case several years ago in which a man with lung cancer coughed so hard he ruptured a blood vessel in his throat. When we found him, there was so much blood flow around his face and head that we initially mistook him for a murder victim.

For actual murder victims, however, blood flow patterns can be very important. Any gaping wounds with no blood flow around the body usually mean that the body has been moved. Also, has the blood around the victim dried and clotted? This can refute statements from a suspect that the event just occurred.

If the lead homicide detective believes there should be blood somewhere in the crime scene, but can't find any visible traces because the suspect has attempted to clean up the scene, the detective may have the crime lab technicians use luminol. This chemical can detect blood that has been diluted up to 10,000 times. Consequently, it can be very helpful in finding blood at a crime scene where the perpetrator has used soap and water and cleaned up all visible signs of the crime. Luminol, when sprayed as a fine mist, reacts with blood and causes it to glow a light blue color. This can only be seen in darkness and may last for only a few minutes. Therefore, the crime lab technician using luminol usually has someone standing by with a camera ready to take photographs of the blood traces.

Finding trace amounts of other bodily fluids can also be crucial to solving a murder. A 2003 report by the U.S. Department of Justice tells about the development at Sandia National Laboratories of a device called the criminalistics light-imaging unit (CLU).[15] This device uses various colors of light to examine evidence. It can be very useful when searching a crime scene for trace evidence not visible to the eye. Recently, using a CLU, investigators were able to detect three tiny samples of semen on a murder victim's body that had not been detectable using a conventional blue light detector and goggles. CLU is also useful for detecting trace amounts of blood and hard-to-find fingerprints.

Along with all of the above, when initially viewing the body, homicide detectives always check for the body's lividity. The law of gravity is universal, and so, after death, when the blood stops flowing because the heart has stopped, a person's blood will be pulled by gravity to the lowest part of the body, discoloring the skin. This purplish discoloration, which is called lividity, will become noticeable usually in one to two hours, and will be completely settled and fixed in about eight hours. However, these times are only approximate because a number of variables, such as temperature, blood pressure, and body heat, can alter them. Finding lividity on the upper surfaces of a murder victim's body, however, means that the body has been moved after death. Being able to prove movement after death can often help to refute statements given by suspects.

In addition to lividity, homicide detectives also look for any signs of rigor mortis. Soon after death the body begins to stiffen. While the body stiffens at an equal rate all over, it can often be detected first in the jaw area because the muscles there are so small. While air temperature, body weight, clothing worn, and other variables can affect the time, under normal conditions a body will become fully rigid at around twelve hours after death and will stay this way for approximately twenty-four to thirty-six hours, after which the stiffness will disappear. Because of all the variables that can affect the onset of rigor mortis, these times are only approximate, but still they can be used in conjunction with other evidence to tell a homicide detective something about the crime. For example, if rigor mortis is present, it must fit the position the body was found in or the detective will know that the body was moved twelve to thirty-six hours after death. I recall a case we had in which a jogger found the body of a murder victim lying in the middle of a road. When I saw the body I knew the victim had been killed elsewhere and dumped in the road. While the young murder victim lay on his back, he had one hand raised straight up in front of him.

Homicide detectives also look for any vomit when examining the body, which can mean many things, such as an overdose of drugs or alcohol, or various illnesses. Detectives additionally check for froth around the nose and mouth, which can also mean many things, such as drowning, sudden infant death syndrome (SIDS), or heart failure.

Once the preliminary look around the crime scene has been completed, the lead detective then has photographs and usually a video made of the crime scene, if someone hasn't already done it. This is important in order to document what the scene looked like before being processed. All of the photos taken are recorded in a log so that the lead detective can be certain everything of importance has been photographed. Along with photos of the crime scene, which include all rooms in a house, whether connected to the crime or not, photos are also taken of the closest street signs, the entry into the crime scene, street addresses, and any other photos that can ground the crime scene to a specific location.

Homicide detectives always have close-up photos taken of the body and any obvious evidence. It is important to photograph every piece of evidence before moving or processing it, because at the trial, the location and appearance of evidence at the crime scene can be crucial to a conviction. Consequently, other than the exceptions given earlier, there is never any reason to move evidence before it has been properly photographed. Then, after being photographed, if any additional evidence, such as finger-prints, fibers, or bodily fluids, needs to be recovered from the original piece of evidence, a crime lab technician either does it at the scene or securely bags and marks the evidence for later processing. In addition, it is important to photograph and examine not just the body, but also the area the body occupied before being moved. Is there blood or other evidence there?

Film and videotapes, homicide detectives find, are cheap compared to the cost of not recording or taking a photo of something that could prove crucial later. Consequently, a detective cannot have too many photographs taken or too much videotaping done of a crime scene. Fortunately, many police departments are now using digital cameras, which allow the photos taken to be viewed at the scene to be certain they came out and include everything that needs to be included.

Whenever a witness tells the police that he or she stood in a certain spot and saw something important in the investigation, a photograph is taken from this point of view in order to confirm or refute that what the witness said could be true. It can also be helpful to take photographs of the crowd that inevitably gathers at any murder scene. Often the murderer will be there, standing back in the crowd, attempting to find out how much the police know. These photos of the crowd can also help counter any alibi claims that suspects at the scene may later try to establish.

In addition to photographs and video, the lead homicide detective will also make a sketch of the murder scene. A sketch includes only the important items of a crime scene and therefore doesn't contain the clutter that many crime scene photographs do. On the sketch the detective will note the placement of key elements of the case, including the location of the body, the location of evidence, the entry and exit points to the scene, and any important structures. Careful measurements are taken of the crime scene that will then be included on the sketch. Distances in photographs can often appear distorted depending on how the pictures were taken, and so the sketch will be used to document these.

During the investigation at the crime scene, the lead homicide detective also writes or dictates into a tape recorder a narrative of the investigation. This can be invaluable later when the detective writes his or her report of the murder. This narrative includes such things as the case number or other identifier, the date and time, location of the murder scene, the weather, the lighting, the victim's name if known, witnesses identified, all evidence found, and the names of other officers and specialists who assisted in the investigation.

At murder scenes where a body is still present, a deputy coroner or medical examiner will be called and he or she will be the one to pronounce the person dead. A medical examiner is a physician who has usually specialized in pathology, whereas a deputy coroner works for the county coroner, who is an elected official. This person may or may not have extensive medical experience, though in most large jurisdictions he or she does receive considerable training.

"Training for medicolegal investigators is paramount to a thorough, consistent, and professional investigation," Marion County (Indiana) Coroner John P. McGoff, an emergency room physician, told me. "Two letters describe how a botched crime scene investigation can let a killer go free: O. J."[16]

Whichever one of these is called to the scene, this official is the one who moves and examines the body, with the homicide detectives assisting. The deputy coroner or medical examiner will inspect the body for obvious injuries, take and secure any property the body has on it, and assist the homicide detectives in preserving any evidence that could be important. For example, if the lead homicide detective believes that possibly important evidence may be on the victim's hands or feet, such as blood, gunpowder, or skin under the fingernails, the deputy coroner or medical examiner will put protective bags over them. The deputy coroner or medical examiner will also remove any fragile items of evidence that might be lost when transporting the body, such as hairs, fibers, or bodily fluids on open surfaces. If the identity of the victim is not known, the deputy coroner or medical examiner may take a thumbprint from the victim for identification purposes. The body is then placed in a plastic body bag.

Verifying the identity of a murder victim is extremely important, not just because it can be very traumatic for family members to discover from watching the news that a loved one has been murdered, but knowing the identity of a murder victim is a starting point for the homicide detectives. From this, the detectives can begin to uncover a motive for the murder, find out the victim's movements just before the murder, who the victim's friends and acquaintances are, who last saw the victim alive, and who might want to kill the victim.

If the victim's fingerprints are not on file, if no one at the crime scene knows his or her identity, and if the body carries no identification (a much more common experience than most would suppose), the police will usually take a picture of the victim's face if not disfigured and use it for identification purposes, occasionally putting it or a representation of it on the news. If these methods don't work, detectives can use dental records, x-rays to look for old injuries or operations, scars, tattoos, deformities, birthmarks, and even a DNA comparison. Sadly, however, every year police departments across the United States have murder victims who are never identified.

When, as occasionally happens, only a skeleton remains of the victim, a number of police departments have had luck in having a forensic anthropologist build a clay model of what the victim's face likely looked like, using age-range averages for the thickness of various parts of the face. We had a case here in Indianapolis in which a murder victim who had been set on fire sat unidentified for over a year. After a forensic anthropologist built a clay model of his face and we distributed pictures of it to the press, family members recognized him. Apparently, the man had been unstable and would often stay away for long periods of time, and so family members hadn't been overly concerned about his absence.

After the body has been examined at the crime scene and any evidence recovered or protected, the deputy coroner or medical examiner will then have the body transported to the morgue or some other similar facility. In most instances an autopsy, which we will discuss in the next chapter, will be performed on the body. An immense amount of information can be obtained from an autopsy.

While it is important to note and collect any evidence on the body of a murder victim, it is just as important to examine what is left after the body is removed. Often, homicide detectives will find that the victim has been lying on something important to the case. The discovery of a gun under a victim, for example, can change the investigation from one of a murder to perhaps a suicide or self-defense. Other evidence left after a body is moved can include anything that fell off of the victim when he or she collapsed to the ground, such as fibers or hairs.

There are three ways to solve and prove a murder. Two of these, witness statements and confessions, require corroboration to be valid. The third way, physical evidence, doesn't need corroboration. Physical evidence speaks for itself. Often, a single piece of physical evidence can be the key that convicts a murderer.

"Normally, when you search for something, it is a particular item that is missing, but not so at a crime scene," Michael Taylor, a former police officer and now crime scene technician, told me. "Crime scenes produce 'found items' that need to be investigated for evidentiary value. Thus, you never know what is evidence, and consequently a thorough crime scene search is paramount."[17]

After the body is removed, an extremely thorough search must be made of the murder scene in order to recover not just the obvious physical evidence, but also that evidence that can be hard to find or perhaps even invisible to the naked eye. Naturally, the lead homicide detective will have the most fragile and transient pieces of evidence photographed and processed first. At any murder scene, an evidence log must be maintained. In this log, every piece of physical evidence is recorded, including information on what it is, who found it, and where. While I will discuss at length in a later chapter what this physical evidence is and how it is recovered, no crime scene can be released until the detective is certain that every bit of physical evidence, no matter how small, has been found and recovered.

How does a detective do this? He or she does it by conducting a methodical search of the crime scene, paying particular attention to possible entry and exit points, where perpetrators many times drop or throw away valuable evidence. Often also, witness statements at the crime scene can guide the detective in the search for evidence. Witnesses are often able to tell the detective what to look for and where it might be. Depending on the size of the crime scene, various methods can be used to search it, including breaking the murder scene into grids and strips, spiraling outward from the body, or using a point-to-point search, in which the detective moves from one piece of evidence to another.

When vehicles are evidence, before searching them homicide detectives note whether there is a key in the vehicle, what position the key is in, the odometer reading, the position of the gear shift, how much fuel is in the vehicle's tank, whether lights are on or off, the vehicle's license number, and the VIN (vehicle identification number, located on the dash and visible through the driver's side windshield). In searching homes, detectives will first note whether the lights were on or off, windows and doors open or closed, windows and doors locked or unlocked, the thermostat reading, newspaper and mail collected or not, and any other conditions that might tell when the murder possibly occurred.

In crime scenes that involve wooded or high-weed areas, an entrance and exit to the crime scene must be designated, as well as a pathway through it. Otherwise it becomes too easy to step on evidence that may be hidden by weeds or leaves. Many times in such a crime scene, metal detectors must be used in order to find metallic evidence that might be hidden in the leaves or high weeds.

Along with looking in the obvious places for physical evidence, homicide detectives must also consider all of the less-than-obvious places a murderer might have tried to hide evidence, for example, down sewers, in car wheel wells, in bushes, under leaves, and so on. There was a murder case in Wyoming in which the murderer hid a young child's body in a trash Dumpster. However, rather than just throwing the body in the Dumpster, he put it inside of a canvas bag, which he then put inside of a regular plastic trash bag. When the police searched the Dumpster they didn't see a body, only trash bags, and overlooked the possibility that the victim might be inside.

Homicide detectives find that searching through the trash at a crime scene, as in the case above, can occasionally turn up valuable clues. According to an article in *Law Enforcement Technology*, "While conducting 'Trashology' workshops, [the instructors] found that students didn't go far enough to find evidence. This was especially true if evidence was hidden in something really nasty, like a dirty diaper, moldy sandwich, or used tissue. 'The nastier the trash, the more likely that's where the actual evidence will be, because that's where people think you would be least likely to look,'" says one of the instructors in the article.[18]

Experienced homicide investigators, when looking for physical evidence, also always have the sink traps examined in the event the murderer has tried to clean up the scene. Blood, hair, and the like will often end up in the sink trap.

Homicide detectives, when searching murder scenes, particularly look for anything that appears out of place. This can often help point them toward the murderer, and may include such things as items overturned, items obviously moved, and items that don't appear to belong to the victim, such as cigarette butts or bodily fluids. Detectives are additionally taught to remember that crime scenes are three-dimensional. Murderers have often been known to throw valuable evidence up onto roofs when leaving crime scenes.

Finally, in addition to all of the above, when looking for physical evidence, homicide detectives always search the crime scene for bullet holes, which can tell them the type of weapon used and the trajectory of the bullet. While I will discuss bullet trajectory in the chapter on evidence of murder, finding bullet holes can be vital to a murder case because they can tell homicide detectives the likely spot from where the murder weapon was fired.

In addition to recovering physical evidence, often samples of the soil around crime scenes will also be collected. This can become important later if a suspect, who claims to have never been in the area of the murder, has matching soil on his or her shoes or clothing. Detectives likewise collect samples of other items that might turn up on a suspect, such as carpet fiber, animal hair, and sometimes even dust that is specific to the area.

Of course, just as important as the evidence found at a murder scene is what isn't found at the scene. Is the victim's wallet or purse missing? Has the victim's car disappeared? Is there a white area on the victim's wrist but no watch? The police have found that occasionally murderers will take a souvenir of their crime. Therefore, it is important for homicide detectives to consult with family members of the victim in order to ascertain what property of the victim may be missing. Something as small as the charm from a charm bracelet can connect a suspect to a murder.

Another important part of processing a crime scene is the neighborhood canvass. This consists of detectives knocking on the doors of every apartment or house within a certain radius of the crime scene and asking the people there whether they heard or saw anything connected with the murder. How big the canvass is depends on the peculiarities of the murder. A long chase before the actual murder, for example, will require a larger canvass. Quite often during a canvass, detectives will find people who have seen or heard something that they didn't realize the significance of at the time, or they will find people who know the victim and can give the police additional information about him or her. The canvass is often repeated the next day and a week to a month afterward in order to catch the people who weren't at home when the first canvass was conducted. Often also, people don't want to talk to the police on the night of the murder because they fear they will be labeled as snitches, but they feel safer a week or a month later, when the excitement is over and the crowd is gone.

"A total and documented canvass is crucial, not just for witnesses but also for a victim profile," Detective David Hatch of the Las Vegas Police Department told me. "The initial canvass can locate eye witnesses and it can also locate witnesses who are unaware of the importance of what they saw prior to and after the crime."[19]

The final act at a murder scene is the crime scene debriefing. At this gathering, everyone involved in working the crime scene discusses what was found and what he or she personally did. During the crime scene investigation, the lead homicide detective designated someone to keep a list of every person who entered the crime scene and a chronology of the crime scene activities. These are reviewed during the debriefing. Consequently, the debriefing can be invaluable in determining whether anything has been forgotten or overlooked. Many lead detectives, following the debriefing, will take one last look around the crime scene to be absolutely certain that nothing has been missed or left behind. In addition, lead detectives also often have photographs taken of the crime scene just before leaving, in order to counter any possible defense claims that evidence was missed or purposely ignored. This action also can refute any claims of the property owner that the police damaged property they actually didn't.

The length of time homicide detectives spend at a murder scene naturally depends on the size of the crime scene and the complexity of the crime. This can run from a few hours to a day or longer if very large areas are involved. The detectives must stay at the crime scene until every bit of evidence has been found, recorded, recovered, and sent in for analysis. In many locales it often is impossible to come back and re-work a crime scene once the barriers have been taken down. Residents will many times clean up the area, evidence can be inadvertently destroyed or carried away, and the value of anything found afterward naturally decreases dramatically.

Upon finishing with the crime scene, however, the lead homicide detective isn't even close to being finished with the case. He or she then moves on to the next most valuable source of evidence about a murder: the body.

CHAPTER 3

The Body

After searching and processing the scene of fifty-five-year-old Ted Binion's death, the police at first believed that the former Las Vegas casino operator had died from simply an accidental overdose of heroin and Xanax. Found lying on a sleeping bag in the den of his Las Vegas mansion on September 17, 1998, Binion had been well known among Nevada's gambling elite as a man with a serious drug addiction. In 1997, the Nevada Gaming Commission had suspended his gambling license because of it. As a result, the management of Binion's Horseshoe Casino in downtown Las Vegas was turned over to Binion's sister, Becky Behnan. Many of the people who knew Ted Binion were not surprised at all by his death, but simply figured that his lifestyle had finally caught up with him.

"He had all the money anyone could want," said Nevada Gaming Commission member Augie Gurrola, "and for some reason it just didn't seem to be enough."[1]

The Las Vegas police at first agreed that Binion's death appeared to be an unfortunate and accidental result of his dependence on drugs. "At first glance it appears accidental and not an intentional act," said Las Vegas police sergeant Jim Young. "While it's suspicious, it's not suspicious to the point where we're talking about criminal activity."[2]

Binion had left no note, and interviews with his family members didn't indicate that he had talked about suicide or made any plans for it. Also, the home showed no signs of a break-in, so the police at first ruled out both suicide and murder, and settled on an accidental overdose as the cause of death.

However, a closer examination by a pathologist hired and brought in by the Binion family—who, unlike the police, hadn't ruled out murder—told a different story. Dr. Michael Baden, a former medical examiner in New York City who had conducted over 20,000 autopsies, found abrasions on Binion's wrists that appeared to have been caused by handcuffs. In addition, he determined that a red mark found on Binion's mouth had likely come from pressure applied there by a hand or some other object. Also, he discovered several small, round, red marks on Binion's chest that he believed had been caused by the buttons on his shirt being violently pressed into his chest. All of this evidence made Dr. Baden conclude that Binion had been "burked," which is slang for a method of suffocation that killers often believe won't be recognized as a murder, but will appear instead as a natural death. Dr. Baden stated it was his belief that someone had covered Binion's nose and mouth and then applied heavy pressure on his chest until he suffocated to death.

The Binion family, in addition to hiring Dr. Baden, also hired private detective Tom Dillard, a former police homicide detective. Dillard became instrumental in helping the Las Vegas police collect the vital evidence needed to show that Binion's death was not accidental, but indeed a murder.

On June 24, 1999, nine months after the murder, the police arrested Sandra Murphy, a former topless dancer who had been Binion's girlfriend at the time of his death, and Rick Tabish, a convicted drug dealer and friend of Binion's. During their investigation, the police discovered that Murphy and Tabish were lovers, and very possibly had been lovers when Binion was murdered. The police charged both of them with murder and robbery. Interestingly, Tabish had already been arrested for another crime involving Binion. The police had arrested Tabish, along with two other men, less than forty-eight hours after Binion's death when the police caught them attempting to truck away twenty-three tons of silver that Binion had stored in an underground vault near Pahrump, Nevada, about fifty miles west of Las Vegas.

The police, during their investigation of Binion's death, which had now become a murder investigation, took a statement from Jason Lee Frazier in February 2000. Frazier told them that he had been involved in a plot to pay several individuals to provide an alibi for Tabish during the time of Binion's death. Along with this, in March 2000, Tabish's brother-in-law told the police that Tabish had given him a collection of silver coins to repay a loan he'd made to him. The police determined that the coins had been stolen from the Binion estate. "If I was caught with the silver, it wouldn't look good," Tabish reportedly told his brother-in-law.[3]

Eventually, Murphy made bail, thanks to $300,000 put up for her by a Las Vegas businessman. Although placed on home detention by the court, Murphy violated it several times to go shopping or to dinner with friends. One time she even spray-painted the ankle alarm bracelet she wore (which alerts the authorities when someone on home detention leaves the house) to match a dress she wore to court.

At the trial for Ted Binion's murder, which began on March 25, 2000, the prosecution presented evidence that Murphy had told her manicurist that Binion would die soon from a drug overdose and that when it happened she and her new boyfriend would get the silver Binion had hidden in the desert. The Binion gardener also testified at the trial and said that the blinds at the Binion mansion had been shut the day Binion died. He told the court that in all the years he had worked there, he had never seen them shut. Police believe it was the gardener's attempt to peek through the blinds that made the murderers decide to suffocate Binion rather than to wait and let him die of the overdose. Following this testimony, the Binion maid also testified that Murphy had inexplicably told her not to come to work the day Binion died.

Interestingly, along with Dr. Baden's testimony about his belief that Binion had been "burked," the local medical examiner also testified, saying that he believed Binion had been forced to take the lethal amount of drugs that were found in his body. Finally, Binion's attorney, James Brown, told the court that the day before his death Binion called him and said, "Take Sandy out of the will if she doesn't kill me tonight. If I'm dead, you'll know what happened."[4]

At the conclusion of the testimony, the jury took eight hours to discuss and review the case before returning with a finding, on May 19, 2000, that Murphy and Tabish were guilty on all counts. A number of people watching the trial had felt certain that Murphy and Tabish would be acquitted.

The jury felt different, however. Probably the most critical evidence presented, according to the jury foreman, was Dr. Baden's testimony, in which he explained about the autopsy results that showed Binion had been suffocated. "Doctor Baden was more believable than anyone else," the jury foreman said.[5]

In addition to the murder charges, the jury also found Tabish guilty on five counts involving an extortion plot in 1998. In this case, Tabish had reportedly held a man against his will and tortured him in an unsuccessful attempt to get the man to sign documents that would allow Tabish to control his business. Both prosecutors and the police believed that the Binion murder was planned because Tabish needed cash in order to buy out the business.

On May 24, 2000, the judge in the case sentenced Murphy to life imprisonment with the possibility of parole, which under Nevada law meant that Murphy could apply for parole in twenty years. Tabish received the same sentence for the Binion murder, but then he also received additional prison time for his convictions in the failed extortion plot.

However, on July 14, 2003, the Supreme Court of Nevada overturned their murder convictions and ordered a new trial for Tabish and Murphy. The Supreme Court found that the trial judge had erred in allowing Tabish to be tried for the extortion plot and Binion murder at the same time, since they weren't connected. The Supreme Court felt that doing this might have prejudiced the jury against both Tabish and Murphy. But the prosecution, as stated above, felt that the crimes were connected since it believed Tabish committed the Binion murder in order to obtain enough money to buy control of the business he had attempted to extort. The Supreme Court also found that the trial judge had erred in not instructing the jury on how much weight they should give to attorney James Brown's testimony concerning his conversation with Binion the day before he died.

Following the Nevada Supreme Court decision, a local court set Murphy's bail at $300,000, which a Las Vegas businessman again put up for her. The court denied bail for Tabish, however, because the Supreme Court, though ordering a new trial on the Binion murder charges, had allowed his extortion conviction to stand. The Las Vegas prosecutor's office stated that it believed it would have no problem convicting the pair of Binion's murder again in its new trial.

The human body is an astounding organism. It can be amazingly resilient and able to survive unbelievably severe injury, yet occasionally it can also die from what appears to be, from visual inspection, only minor injury. A dead human body, however, can usually tell a homicide detective volumes about what happened to cause its death.

Homicide detectives generally want to know two things immediately about a dead body they are called to investigate: the cause of death and the manner of death. The cause of death can be divided into two parts: the proximate cause, or the initial event that led to the death; and the immediate cause, or the last thing to happen to the body just before death. For example, a proximate cause of death could be a stab wound, but the immediate cause of death could be a loss of blood or even an infection from the stab wound that killed the victim days, weeks, or months later.

Manner of death can usually be classified into one of five categories: natural, homicide, suicide, accidental, or undetermined. While the first four categories are self-explanatory, the final category covers deaths for which the pathologist can find no apparent cause. This happens particularly when a body is badly decomposed or is simply skeletal remains. It can also occasionally occur when a person is found dead but an autopsy reveals no apparent cause for the death.

Occasionally, there can be a crossover between the manners of death. For example, if a person dies of a heart attack, the death is usually considered natural; but it can become a homicide if the heart attack was brought on by a crime, for example, through the victim being threatened with a weapon. *A Guide for Manner of Death Classification* by the National Association of Medical Examiners states, "Deaths resulting from fear/fright induced by verbal assault, threats of physical harm, or through acts/aggression intended to instill fear or fright may be classified as homicide if there is a close temporal relationship between the incident and death."[6]

Another important question that homicide detectives often want answered quickly about murder victims, usually at the crime scene, is, when did the victim die? Knowing this can explain many things about a crime scene, can help identify suspects, and, at the same time, can also help eliminate suspects. However, determining exactly when a person died is never as easy or as exact as it appears to be in books and movies. Unless the police have eyewitnesses who saw the murder and can give the authorities the exact time, the time of death will usually be only an estimate.

According to forensic expert Bernard Knight, "Any estimate of the time of death based solely on physical evidence and which does not have a variance of at least one half hour in either direction (an interval of at least one hour) should be viewed as suspect and not trusted."[7] What this expert is saying is that while there are many methods for establishing a time of death, all of them are affected by so many variables that giving an exact time of death to the minute—absent eyewitness verification—is impossible.

However, fixing the time of death to the smallest possible time interval can be crucial to making a murder case because knowing the time of death can establish a person's opportunity to commit a murder. Knowing the time of death to the closest approximate time span can also help the police negate a suspect's alibi. Therefore, there are a number of methods and visual clues that a medical examiner or deputy coroner will use to establish an approximate time of death to the closest possible time span.

Soon after death, for example, a thin film forms over the eyes, which will usually appear cloudy in about three hours. Also, under most conditions, after about forty-eight hours bacterial action will often cause the skin of a dead person to turn a greenish hue, followed by a bloating caused by bacterial gas formation. As another measure of time of death, blood will usually dry in one half to four hours. There was a case in Florida, for example, in which a man claimed that his murdered wife had preceded him into their home by just a few minutes, yet her blood was dry when the police arrived only minutes after that.

The state of the body's rigor mortis can additionally be used as an estimate of the time of death. However, the onset and cessation of rigor mortis, like most measures of time of death, are affected by many variables. As stated in the last chapter, under ideal conditions, full rigor of a dead body usually takes ten to twelve hours, the body then remains stiff and rigid for twenty-four to thirty-six hours, and after this goes flaccid again.

Livor mortis, or lividity, which is a settling of the blood after death due to gravity, can also be used as a measure of the time of death. The discoloration of the skin due to this becomes apparent approximately one hour after death and becomes set or fixed in approximately eight hours. However, variables such as the air temperature can affect these times. Another method for estimating the time of death, this one used at the autopsy, is an examination of the stomach contents. For example, undigested breakfast food in the stomach suggests that the person likely died soon after breakfast.

The most common method used to determine how long a body has been dead is algor mortis, or body cooling, which medical examiners or deputy coroners determine by measuring the body's core temperature. They measure this temperature by inserting a thermometer either into the rectum or into the liver through an incision made in the chest wall. While under perfect conditions a body will lose 1.5 degrees Fahrenheit every hour until it reaches the surrounding air temperature, this average temperature loss can be affected by body size, type of clothing worn, humidity, movement of air, the surrounding air temperature, and whether or not the body was submerged in water.

For bodies that have been dead several days to several weeks or longer, determining a time of death can become much more challenging. One method, however, for estimating the time of death in these cases is examining the remains for insect larva. A dead human body very quickly becomes an attractive medium on which insects lay their eggs.

"The first witness to a death is usually a fly," said Mike Sarna, director of exhibits at the Peggy Notebaert Nature Museum, which in July 2004 opened an exhibit on crime scene insects. "Their sense of smell is so acute that they've been known to fly two miles to get to a fresh corpse."[8]

Scientists have found, however, that different types of insects, along with flies, are attracted to decaying bodies at different stages of decomposition, and that each insect type has a distinctive maturation time. Therefore, by identifying the type of insect infesting a human body and its state of maturation, a time of death can be estimated.

Since all of these methods, no matter how precisely done, eventually become only estimates of the time of death, homicide detectives use other investigative techniques to narrow the time span estimate. Homicide detectives do this by checking on such things as when the mail and newspaper were last picked up, the last time someone saw the victim alive, what clothes the victim wore (work clothes, pajamas, and so on), the victim's last use of e-mail or the telephone, whether the lights around the crime scene were on or off, whether appliances were turned on or off, or whether some task being done by the victim was only half completed.

Whenever a body has been buried or has lain somewhere for such a long time that the flesh has decomposed beyond the point of insect infestation, or has decomposed to only bones, homicide detectives may call for a forensic anthropologist. While in these cases a cause of death can occasionally be surmised from holes in the skull or severe damage to other bones, many times determining the cause of death can be extremely challenging or perhaps even impossible. However, in these cases forensic anthropologists can still usually determine the age range, sex, and race of the remains. Often a forensic anthropologist can also give the homicide detective a rough estimate as to how old the bones are. Also, the bones, particularly scattered bones, may not even be human, but of some animal. Again, a forensic anthropologist will be able to tell this.

To assist in the training of these forensic anthropologists, the University of Tennessee at Knoxville has established a unique facility named the Forensic Anthropology Center, or the "Body Farm," as most people at the university call it. This three-acre outdoor facility studies the various factors affecting the decomposition of human bodies. Using donated corpses, the Body Farm tests such things as the effects of various types of clothing on decomposition, and how much sun and shade increase and decrease decomposition. The Body Farm is also involved in improving estimates for the time of death, using such measurements as the intensity of volatile fatty acids and the ratios of amino acids in the major body tissues of decomposing bodies.

Additionally, the Body Farm at the University of Tennessee is also involved in developing methods for finding hidden graves, using machinery that can detect distinctive human decomposition odors. Already pursuing this end, however, a number of jurisdictions have dogs that are trained to locate human remains. Many of these dogs are so well trained they can distinguish between human and animal remains.

We had a case recently here in Indianapolis that demonstrated the ability of one of these highly trained canines. A woman on the West Side of Indianapolis let her two dogs out one morning, and when they returned a few hours later she found to her horror that one of the dogs carried a fresh human arm. She naturally called the police, and, though my detectives made a thorough search of the area, they couldn't find the body the arm had come from. However, just a few minutes of searching by a human remains detection dog turned up the body. A young girl, minus the arm chewed off by the dogs, lay hidden under some heavy underbrush less than a block away from the home of the woman who had called the police.

Once the homicide detective and medical examiner or deputy coroner have finished their investigation of the body at the crime scene, the remains of the murder victim are usually sent to the county morgue or some similar facility, where they are stored until the autopsy, a word that literally means "seeing for yourself." While people can watch movies or view depictions on the Internet of an autopsy, there is no way to show the reality of what it is like to attend one in person and actually witness the autopsy of a human body. Although I suppose it becomes possible after attending enough autopsies to distance oneself from what is happening, the first few times viewing one can be very challenging. Still, often information crucial to a homicide investigation can come only from an autopsy, and so consequently the homicide detective assigned to the case must attend it.

"I'm continually amazed at how much you can learn from the body of a murder victim," Marion County, Indiana Chief Deputy Coroner Frances Kelly told me. "As coroners, we are the last advocate to speak for the dead. The details and evidence that are on the body are the deceased's way of speaking to us."[9]

Witnessing my first autopsy took place, unfortunately, right after lunch. I found upon entering the autopsy room that someone had set a stick of incense to burning. Earlier that morning, they told me, they had done the autopsy of a man who had been found in an advanced state of decomposition. Regardless, I felt grateful to whoever had thought of doing this.

My first autopsy brought with it several surprises. I was amazed, even though the body had been dead for about eighteen hours, how much liquid blood there was, and how it still ran out of the bullet holes when the morgue attendant moved the body. Also, the tools the pathologist used, I found, were not the delicate instruments that a surgeon might use, but much sturdier devices meant to get the job done without too much worry about tissue damage or surface marks.

After my murder victim's body had been washed and dried, the pathologist took an hour or so measuring and photographing the bullet holes and checking with the x-rays taken earlier to determine where the one bullet still in him had ended up. Following this, the morgue attendant placed a block under the dead man's back to raise him up off of the metal table, and then the pathologist picked up a scalpel and made a large Y-shaped cut from the chest down to the groin. Continuing to wield the scalpel, the pathologist further cut loose the skin and fat and then spread the Y-shaped cut open. After this, the pathologist, using an electric saw, cut and lifted off a large, shield-shaped segment of the rib cage, exposing all of the internal organs of the chest.

Since my murder victim had been shot through the lung and had bled profusely internally, the pathologist used a metal cup to scoop the blood out of the chest cavity. She then poured the blood through a strainer in order to find the bullet that the x-rays had shown still sat in the victim's chest. When the pathologist finally recovered the bullet, she noted it in her report and began the chain of custody (a record of where the evidence came from, where it goes to, and who has access to it) for this piece of evidence, which would later become extremely valuable when we arrested the murderer still in possession of the firearm it had come from.

Along with evidence such as the bullet above, however, what else is a pathologist who performs an autopsy looking for? He or she is, of course, looking for the cause of death. But the pathologist is also looking for any other evidence on or in the body that will assist the homicide detectives in determining what happened, how it happened, when it happened, where it happened, and who caused it to happen.

Because of the importance of any evidence recovered, the pathologist or an assistant will photograph the autopsy throughout in order to document what is found. Before the autopsy begins, the pathologist measures the person's height and weight, and notes the general condition of the body. He or she also notes any tattoos, scars, or deformities. Usually the pathologist takes the person's fingerprints and, if any imprints of bare feet were found at the crime scene, will also take inked footprints.

In determining what has happened that caused the person to die, and how it happened, the pathologist examines the total exterior of the victim's body, looking for puncture wounds caused by bullets, knives, or needles. The pathologist also looks for blunt force injuries such as abrasions and bruises. He or she will additionally examine the body for defensive wounds, such as bruises on the arms received while attempting to block a blow, or cuts on the hands and fingers from grabbing and trying to stop a knife. The body from the first autopsy I attended had just such a defensive wound, a bullet hole through the hand, where he had raised his arms to cover his face when being shot at. The pathologist also looks for ligature marks on the neck and the wrists and ankles. When on the neck, these can show that the victim was possibly strangled, or forcibly restrained (by handcuffs, rope, and so on) if on the wrists and ankles. If it is believed that the victim was strangled, the pathologist will carefully inspect the neck. He or she will cut into and examine the bones in the throat to determine whether they are crushed or broken.

During the autopsy, the pathologist will often extract and send blood, hair, bile, urine, and occasionally the fluid from the eyes to a laboratory for toxicology studies to detect drugs or poison. In addition, the pathologist may take swab samples from the mouth, rectum, and sexual organs.

As stated above, most murder victims, prior to the autopsy, are x-rayed in order to find any bullets, bullet fragments, broken knife blades, and so on inside them. X-rays, however, can also show major internal injuries, such as bone fractures and punctured or torn organs.

The pathologist, though, pays particularly close attention to gunshot wounds. A close examination of these can often tell how close the gun was to the victim when fired. For example, if a murderer presses a gun up against a victim's skin before firing it, the wound will have burned or seared edges, and sometimes the area around the wound will be bright red from the carbon monoxide expelled by the gun. (Individuals who commit suicide using carbon monoxide are readily distinguishable by the bright red hue of their skin.) A gun barrel pressed against the skin before firing will also cause pressure that can rupture and tear the entrance wound and increase the internal damage the bullet does.

A bullet fired close to, but not directly in contact with, the skin will usually leave what is called stippling around the wound. These are small black dots around the wound that come from pieces of burning gunpowder embedded in the skin. The more sparse and spread the stippling is, the farther away the gun usually was. However, this is not an absolute because the longer the barrel of the gun is, the less stippling there will be since more of the gunpowder will be burned up before reaching the skin.

Knowing the approximate distance a person was shot from can be important to a homicide detective for a number of reasons. Besides telling the approximate locations of the victim and the perpetrator at the time of the murder, guns held close to the victim when fired will often have "blowback" on them, which is the blood and flesh of the victim blown back onto the gun. Using DNA analysis on this blowback, laboratory technicians can show that a firearm found by the police is the murder weapon.

Although the entrance and exit wounds made by a bullet are usually easy to distinguish—entrance wounds being round and smooth and exit wounds rough and jagged—this also is not an absolute. Entrance wounds can become distorted and jagged if, as talked about above, the murderer holds the gun tightly against a victim or if the entrance wound comes from a ricochet, while exit wounds can occasionally look round and smooth if the spot of the exit is pressed up against a hard surface. In addition, guns held at an angle to the victim will usually make an elliptical entrance wound rather than a round one.

Yet, while knowing which is an entrance and which is an exit wound can be important for establishing the likely positions of the victim and murderer when the shot was fired, these likely positions can be misleading and should be used only as a best guess. For example, occasionally people claiming self-defense will insist to the police that the victims were facing them with a weapon when they shot them, yet the pathologist finds that the entrance wound is in the back. This also occasionally happens when police officers shoot an armed felon whom the officers swear was facing them. Are these individuals lying? Not necessarily.

Two researchers, Ernest J. Tobin and Dr. Martin L. Fackler, set out to discover whether it was possible for a person to turn 180 degrees before someone could pull the trigger of a gun. In their study, published in *Wound Ballistics Review*, these researchers found that it took test subjects an average of .31 seconds to turn 90 degrees and .676 seconds to turn 180 degrees. On the other hand, with their finger on the trigger, it took test subjects (who were police officers), upon hearing an auditory signal, .356 seconds to pull the trigger, and .677 seconds to pull the trigger if they didn't have their finger on it, which police officers are trained not to do unless in imminent danger.[10] Keep in mind that in this study the subjects were expecting to hear a signal to pull the trigger, while the signal to pull the trigger in real-life situations is seldom ever that clearcut. What these researchers were able to show, however, is that it is entirely possible for individuals to turn their backs before someone facing them with a gun can pull the trigger. There is an axiom taught in both offensive and defensive tactics training: "Action is faster than reaction." This study clearly shows that.

Regardless of where on their body individuals are shot, however, it is often possible for a pathologist to tell from the wound pattern the type of gun used. For example, non-contact shotgun wounds will usually make many small wounds as the pellets have spread out and will strike the skin individually. Assault rifles, on the other hand, will often do much more damage than handguns because the higher velocity of their bullets give them much more kinetic energy. One of the most gruesome gunshot wounds I ever saw was on a teenage girl who shot herself in the head with an assault rifle. We found pieces of this suicide victim's skull forty to fifty feet from her body.

Interestingly, while individuals with multiple gunshot wounds are seldom believed to be suicide victims, this isn't always true in reality. I have personally seen several cases of suicides that involved multiple gunshot wounds. Often, suicide victims will have a "flinch reaction" when they pull the trigger, causing the bullet to deviate from its intended path, and only wounding rather than killing them. Occasionally this can happen several times before the victims actually kill themselves. Other than a shot in the brainstem, few gunshot wounds, even horrendous ones, can assure instant death.

Knife punctures and other cutting wounds, as opposed to firearms, are much more difficult to trace to a specific weapon. If a murderer plunges a knife straight in and out, a distinctive puncture pattern may be present. For example, single-edged knives will usually leave a wound with one sharp end and one blunt end, while double-edged knives will leave wounds with two sharp ends. However, unless surprised, usually victims attacked with knives are struggling and this movement distorts the wound, as will the assailant twisting the knife while stabbing the victim. These movements will make the size of the wound appear larger than the knife actually is. Usually, the gaping of the wound has more to do with the elasticity of the skin than it does with the size of the cutting weapon. And while it can be obvious that a person was killed with an instrument such as an ax, it is seldom possible to say that a specific ax, absent blood and hair on it, was the murder weapon.

Like a person with multiple gunshot wounds, someone who has suffered multiple stab or slice wounds also would seldom be considered a suicide victim, but again this isn't always true. Often, suicide victims will be seen with one deep, fatal stab wound surrounded by many smaller, non-fatal stab wounds called "hesitation wounds." However, several small cuts around the chin or neck area, rather than suicide, often mean that the murderer intimidated and controlled the victim by holding a cutting instrument close to the victim's neck and face.

To help in determining the cause of death, the pathologist during an autopsy, along with looking for gunshot and stabbing or slashing wounds, also examines the body for any signs of blunt force trauma. Severe blunt force trauma usually results in abrasions, contusions, and/or lacerations. Occasionally, the pathologist finds during the autopsy that a blunt force injury has left a recognizable pattern on the skin, such as the outline of a baseball bat, hammer, or belt buckle.

Pathologists find that blunt force abrasions are usually caused when the skin is scraped away by friction. Often, a pathologist can tell the direction of the abrasion by looking for the wound end with raised skin, which shows that the abrasion started from the other end.

Contusions, or bruises, from blunt force trauma are a bit more difficult to analyze. Because people bruise and heal from bruises at different rates, it is usually impossible to determine how much force caused a bruise or how old a bruise is.

Lacerations from blunt force trauma, pathologists find, usually appear different from lacerations caused by sharp cutting instruments. Blunt force lacerations will often have tissue still connecting the two sides of the wound and will appear much more jagged than lacerations caused by cutting instruments.

Yet, even though deceased individuals may have contusions, abrasions, or lacerations, this doesn't necessarily mean that someone attacked them. People who die from natural causes will often injure themselves when they fall or while flailing around during the throes of death. These injuries will most often be on parts of the body that protrude, such as the eyebrows or nose.

For victims who have died from asphyxia (lack of oxygen to the brain), often an external examination can determine how this occurred. Hanging victims, for example, show distinctive contusion markings that go around the neck and up behind the ear, while individuals strangled by an assailant's hand or an object such as a scarf or rope will usually have contusions that circle the neck parallel to the ground. Occasionally, the object used in the strangulation will leave a contusion reflecting the pattern of the object, such as the weave of a rope. For those victims strangled by hand, many times the assailant's fingerprints can be found on the victim's throat. During an autopsy, pathologists always examine the eyes of individuals suspected of dying by strangulation. The pressure buildup from this act causes the capillaries of the eye to burst and will leave small red spots called petechiae. It should be noted, however, that other injuries besides strangulation, such as rapid chest compression, will also cause petechiae.

Bodies that have been submerged in water for a lengthy period of time can also present a challenge to pathologists. If the cause of death was a gunshot or knifing, the pathologist can usually establish this. However, proving whether a person accidentally drowned or was intentionally drowned can be much more difficult. While a person struggling against being drowned will often have bruises and abrasions, these can also appear on a person who has accidentally fallen into water and is flailing about or is pushed against rocks and other obstacles by the current.

If the location of a murder is unknown, a dead body can often tell an observant pathologist where it met its end. The dirt, industrial chemicals and dust, and plant pollen found on a body can tell a pathologist where the body was prior to its death.

Determining exactly who caused a person's death can also many times come from the victim's body during an autopsy. Bullets removed from a body can be matched to a specific gun, while some wounds can be matched to specific implements used in the murder. Also, fingerprints can be recovered from dead bodies, while bite marks can be matched to the teeth of a specific person. In addition, pathologists routinely scrape under the fingernails of murder victims for any traces of skin from an assailant, while sexual murderers usually leave behind bodily fluids and hair, all of which can be matched to a specific person through DNA analysis.

While the information a murder victim's body gives to homicide detectives will occasionally point them to a specific person, in other cases, rather than to a specific person, a dead body can point the detectives to other sources of evidence that may connect a specific person to a crime. In the next chapter we will look at all of the various types of evidence for murder, where the evidence comes from, how it is found, how it is analyzed and processed, and how it can assist in building a murder case against someone.

CHAPTER 4

Physical Evidence of Murder

Jimmy Parker, sixteen, and Robert Tulloch, seventeen, both came from solid, two-parent, middle-class New England families. They both performed exceptionally well in school, and most of their high school teachers regarded them as intelligent young men with bright, promising futures. These promising futures, however, came to an abrupt end in April 2002 when a court in New Hampshire sentenced Parker to twenty-five years in prison and Tulloch to life without parole. Earlier, they had both pled guilty to the brutal and bloody knife murders of Half and Susanne Zantop, a New Hampshire couple who were professors at Dartmouth College.

On January 27, 2001, Roxanne Verona, a friend of the Zantops, having been invited to dinner, set out for the Zantop home in the small rustic village of Etna, New Hampshire, located just a few miles east of the Dartmouth College campus. At around 6:30 p.m. she pulled her gray Saab into the Zantop driveway. Everything seemed to be fine. However, a few minutes later, after finding the front door unlocked and going inside, she fled from the house in horror. Racing to a neighbor's house, she breathlessly asked to use their telephone, then dialed 911. The Zantops, she told the police dispatcher between gasps for air, had been murdered.

"They were wonderful people," Roxanne would later tell reporters. "They were special—intellectually, humanly, everything."[1]

When the police arrived at the murder scene they immediately noticed that the Zantop house showed no apparent signs of forced entry. Inside the home, everything at first seemed to be in order. In the living room, several pieces of expensive artwork, including a signed statue by Auguste Rodin and an original painting by Abraham van Beyeren, had not been disturbed. In the kitchen, it appeared that someone had been in the midst of preparing a meal. However, the study of the house, the police discovered, looked like a war zone. Officers found blood smeared and spattered everywhere, furniture overturned and broken, and there they also found the stabbed and slashed bodies of Half and Susanne Zantop. Half lay with his head on the bottom shelf of a bookcase, while Susanne lay just inside the door to the study. Huge amounts of blood pooled around both of them.

After securing and documenting the murder scene, the police then began a systematic search. As talked about in the chapter on crime scenes, when searching for evidence, one of the things homicide detectives always look for are items out of place in the location, and which therefore might have been dropped or left by the murderer or murderers. At the Zantop crime scene the police spotted something immediately. On the floor of the study they found two, foot-long, plastic knife sheaths with the letters *SOG* printed on them. Upon visual examination, the police found that the sheaths were empty. However, a search of the house and the surrounding property didn't turn up the weapons they had held.

During a crime scene search the police also always look for any evidence the perpetrators may have left behind that will help identify them. In this case, the police recovered fingerprints from the knife sheaths and from a chair in the study. They also found a bloody footprint on a piece of paper lying on the floor of the study, some human hair, and a bloody trail leading out of the house.

Homicide detectives, in addition to the above, also always search for evidence that will help them reconstruct the crime. In this case, besides noting the body positions, the direction of blood spatters, and the overturned furniture, the homicide detectives found that two extra chairs had been brought into the study. These two chairs indicated that before the murders the Zantops had had at least two visitors.

Finally, and just as important as the evidence left at a murder scene, is the evidence that is missing. The police discovered that Half Zantop's wallet was gone, indicating that robbery may have been the motive for the murders. However, it also indicated that the robbers were amateurs, as they hadn't ransacked the rest of the house and had left behind the extremely valuable works of art talked about earlier.

The police found during their investigation that Half Zantop, a professor for over twenty-five years at Dartmouth College, had been a highly respected member of the community. No one they talked to knew of anyone who didn't like him. "There are a lot of professors whom I respect," said a Dartmouth College senior, "but Half was one whom I admired."[2]

Susanne, likewise, was admired and liked by practically everyone who knew her. "All of us will remember her bravery, her wit, her critical acumen, her ethics, and her loyalty and support of others," said Jeannine Blackwell, chair of German studies at the University of Kentucky.[3]

Because the Zantops had been so well liked and respected, and because the community around Dartmouth College hadn't seen a murder in well over a decade, the police knew they needed to get to work right away on the evidence they had recovered at the crime scene. New Hampshire State Trooper Charles M. West became the lead homicide investigator on the case, and Detective Lieutenant Frank Moran from the nearby Hanover Police Department assisted him.

Once they had finished processing the evidence at the crime scene, the detectives began following where the evidence led. While the police had found fingerprints on the knife sheaths and on a chair in the Zantop study, they also found that these didn't match any fingerprints on file anywhere. The next most obvious pieces of evidence to work on, of course, were the knife sheaths left behind. An autopsy showed that the Zantops had both been stabbed and slashed to death, and so the police naturally surmised that the sheaths had contained the murder weapons.

The homicide detectives, after doing a little checking with knife dealers, found that the sheaths had held knives manufactured by the Specialty Knives & Tools Company of Lynnwood, Washington, and that the initials SOG stood for Studies and Observation Group, an intelligence unit that had operated during the Vietnam War. Their investigation additionally showed that the sheaths had apparently held SEAL 2000 knives, which are extremely sharp and deadly foot-long knives. The sheaths, the detectives' investigation also uncovered, had been constructed of a plastic called Kydex, which had only been in use for a year or so. This, they hoped, would narrow down the possible number of purchasers.

The next logical step in the investigation was to obtain a list of the dealers who sold these types of knives. While the list turned out to be huge, and, of course, there also existed the possibility that the knives might have been bought privately rather than through a dealer, the detectives went to work nevertheless checking with dealers. After considerable work, they finally hit pay dirt. A mail-order knife dealer from Scituate, Massachusetts, reported that just a month before the murders he had sold two SEAL 2000 knives to a Jimmy Parker, who lived in nearby Chelsea, Vermont.

The detectives drove to the Parker household and spoke with sixteen-year-old Jimmy Parker, who admitted to buying the two knives. He told the detectives that he and a friend, Robert Tulloch, had intended to use the knives to cut wood in order to build a fort. He also told the detectives that the knives hadn't worked well for this purpose and so he and Tulloch had sold them to a man they met in an Army/Navy surplus store. He couldn't, however, identify the man and didn't know his name. Since fingerprints had been recovered at the murder scene, the detectives asked Parker and his parents whether it would be all right for them to fingerprint him, which they agreed to. Also, the detectives requested permission to take some of Parker's shoes for comparison with the bloody footprint they had recovered at the crime scene. Parker, wanting to act innocent, and his parents, believing their son to actually be innocent, also agreed to this.

Detectives then talked to Robert Tulloch, who told them basically the same story concerning what had happened to the knives. As with Parker, the police asked for permission to fingerprint Tulloch and to take some of his footwear for comparison. In addition, the police asked for permission to search the Tulloch home. Later, the police would find the two SEAL 2000 knives hidden in a box in Robert Tulloch's bedroom.

However, Parker and Tulloch decided not to hang around. Both young men knew that the police would return as soon as they made comparisons of the fingerprints and footprint. So they climbed into a silver Audi belonging to the Parker family and fled town. Just as the two young men had suspected, New Hampshire courts soon issued warrants against both of them for the murders of the Zantops. A nationwide alert for Parker and Tulloch went out.

Walter Coombs, a Massachusetts state trooper, found the silver Audi parked at a truck stop in Sturbridge, Massachusetts. Upon investigation, the police discovered that Parker and Tulloch, now calling themselves Sam and Tyler, had gotten a ride from a husband and wife truck-driving team going to New Jersey. From there, the police learned, the two young men had gotten a ride with a truck driver heading west. They had told truck drivers at the Travel Centers of America truck stop in Columbia, New Jersey, that they were heading for California.

On February 19, 2001, Sergeant William Ward of the New Castle, Indiana Police Department heard a trucker on the CB radio asking if anyone could give two young men from New Jersey a ride to California. Having just read about the alert for the two young murderers from New Hampshire, Sergeant Ward grabbed the CB microphone and, pretending to be a trucker, said that he would be glad to give them a ride. He said to just drop them off at the Flying J Truck Stop in New Castle. The police then descended onto the truck stop and found the two young men waiting by the gas pumps. A few minutes later, after Parker and Tulloch got confused trying to keep up their aliases, they admitted who they were, and the police took them into custody.

Naturally, the small community around Dartmouth College was alarmed and concerned, and not just by the murders, but also by whom the police had arrested for them. "Everybody's very stunned about it," said Dartmouth sophomore Andy George, "especially the fact that a sixteen- and seventeen-year-old could kill two people."[4]

While Parker and Tulloch at first pled not guilty, they eventually changed their minds and agreed to plead guilty. The evidence against them was overwhelming. The police matched the fingerprints recovered from the chair in the Zantop study and from the knife sheaths left behind at the crime scene to the two suspects. Blood on the knives recovered from Tulloch's bedroom matched Susanne Zantop's DNA, while the police also found her blood on the floormat in a 1996 Subaru used by the two murderers. Laboratory tests additionally showed that the SEAL 2000 knives had likely made the gash marks on Half Zantop's skull and on a bookcase in the study. Finally, a bloody footprint left on a piece of paper at the crime scene matched a pair of hiking boots taken from Parker.

After entering into a plea agreement, for which Parker received a twenty-five-year prison sentence and Tulloch a sentence of life without parole, the two young men told the police that the murder had been part of a plan to raise $10,000 to finance a trip to Australia. Parker said in an interview that legitimate ways to make money were "boring and take a lot of time," and so they had come up with another way—robbery and murder.[5]

During interviews, the two young men also told the police that in the six months before the Zantop murders, they had tried to gain entry into several other homes in the area by pretending to be Dartmouth students conducting an environmental study. However, until they knocked on the Zantop door they had been refused entry everywhere they tried. Reportedly, the two young men had planned to force their victims to give them their credit card PIN numbers before they murdered them, but when Half pulled out his wallet to look for a telephone number, the two young men saw that he had a lot of cash and immediately attacked him with the knives. Susanne, upon hearing the struggle in the study, rushed to her husband's assistance, and Parker and Tulloch also stabbed and slashed her to death.

Following the murders, Parker and Tulloch, covered with blood, grabbed Half's wallet and fled from the house. While they were attempting to wash the blood off of the knives and the floormat of their car, they realized that they had left the knife sheaths behind. However, when they returned to the Zantop house for the sheaths they saw a police cruiser parked in the driveway, and so they quickly left the area. They later burned Half's wallet and some of the blood-soaked clothing they had worn during the murder.

"I really feel that both of these guys are a menace to society and should be taken out of circulation for a very long time," said Audrey McCollum, a neighbor of the Zantops, expressing the general feeling around the community about the suspects.[6]

While the leaving of the knife sheaths at the murder scene made connecting Parker and Tulloch to the murder appear relatively easy, it wasn't. There was still a considerable amount of work that had to be done to positively prove that Parker and Tulloch actually committed the murders: fingerprints had to be compared to those left on evidence and at the scene, blood on several pieces of evidence had to be analyzed to show that it belonged to the victims, markings on bone and pieces of furniture had to be compared to show that they were likely made by the knives found by the police, and so on.

Actually, while leaving the knife sheaths may have seemed very amateurish, practically every murderer leaves something behind at a crime scene, occasionally as large as knife sheaths or firearms and sometimes as small as just a few flakes of dandruff. Edmond Locard's Exchange

Principle states, "Whenever two objects come into contact, there is always a transfer of material."[7] (Edmond Locard was an esteemed early-twentieth-century criminologist who opened his own police laboratory at age thirty-three and became very influential in the field of physical evidence.)

The reason, however, that many murderers will often leave substantial pieces of physical evidence behind at crime scenes, such as the knife sheaths, is because few murders are well planned, and consequently the unexpected happens: the intended victim resists more than expected, a gunshot or knife stab doesn't kill as expected, or someone arrives at the crime scene unexpectedly. In the incident at the beginning of this chapter, for example, the two young murderers expected that one stab or slash would kill instantly, as in movies, but it didn't, and instead a violent struggle ensued. Because of unexpected circumstances such as this, murderers often panic and items are dropped, blood is spattered onto the perpetrators, items are touched and then forgotten, and so on. In the excitement of trying to cope with unexpected events, murderers often leave valuable physical evidence behind.

This is important because, absent eyewitnesses, physical evidence is the best way to show that a person was at the scene of a murder, had the means to commit the murder, and actually did commit the murder. And while the knife sheaths in the incident at the beginning of this chapter very obviously connected the suspects to the Zantop murders, almost all murderers, as stated above, leave something behind that will identify them and connect them to the crime. This evidence simply waits for a detective to find it.

Respected criminologist Herbert Leon MacDonell had this to say about physical evidence: "Physical evidence cannot be intimidated. It does not forget. It doesn't get excited at the moment something is happening—like people do. It sits there and waits to be detected, preserved, evaluated, and explained. This is what physical evidence is all about. In the course of a trial, defense and prosecuting attorneys may lie, witnesses may lie, the defendant certainly may lie. Even the judge may lie. Only the evidence never lies."[8]

Physical evidence of murder, the police find, can take many forms. It can be, as discussed above, any item that shows that a murder was committed, that helps reconstruct the murder, and/or that connects a specific person to a murder.

Blood, as demonstrated in the case of the Zantops, can be one of the most important pieces of physical evidence found at a murder scene. It can reconstruct the crime and can also connect a specific person to the crime scene. For example, in the Zantop case at the beginning of this chapter, finding samples of one of the victim's blood on the knives discovered hidden in one of the suspect's bedrooms, and also finding it on the floormat of a car used by the suspects, became damning evidence. With the new DNA analysis techniques available, it is now possible, as happened in the Zantop case, for an expert to testify in court that the blood recovered during a murder investigation belongs specifically and uniquely to a certain person. DNA, of course, is the blueprint of a human body that is contained in almost all human cells. Like fingerprints, each person's DNA is unique.

Evidence of blood at a crime scene, however, can include not just the victim's blood but also blood from the murderer. Particularly when the murder involves a violent struggle, murderers will often become injured and leave some of their own blood behind. Most states either now have or are in the process of setting up DNA banks in which they store samples of the DNA of violent felons. Blood found at the scene of a murder that doesn't belong to the victim can be run through this collection and checked to see whether it matches that of anyone registered in the DNA bank. I will discuss this at length in the chapter on developing suspects.

But just as important as the presence of blood at a crime scene is the absence of it. Victims with gaping wounds but very little blood in the area around them usually mean that the victims have been moved from the original murder site. Likewise, missing blood spatters mean that something or someone, usually a perpetrator, blocked the blood spatters. For example, whenever a homicide detective finds a trail of blood spatter on a wall that stops abruptly and then starts again, he or she knows that this means someone or something stood in the way and collected the blood spatter. This can help reconstruct the crime scene by telling the detective where a suspect possibly stood, and naturally the homicide detective will be certain to search the clothing of any suspects for evidence of this blood spatter.

The pattern and shape of blood spatter can also tell a homicide detective about what happened at a murder scene. "Bloodstain patterns define the nature of the event that created them," said Ross Gardner of Gardner Forensic Consulting.[9]

An article on the interpretation of blood spatter that appeared in *Law Enforcement Technology* stated, "When a victim sheds blood, whether the result of a homicide or a car accident, the bloodstains and patterns formed are characteristic of the physical forces that created them.... When blood leaves the body, it acts as any liquid and forms round drops that are affected by gravity and the velocity at which they are propelled through the air."[10]

Using this principle, a homicide detective, by examining the shape and size of blood spatter at a murder scene, can tell the velocity of the spatter, which then often tells the detective how the wound occurred (blood spatter from a gunshot wound, for example, because of the high velocity of the impact, will produce blood spatter with a high percentage of fine, or atomized, specks of blood). The shape of the blood spatter can also tell the homicide detective from which direction it came. Blood spatter that is circular, for instance, means that the blood dropped perpendicular to the surface it was found on. Blood striking a surface at any other angle will leave a drop in an elliptical shape, and blood spatters formed into long, thin elliptical shapes will have a tail that points in the direction the blood traveled.

By measuring the length and width of a blood spatter drop and then inserting these figures into a mathematical formula, a crime scene technician can determine the angle at which the blood drop struck the surface. By attaching strings to several blood spatter drops at the angles in which they struck the surface, a crime scene technician will find that they all meet at a certain point, which will be where the source of the blood (i.e., the victim) was when it spattered. There are now even computer programs available that allow crime scene technicians to find the direction the blood spatter came from and, using this information, generate a three-dimensional model of the crime scene, showing the location of the source of the blood and consequently often also where the suspects likely stood. Many times, knowing where the participants were during the commission of a murder can show that a suspect's story about what happened couldn't possibly be true, and may therefore elicit a confession.

In cases in which the murderer kills a victim with a blunt object or a stabbing/slashing instrument, the pattern of the blood spatter that is thrown off of the weapon as it is raised to strike can show where the murderer stood, whether the attacker was right- or left-handed, and how many times the weapon was used. A blood track to the right when facing the victim, and which goes away from the victim's position, shows the detective that the attacker swung the weapon with his or her right hand. Also, finding several of these tracks of blood means that the perpetrator raised the weapon to strike several times, which can counter a suspect's story of only striking the victim once. In addition, the width of the blood track can indicate the type of weapon used. For example, a knife will throw off a much narrower track than will an ax or a baseball bat.

In addition to the above evidence, people who are shot or stabbed usually grab the wounded area, so bloody handprints found at a murder scene are usually, but not always, the victim's. Still, this evidence can help reconstruct what happened. Also, blood spatters at a crime scene, along with coming from the wound or the assailant's weapon, can also come from a victim flailing a bloody hand or arm.

While blood spatter evidence can be valuable, finding these traces of blood can often be difficult, particularly if the murderer has meticulously cleaned up the crime scene. Difficult but not impossible. The police have a number of methods for finding blood traces not visible to the eye. One is through the use of luminol. As talked about earlier, this is a chemical that, when sprayed around a crime scene, will cause minute traces of blood to glow. However, luminol will only show up in totally dark areas and only for a short time. Therefore, crime scene technicians have other devices they can use for finding blood, such as high-intensity lighting filtered to shine a violet beam, and other assorted specialty lighting devices.

Along with blood, another of the most telltale and damning clues murderers can leave at a crime scene or on a crucial piece of evidence is their fingerprints. This is particularly true if the fingerprints are left on the murder weapon or the victim, and even more so if the murderers deny being at the crime scene and have no legal reason for their fingerprints to be there. As we will discuss in the chapter on interview and interrogation, being able to show suspects that the police can positively place them at a crime scene will often lead to a confession.

Fingerprints left at a crime scene can be grouped into one of three types. The first are patent fingerprints, which occur when a fingerprint is transferred onto a surface through a foreign substance on the fingers, such as blood, paint, or tar. The second type are plastic or molded fingerprints, which occur when a person presses a finger into some soft substance, such as clay, wet paint, or mud. The third and most common type of fingerprints left at a crime scene are latent fingerprints. These occur when the perspiration and oils that normally coat the skin are transferred onto another object.

However, despite what a reader might see on television or at the movies, fingerprints can't be recovered from absolutely anything touched. Some surfaces simply don't retain fingerprints. Still, many surfaces do, and at a crime scene one of the most important jobs of the homicide detective is to locate objects that may contain fingerprints, and then to protect them until the fingerprints can be processed by a crime scene technician.

The usual methods for collecting and preserving patent and plastic or molded fingerprints are to photograph them and, if possible, take as evidence the objects they are on, whereas the usual method for recovering latent fingerprints is for a crime scene technician to brush fingerprint powder onto the surface believed to contain the fingerprints. In doing this, crime scene technicians use very soft brushes so as not to distort the fingerprints and very fine powder that will stick to the body oils that make latent fingerprints. Fingerprint powder, while usually black, also comes in various other colors in order to provide contrast to the surface the fingerprints were found on. Once photographed, crime scene technicians lift the latent fingerprints from the surface using wide, clear, low-tack tape, which is then transferred to a fingerprint card on which pertinent information about where the fingerprints were found, when they were found, and who found them, can be recorded. For surfaces on which this tape won't properly lift a fingerprint because of surface irregularities, a type of putty called Mikrosil can be pressed onto the area and the fingerprint lifted off.

Recent scientific advances have now made it possible to find and recover fingerprints from surfaces that, while able to retain fingerprints, do not show the fingerprints when visually inspected. Crime scene technicians use various alternate lighting systems that emit spectrums of light other than visible, and under which fingerprints undetectable in normal light become visible and can be recovered.

Along with these alternate lighting systems, another way to bring out visually undetectable fingerprints is through the use of one of the key ingredients of Super Glue, a chemical called cyanoacrylate. It has been found that cyanoacrylate, when heated in a closed container, will stick to visually undetectable fingerprint residue and consequently make it visible. The police in Los Angeles solved the case of the infamous Night Stalker murders using this method. The police had recovered a vehicle used by the Night Stalker, but didn't see any detectable fingerprints. So they constructed a building around the vehicle and filled it with heated cyanoacrylate fumes, which eventually adhered to and made visible a fingerprint that led to the apprehension of the Night Stalker. There is even a device that uses cyanoacrylate fumes to find fingerprints on corpses, and a robot that can spray cyanoacrylate fumes onto suspected bombs.

Along with cyanoacrylate, scientists have found other chemicals that will also enhance fingerprints. For example, on porous surfaces such as paper or wood, the chemical ninhydrin will react with the amino acids in perspiration and turn any fingerprints a violet color. Occasionally, crime lab technicians will also use iodine fuming to bring out undetectable fingerprints.

Shoe prints, tire tracks, and footprints can be just as crucial as fingerprints in showing that a person or vehicle was at a murder scene or took part in the crime; and just like fingerprints, shoe prints, tire tracks, and footprints are individual and distinctive. On May 1, 2004, homicide detectives in Edmond, Oklahoma, solved an eighteen-year-old murder case when they found that the footprint of a man caught window peeping matched the footprint left by a murderer eighteen years before.

Similar to looking for fingerprints, the lead homicide detective, when inspecting a crime scene, searches carefully for shoe prints, tire tracks, and footprints; and, when found, protects them until they can be photographed and often a plaster cast made of them. Because shoes and automobile tires wear in a unique way, it is often possible, through cuts and worn sections, to show that a specific shoe or automobile tire made the impression left at a crime scene. And while making a plaster cast of shoe prints, tire tracks, or footprints in snow was difficult and sometimes impossible in the past because hardening plaster created heat that deformed the impression, there is now available a substance called Snow Print Wax. This substance can be sprayed into the impression and will protect the imprint while the plaster cast is hardening.

It is now even possible, besides just photographing them, to recover shoe prints, tire tracks, or footprints made by dust. Crime lab technicians recover them using a device called an electrostatic dust print lifter. This device employs a high static-electric charge to lift the dust print and transfer it onto a piece of film for a permanent record of the impression.

Once homicide detectives have a record of shoe prints or tire tracks, they can then compare these patterns to known patterns using one of several computer programs that will match the patterns found to a specific brand of shoe or tire. Then, as in the Zantop case at the beginning of this chapter, if a suspect has been identified, a comparison can be made to the suspect's shoes or to the tires of a car the suspect may have used. Footprints, of course, can be compared by taking an inked impression of any suspect's feet.

Of course, in addition to identifying a murder suspect, finding shoe prints, tire tracks, or footprints can also show homicide detectives the suspect's route in, around, and out of the crime scene. This can help tremendously in reconstructing the crime and, in the case of multiple shoe prints, tire tracks, or footprints, can tell homicide detectives at a minimum how many suspects they may be dealing with.

Tool marks found at a crime scene can also be very useful when homicide detectives attempt to reconstruct a crime. These include marks made by screwdrivers forcing open windows, bolt cutters clipping through padlocks, wire cutters severing telephone lines, and so on. Many times they can show how a suspect entered the crime scene, and they can also show some of the activities at a crime scene. Occasionally, it is even possible to show that the tool markings found at a crime scene were made by a specific tool, which can often bring about a confession if the tool belongs to the suspect. Sometimes when a tool breaks while being used at a crime scene, and the police recover the broken piece, the crime laboratory can show that the broken piece belongs to a specific tool.

Along with all of the above, the police find that whenever a murder involves a violent struggle, murderers almost always lose some hair, whether from their head, arms, legs, or chest. Of course, the crucial aspects in obtaining this type of evidence, since it so small and light, are for homicide detectives to find it and then protect it until a crime scene technician can recover it.

"If a bloodstain sticks to a piece of clothing, it's dried there," said Max Houck, director of the Forensic Science Initiative at West Virginia University. "If a hair gets transferred to a piece of clothing, you've got to collect that first. The blood will be there after a lot of handling, but the hair is going to get lost right away."[11]

It is for this reason that homicide detectives and medical examiners or deputy coroners carefully examine the body of a murder victim at the crime scene for hairs that don't appear to belong to the victim, and then immediately recover them. Using DNA analysis, these hairs can be traced to a specific person. The same is true for skin cells found either on a murder victim or under the victim's fingernails.

Today's homicide detectives know that, like suspects leaving fingerprints behind, with the recent advances in DNA technology it is now possible to positively connect a person to a murder through the identification of any DNA left behind. DNA can be retrieved from such things as sweat, skin cells, blood, hair, semen, dandruff, mucus, and earwax. Almost any bodily part left behind, no matter how small, will contain DNA. In addition to all of the above, homicide detectives also search for any object that might contain a suspect's saliva, which can also be analyzed for DNA. This saliva can come from envelopes licked, bite marks on the victim, food the suspect may have tasted, or from cigarette butts.

In sexual murders, the police find, the killers almost always leave some bodily substance behind, even if the sexual murderers wear condoms. Consequently, at the autopsy, pathologists always comb the pubic hair of sexual murder victims because they find it will often contain strands of the murderer's pubic hair. For sexual murderers who don't wear condoms, the semen left in a victim can be analyzed for DNA, as can be saliva often left on the murder victim's body.

Along with criminals leaving biological residue, individuals are continuously in their daily lives picking up and losing fibers from clothing, from furniture, or from carpeting. These can become crucial pieces of evidence that will connect a person to a murder by showing that he or she was at the crime scene. For example, a suspect can often be connected to a murder scene if it can be shown that a certain garment the suspect owns or the carpeting in a suspect's home has fibers that match those left at the crime scene; or the police can often show that suspects have fibers on them that originated at the crime scene. This can be particularly damning when the suspects claim to have never been at the scene. As with looking for hair, homicide detectives and medical examiners or deputy coroners closely examine murder victims at the crime scene for fibers that could be lost when transporting them to the morgue. Collecting fibers that are visible is just a matter of using tweezers and then placing the fibers into an evidence envelope. For those surfaces on which fibers are believed to be but are not readily visible, wide strips of transparent tape can be used to collect them.

Like fibers found at a crime scene, dirt, dust, and pollen can be brought into a crime scene or taken away from it. Also, collecting dirt, dust, or pollen from a murder suspect in those investigations where no body has yet been found can often prove helpful in that some dirt, dust, and pollen can be specific to certain geographical areas, and may therefore give the police leads as to where they need to search for the victim.

Broken glass at a crime scene can also tell a homicide detective many things. It can show the point of entry or exit to a crime scene and can often be used to show what happened at a crime scene. Whenever detectives find broken glass at the scene of a murder where a suspect has been identified, the police will search the suspect carefully for any small shards of glass that often stick to a suspect's clothing or shoe soles. These can many times be connected to the broken glass at a crime scene. Recent scientific research has shown that a process called inductively coupled plasma-atomic emission spectroscopy can prove that glass found at a crime scene matches glass recovered from a suspect's clothing, vehicle, and so on. Also, freshly broken glass can be distinguished from other, older glass fragments at a crime scene because the freshly broken glass will usually not be totally coated with dirt, and will still have extremely sharp edges.

Naturally, the police are very interested in any devices that can show who the victim had contact with, or who attempted to contact the victim, just before the murder. These include caller ID devices, cell phones, and answering machines. Knowing this information can often lead the police to suspects they may not have known about.

In addition, sometimes the most innocent-appearing documents at a crime scene can provide crucial information about who the murderer is. For this reason, detectives take any notes, journals, or diaries found at the crime scene or which belong to the victim.

Computers can also provide important information. Documents on a computer and recent e-mail messages will often direct homicide detectives toward possible suspects. In addition, readers would be amazed at how many murderers put their hatred of the victim, and even their plans for the murder, on their computers. And while the suspects may delete these files, that doesn't mean the files are no longer accessible as evidence. Forensic computer specialists have software programs that can often recover deleted files.

Vehicles, like computers, can often provide important evidence in murder cases. These vehicles include both the victim's and the suspect's.

Homicide detectives usually impound these vehicles and then thoroughly search them for shell casings, traces of blood, hair, fibers, and so on. Often, if the victim was transported in a vehicle after being murdered, some evidence will be left behind, particularly if the victim was bleeding. Searching a vehicle for evidence is similar to searching a crime scene. Photographs will be taken first; and then a careful, methodical search will be made using a specific search pattern, such as dividing the vehicle into grids, so that no area of the vehicle is overlooked. Since vehicles contain many smooth surfaces, they become prime candidates for fingerprints.

Of course, of all the types of physical evidence that homicide detectives search for at crime scenes, one of the most important is the murder weapon. While it is often apparent what type of weapon caused the death of a murder victim, occasionally homicide detectives must wait until the autopsy is complete before they find out what killed the victim. This is especially true in cases of asphyxiation, poisoning, and other deaths where the victim's body shows no apparent trauma. In these cases of unknown means of death, homicide detectives simply have to take everything at the crime scene that might have been used in the murder and then later release any property found not to have been a part of the crime. This is much easier than homicide detectives leaving important evidence at the crime scene and only later realizing that they need it.

However, as stated above, the type of weapon used in a murder is usually very apparent. According to the FBI's *Crime in the United States*, in 65.1 percent of the murders for the five-year period between 1998 and 2002, the killers used firearms. Of these firearms, the majority, 78.3 percent, were handguns. Also during this five-year period, murderers used knives or other cutting instruments to kill the victims in 13.1 percent of the murders, blunt instruments in 5.1 percent, and in 6.8 percent of the murders in the United States the killers beat the victims to death with their hands, fists, or feet. The majority of the remainder of the murder victims during this five-year period died from poisoning, explosives, fire, narcotics, drowning, strangulation, and asphyxiation.[12]

Yet, while the above are the most common means of murdering someone, occasionally the police will run into a murder committed in a new or very innovative way. For example, in October 2003, British police arrested two nineteen-year-old men for the murder of Stephen Hilder. The two men arrested had been good friends with Hilder and had even been pallbearers at his funeral. The three men all belonged to a skydiving club, and on July 4, 2003, Hilder plunged 13,000 feet to his death when both his main and reserve parachute failed to open. During their investigation of Hilder's death, the police found that someone had unpacked his parachute, cut the cords to both the main and reserve parachute, and then repacked it.

In Los Angeles in January 2004, Angela Rodriguez received the death penalty after being convicted of killing her husband. Prosecutors showed during her trial that in an attempt to collect his $250,000 life insurance policy, Angela had slipped some poisonous oleander plant into his food. When this made him extremely ill, she then finished him off by lacing his Gatorade with antifreeze.

On May 8, 2002, a jury in Johnson County, Indiana, found Ronald Shanabarger guilty of killing his infant son, Tyler. Ronald's wife, who divorced him, testified at his trial that Ronald confessed to her that he had killed Tyler. She told the jury, "He said, 'I killed Tyler.' I said, 'How?' And he said, 'With Saran Wrap.'" Apparently, Ronald covered Tyler's face tightly with plastic wrap until the infant suffocated.[13]

When the police, upon questioning Ronald, found out the motive for this murder, it turned out to be just as bizarre as the murder itself. Ronald told the police that when his father died in October 1996, he asked his wife (then his fiancée) to cut short the cruise she was on with her parents and come home to be with him. When she refused, he said he became enraged and began planning his revenge, which involved marrying her, having a child, allowing enough time to pass for his wife to bond with the child, and then murdering this child.

The above murders aside, in 2002, as might be expected, for murder victims in the twenty- to twenty-four-year-old age range the most often weapon used was a firearm. This age group also showed the most victims killed by knives and other cutting instruments. Interestingly, though, for death by manual strangulation the most likely victims fell into the thirty-five- to thirty-nine-year-old age group. For asphyxiation, unfortunately, the largest group of victims were individuals under one year of age.[14]

Since murderers kill almost 80 percent of their victims every year with a firearm or cutting instrument, and these types of wounds are usually apparent, homicide detectives naturally want to locate any such firearm or cutting instrument at the crime scene. In those cases, though, in which they can't find the actual murder weapon itself, homicide detectives search the crime scene for any evidence that would link the murder to a specific weapon, such as shell casings, spent bullets, knife sheaths, or parts of broken knife blades.

Using modern technology, both bullets and bullet casings can be shown to have been fired from a specific gun. The insides of the barrels of most firearms have spiraling grooves, called rifling, that are cut into the metal. These grooves give a bullet a spin when fired that greatly increases the bullet's accuracy. They also carve unique marks onto the bullet. For spent bullet casings, on the other hand, the firing pin of every gun makes a unique imprint on the metal cover of the primer. By comparing spent bullets or bullet casings found at a crime scene against bullets test-fired from a gun suspected of being used in the murder, crime lab technicians can determine whether or not these items came from the same gun.

For knives it becomes a bit more complicated. A friend told me that he saw a fictional police program recently on television that involved a stabbing victim. The crime lab technicians poured some type of liquid resin into the stab wound and minutes later pulled out a hardened mold of what the killer's knife looked like. Real crime lab technicians wince and groan when they see something like this because they know viewers believe that crime labs can really do this. Actually, the human body is very elastic and a stab wound would never hold the shape of a knife. However, it is still extremely important to locate any murder weapon used in a stabbing or slashing death because the crime lab can likely find traces of the victim's blood on it, even if the knife has been washed off.

In addition to all we've talked about in this chapter, there are literally thousands and thousands of other types of physical evidence that can be used in a murder investigation. There is no way to list all of these items because the list would be longer than this book. Put simply, any item that can reconstruct the murder or point to a specific person as the murderer can be used as evidence. This evidence has been as diverse as a peculiar scent at the crime scene to a dropped driver's license. When experienced homicide detectives search a crime scene, they try to never overlook anything that will help them reconstruct the crime or pinpoint the murderer.

However, once evidence has been recovered during a murder investigation it is crucial, if this evidence is to be used in court, to establish and maintain a chain of custody. What this means is that homicide detectives must be able to testify in court that the item presented as evidence is the same item that they found during the investigation, and that it has been stored in a secure facility since then. Homicide detectives at a crime scene, therefore, must secure evidentiary items recovered there, mark the evidence uniquely in some way (e.g., with the detective's initials and the date), record information about the evidence in their report, and then send this evidence to the police department property room or some other secure storage facility. Afterward, if anyone, such as crime lab technicians, wants to examine the evidence, they must sign the evidence in and out and state their purpose for obtaining it. A proper chain of custody establishes exactly where the evidence has been at all times and who has had contact with it.

Finding all of the physical evidence at a crime scene and then maintaining a chain of custody can be crucial in solving a murder. Even the smallest of evidence can often prove vital in bringing about a confession or in identifying a suspect. Paul L. Kirk, in his book *Crime Investigation: Physical Evidence and the Police Laboratory*, said this about physical evidence:

> Wherever he steps, whatever he touches, whatever he leaves, even unconsciously, will serve as a silent witness against him. Not only his fingerprints or his footprints, but his hair, the fibers from his clothes, the glass he breaks, the tool marks he leaves, the paint he scratches, the blood or semen he deposits or collects ... all of these and more bear mute witness against him.... Physical evidence cannot be wrong; it cannot perjure itself, it cannot be wholly absent.... Only human failure to find it, study and understand it, can diminish its value.[15]

As the above quote indicates, while physical evidence can often be the best evidence to use when investigating and prosecuting a murder, homicide detectives have found that witness testimony and suspect statements can also be compelling to jurors, particularly if they are backed up by solid physical evidence that supports them. However, obtaining good witness testimony and suspect statements is not simply a matter of just talking to people. Meaningful testimony and statements, as we will see in the next chapter, can be obtained only by detectives skilled and experienced in the art of interview and interrogation.

CHAPTER 5

Interview and Interrogation

Hawaiian police officers weren't overly concerned and didn't think it much out of the ordinary when, on May 8, 2002, they found a black 2001 Honda Civic abandoned in a ditch in the Ka'u district on the island of Hawaii. It appeared to them that the car had simply gotten stuck in the ditch, and they believed the owner would probably soon come back for it. They could find no signs it had been stolen, and, though they attempted to locate the car's owner, twenty-year-old Cassidy Matthew Toole, they couldn't find him.

Eventually, however, when his mother reported him missing, the police put Toole on their missing persons list. However, Toole's mother, concerned because she knew of no legitimate reason why her son should be missing, put up a reward for information about him. Soon after this, apparently suffering from an attack of conscience, twenty-year-old Kyle Hill contacted Mrs. Toole and told her that her son and a friend of his, nineteen-year-old Wesley Alan Matheson, had been murdered. He implicated himself and his friend, nineteen-year-old John McGovern, in the murders.

Officers brought McGovern to the police station and interrogated him about his involvement in the disappearance of Toole and Matheson. On a videotape the police made of this interrogation, McGovern denied any knowledge of, or involvement in, the disappearances of Toole and Matheson.

Soon afterward, though, upon discovering the murdered bodies of Toole and Matheson in a vacant lot, and after gathering evidence that put McGovern at the scene of the murder, the police again brought McGovern in for questioning. On the videotape of this second interrogation, McGovern changed his earlier story and told the police that he had accidentally stumbled onto the scene of the murders immediately after they occurred, but again claimed not to have had anything to do with the murders.

However, when Kyle Hill entered into an agreement with the prosecutor to plead guilty to two counts of second-degree murder and to testify against McGovern, the police once again brought McGovern in for questioning. This time in his videotaped statement, McGovern, faced with mounting evidence of his involvement in the murders and the possible testimony of Hill, admitted to his role in the killing of Toole and Matheson. Although he tried to claim that he killed them because he was afraid that Toole and Matheson might want to harm him because of an earlier drug deal gone bad, he also later admitted wanting to steal both drugs and extensive marijuana-growing equipment owned by the two murder victims.

McGovern told the police during the third interrogation that he had borrowed a .22-caliber rifle from a friend and that he and Hill took it with them to a house occupied by Toole and Matheson on the pretext of using it to do some target practice. However, when McGovern went into the house with Toole, Hill reportedly shot Matheson in the back of the head and, thinking him dead, took the rifle into the house and gave it to McGovern, who then shot and killed Toole as he sat on a couch.

Hill would later tell a jury during McGovern's trial, "John took the gun and shot Wes. He told him, 'Sorry, friend, I didn't mean to do this.'"[1]

After killing Toole, McGovern told the police, he went outside to see the body of Matheson, whom he found still alive and on the ground convulsing. McGovern shot him in the head and killed him. Hill and McGovern wrapped the two corpses in plastic, loaded them in a car, and then, after taking them to a nearby vacant lot and unwrapping them, dumped the two bodies into a hole. Afterward, Hill and McGovern went back to the victims' house and poured bleach in the bathtub, soaking the plastic they had wrapped the victims in. They also used a garden hose to wash away the blood inside the house. When they'd finished cleaning up the murder scene, McGovern told officers during his interrogation, they loaded the two murdered men's marijuana plants into Toole's black Honda and took them home. They returned after this and carted away all of the marijuana-growing equipment. Two days later, Hill and McGovern accidentally ran the Honda into a ditch and abandoned it there.

Following his confession to the police, McGovern took homicide detectives to the murder scene and reconstructed the crime for them. "He showed us the trail and pointed out the area where the bodies were found," said Detective Richard Miyamoto.[2]

Recounting at the murder scene how they had wrapped the two murder victims in plastic, McGovern told the police, "I did Cass and he did Wes."[3]

Even though McGovern admitted his role in the murders during the interrogations by the police, at his trial he pled not guilty to the charges of first-degree murder. His attorney attempted to argue that McGovern was "in distress" at the time of the murders, and that he felt afraid and pressured after Hill had shot Matheson. Because of this, McGovern's attorney told the jury, his client should be found guilty only of second-degree murder or manslaughter, both of which carry a lighter sentence than first-degree murder, and which would mean his client could eventually be paroled.

"If all you do is look at the surface, all you see is two people shot, two people confessed," said McGovern's attorney, Keith Shigetomi.[4] He added that he hoped the jurors would look deeper into what kind of stress McGovern was under at the time of the shootings.

However, during the trial the prosecution played the videotapes of McGovern's three police interrogations. On one of these tapes, McGovern talked about taking drugs from the house and then coming back to haul away the marijuana-growing equipment.

"It was all about greed," said Deputy Prosecutor Jack Matsukawa.[5]

After the close of final arguments, it took the jury only three and a half hours to reject McGovern's argument of distress and find him guilty of first-degree murder. In Hawaii, this carries a mandatory sentence of life in prison without parole.

Along with collecting physical evidence, one of the most important aspects of a homicide investigation is the gathering of witness statements and the interrogation of possible suspects. Actually, the collection of physical evidence and the gathering of testimony are usually complementary because their value, the police find, often depends on each other. Physical evidence can support and corroborate witness and suspect statements, and witness and suspect statements can support and corroborate physical evidence. In addition, the gathering of one can often bring an influx of the other. As the incident at the beginning of this chapter demonstrated, as more and more physical evidence began accumulating, the suspect's original statement to the police kept changing in an attempt to appear consistent with the new evidence, finally resulting in a confession when the physical evidence and his partner's statements forced the suspect to see that further lying was futile. But along with this, occasionally the police discover through talking to witnesses or suspects that there is a vital piece of physical evidence that has been overlooked. Consequently, the police will return to the crime scene or other location, usually with a search warrant, and confiscate this physical evidence.

While during a trial the jurors naturally give a considerable amount of weight to physical evidence that connects someone to a crime, homicide detectives find they also listen attentively to the testimony of witnesses and defendants. Therefore, collecting recorded statements from witnesses and suspects before a trial can be crucial to the success of the prosecution, as months later during the trial, individuals often tend to change or distort testimony given right after a murder. Murder trials, unfortunately, usually don't take place until a year or so after the crime, and many circumstances can change during this time that make individuals want to modify or even deny things they may have said to the police right after the murder. That is why it is vital to obtain and document statements as soon as possible after a murder.

Obtaining verbal information about a murder can come in one of two ways: interview or interrogation. The police use interviews to obtain information from witnesses and others not directly connected with the crime, while they use interrogations to obtain admissions and confessions from suspects. Consequently, their formats differ.

At a murder scene, homicide detectives routinely interview the witnesses to find out what occurred. One of the first things uniformed officers are taught about responding to crime scenes is that as soon as the scene has been secured, their next job is to locate and separate witnesses. As talked about in a previous chapter, witnesses must be separated from each other because if they are allowed to talk and discuss a murder, their testimony can become contaminated. Often, it has been found, if witnesses are allowed to talk with each other, events about which they aren't positive are many times told exactly the same way by several others at the scene and the unsure witnesses then do become positive about how the events occurred, using the majority version rather than what they actually remember. From the opposite view, if a witness saw something that no one else seemed to have seen, this witness can then become less convinced of what he or she saw, and may instead report the event using the view the majority seems to hold. There is also always the possibility that the witnesses will know some of the people involved in the murder well enough to want to help them. Separating the witnesses lessens the chances of them being able to develop a common story that they will all tell the police.

For many witnesses at a murder scene, particularly minor witnesses, the interview will be conducted right away near the crime scene. It is important to talk to these witnesses not just while the event is fresh in their minds, but also before they have had time to worry about whether or not they should become involved. If interviews are conducted a day or two later, the shock and excitement of the crime have worn off and the person often isn't as willing to tell everything he or she saw. Homicide detectives conduct these on-the-scene interviews one-on-one, usually in a police car or at some other location where the interviewee and detective won't be disturbed, and most are tape-recorded.

Interviewing witnesses well requires skills that homicide detectives acquire only through years of experience. Starting off immediately by asking witnesses what happened often won't get the information the detectives need. Homicide detectives must first take the time to establish rapport with the witnesses by being friendly and cordial, and often by inquiring about their welfare. Once they have established rapport, though, homicide detectives must then ask open-ended questions that will elicit the witnesses to talk about what they have seen. This is much preferred to just having the witnesses give short answers to specific questions, which can often result in them leaving out valuable information.

A report by the U.S. Department of Justice states, "Because the witness, rather than the interviewer, possesses the relevant information, the witness should be mentally active during the interview and generate information, as opposed to being passive and waiting until the interviewer asks the appropriate question before answering. The interviewer can encourage the witness to be mentally active by directly requesting this activity or by asking open-ended questions."[6]

Homicide detectives, however, must be aware that all individuals like to think of themselves as rational and clear-thinking, and no one wants to appear to have been a sucker or look foolish. Therefore, witnesses will seldom tell any part of a story that would make them look that way. Experienced interviewers, if they suspect this is the case, can overcome it by establishing good rapport with witnesses and by telling them of times in the past when they were suckered or made to look foolish, even though their actions and motives were pure. Misery loves company, and people feel much more comfortable talking about an embarrassing situation if they think the person they're talking to has experienced the same thing.

Establishing rapport with individuals being questioned, while not only vital, is also a skill that can usually only be developed through experience and practice. For rapport to be built, the detective, no matter what the demeanor of the person being questioned, must appear cordial and friendly. The detective must also appear non-judgmental and fair, seeming to be interested only in arriving at the truth and clearing up the matter under investigation. Establishing good rapport means never talking down to people or appearing to look down on them and their lifestyle. Quite the opposite, building rapport means appearing to those being questioned as a person holding values very similar to theirs.

Occasionally, though, homicide detectives find, witnesses will not want to disclose all they know about a murder because of the fear of harming others, including the possible murderer (particularly if the victim, in their opinion, deserved what he or she got). Sometimes also, witnesses don't want to talk because they are worried about the reputation of the victim, particularly if they know the murder occurred because he or she was involved in something illegal or simply bad. Good rapport can also overcome these problems. After establishing this rapport, detectives explain that they need to know all of the facts of the case before it can be cleared up, and that anything bad said will likely not be made public or attributed to the witness. Also, good rapport can convince interviewees that their truthful cooperation will likely serve everyone's best interests in the end. Good rapport will make witnesses like and trust the detective, who must then do everything he or she can to show that this trust was well founded.

Usually, the police tape record on-scene witness interviews so that the lead homicide detective can review them later, since assisting detectives are the ones who often conduct on-scene witness interviews. A tape recording can also be valuable later if witnesses give a different statement or testimony in court, and can be used before the trial as verification of what they said. Often, days or weeks after a murder, or during the trial, witnesses may attempt to deny saying what they said to the police at the murder scene. And of course, detectives always verify the identity of all witnesses talked to at the murder scene since the lead detective will often want to contact them later with follow-up questions.

If witnesses, however, appear to have very valuable and pertinent information about a murder, they may be taken to the police station for questioning. Here, of course, the police have a much more controlled environment. Homicide detectives also usually have witnesses transported to the station if they believe the witnesses have more information than they are giving on the scene or if the homicide detectives believe the individuals may be more involved in the murder than just as witnesses. When at the police station, many homicide detectives, along with gathering as much pertinent personal information as possible about critical witnesses to a murder, such as name, address, place of employment, and so on, also often like to take a photograph of them. This way if an arrest is made in the case years later, locating the critical witnesses can be much easier, as people often change jobs, addresses, and even names.

Witnesses who saw a murderer whose identity they and the police don't know will usually be asked to view mug shots of possible suspects. Most large police departments now have these computerized, so that rather than looking through large books, witnesses view the mug shots on a computer screen.

If the police, on the other hand, do have a definite suspect in the case, they may ask witnesses to view a photo lineup. In this instance, the suspect's photograph is inserted with a half dozen or so other photographs, and the witnesses are asked to see if they can pick out the person they saw at the murder scene. To be valid, the suspect's photograph must not stand out in any significant way from the other photographs, and the individuals in the other photographs must resemble the suspect in significant features. For example, the suspect's photograph must be the same size and format as the others, and it wouldn't be valid to have the photograph of a bald suspect put in with photographs of individuals having full heads of hair, and so on. Our computer program at the

Indianapolis Police Department has a feature that allows us to let the computer randomly select photographs of other individuals who match the significant features of the suspect.

In the event a live lineup of suspects is used, the same safeguards apply. The other individuals in the lineup must generally fit the suspect's physical features. Most detectives, however, find that they often have better luck getting an identification from a photo lineup than from a live one. Even though the live lineup subjects cannot see the witness, a live lineup is much more stressful for a witness. Also, a photo lineup is naturally much easier and less costly to put together than a live lineup.

Before a photo or live lineup can be conducted, however, the police must first interview the witnesses. Homicide detectives conduct most of these witness interviews with only a little advance planning, since the most they hope to gain from these is general information about what happened. They will plan a little more for interviews with critical witnesses, such as those who saw a suspect. However, they plan most suspect interrogations in great detail, since the detectives hope these will generate important information, small admissions, or perhaps even a confession. Before going into a suspect interrogation, homicide detectives usually attempt to find out all they can about the suspect: his or her background, criminal record, level of involvement in the murder, and what physical evidence and testimony connects the suspect to the crime. Also, homicide detectives must always be up to date on the latest street slang so they won't misunderstand what a suspect is saying.

"The most productive interviews are planned well in advance," said an article in the *FBI Law Enforcement Bulletin*. "Except in exigent circumstances, competent investigators have learned to invest time in the initial information gathering process."[7]

Some homicide detectives even use a checklist to make certain they have investigated the suspect's background and lifestyle thoroughly. It is important in an interrogation to have facts about a suspect that can counter, if necessary, any information the suspect offers. These facts can include, besides the items mentioned above, such things as job performance, demeanor at work and home, relationships with others, financial and personal problems, and so on. It is also important to know about the suspect's temperament and likely attitude before the interrogation begins. With these facts, a homicide detective can decide on the best way to approach and break down a suspect.

Before actually conducting an interrogation, some homicide detectives like to have an informal interview first with possible suspects. During this informal interview the detectives can attempt to establish rapport and can also obtain any information on likely alibis, motives, and the suspects' opportunity and ability to commit the murder. In addition, all of the information gained in these pre-interrogation interviews can then be used in the planning of the formal interrogation.

However, as talked about with physical evidence, information from witnesses and suspects should be collected with the intent of arriving at the truth in an investigation, and not just supporting a belief already formed by the investigator about who is guilty. Until an unrefutable conclusion of guilt is reached, experienced homicide investigators know that they must keep open minds and, though they may develop theories during their investigation, they should be ready and willing to replace or modify these theories upon the discovery of any reliable witness or suspect statements that contradict them.

In the interrogation of a murder suspect, the actual questioning almost always takes place at the police station, and usually in an interrogation room. These are rooms the police have specifically designed for interrogation use. The rooms must ensure privacy, have good lighting, be painted neutral colors, and allow nothing to interfere with or disturb the interrogation. Ours at the Indianapolis Police Department, for example, have all of the above conditions, and are also set up so that the suspects sit against a wall where they and the detectives are visible in the videotape being made of the interrogation.

Making a videotape of an interrogation can be extremely helpful, particularly if a suspect confesses or makes incriminating statements. Often later, regretting having said anything, suspects will deny making a confession or will claim that the police coerced the confession from them. Having a videotape to play at the trial can quickly deflate these types of charges.

"Electronic taping will solve once and for all, did he say or not say it," said Rob Warden, executive director of Northwestern University's Center on Wrongful Convictions.[8]

"(Taping) would eliminate a lot of miscarriages of justice, a lot of frivolous claims of police misconduct," said Professor Richard Ofshe, an expert on police interrogation and false confessions.[9]

In addition to the audio- and videotaping of interviews and interrogations, many homicide detectives also maintain an interview log. This log lists everyone interviewed during a murder investigation, and contains not only specifics about the case but also about each person interviewed or interrogated, such as the date and time of the interview or interrogation, interviewing officer, location of interview or interrogation, and any specifics about the interview or interrogation that might have a bearing on the case.

An interrogation of a murder suspect, homicide detectives find, must be set up and staged as well as any performance given in a theater. During the questioning of a murder suspect, the interrogators sit so that nothing behind them distracts the suspect. The only things to look at are the interrogators. They also sit in positions that allow them to move closer to the suspect when it becomes appropriate. The suspect, however, is seated with limited room to move away from the interrogator.

Exactly how the interrogators and suspects sit in relation to each other at the start of the questioning, however, depends on the preferences of the interrogators. Most like to start with them and the suspects about six feet apart and with nothing blocking the full view of the suspects, since good interrogators want to watch the total body for body language signs. Some interrogators also like to start off sitting at a forty-five-degree angle to the suspects so that the interrogation doesn't begin confrontational. As mentioned earlier, the room and seating arrangements must be designed so that as the interrogation continues, the interrogators can move their chairs closer to the suspects, but the suspects cannot move away from the interrogators. Moving closer to the suspects allows the interrogation to become more intimate, and also allows a light touching of the arm or shoulder if indicated during the most emotional parts of an interrogation.

Although good interrogators maintain eye contact with the suspects during an interrogation, they don't stare at them, as the suspects can view this as threatening. An occasional break of eye contact can actually facilitate rapport building. Also, good interrogators never cross their legs or fold their arms. This can also appear confrontational. Instead, experienced interrogators sit with their feet on the floor, palms visible, and arms open.

"Perceptive interviewees can sense your attitude as it is expressed through the formulation and presentation of your questions and the way you listen to the responses," said ex-FBI agent Charles L. Yeschke. "They are keenly aware of verbal and nonverbal signals expressing negative attitudes."[10]

Interrogation is an art form that most in police work say usually comes only from years of practice. "It is a skill learned through the conduct of a great many interviews and the patient and continuing observation of human nature," said retired FBI agent John E. Hess in his book *Interviewing and Interrogation for Law Enforcement*. "The wise investigator knows that the development of interview skills is a life-long process."[11]

However, it has been my experience after thirty-six years as a police officer that some people are simply able to become much better interrogators than others. This is because a good interrogator must also be an astute actor and salesman. Good interrogators must be able to persuade murder suspects that they are individuals the suspects can trust, who feel empathy for them, and who understand what they went through that led them to commit the crime. At the same time, good interrogators must be able to sell suspects on the idea that confessing to the crime and telling the police all about it are in their best interests.

Along with the above, being a good interrogator also comes from being able to establish rapport with all types of suspects, which is not an easy task considering the heinous crimes many of them have committed. To establish this rapport, though, interrogators will often attempt to show some general similarities between them and the suspects, using such statements as, "I've done a lot of stupid things in my life, too," or "I'm not sure how I would have acted under that much stress myself." But most important, good interrogators must show respect for suspects and treat them simply as good people who have done a bad thing.

"Convicted felons have explained that they more likely would confess to an investigator who treated them with respect and recognized their value as a person," said David E. Zulawski and Douglas E. Wicklander in an article in *Law and Order* magazine.[12]

However, a trait also extremely important for good interrogators is the ability to be flexible and ready to change tactics if it becomes apparent that a tactic being used isn't working. No one interrogation technique will work with all suspects. That is why it is important for an interrogator to research a suspect beforehand and to plan the interrogation tactics, and alternate tactics, based on the crime, its specifics, and the background and temperament of the suspect. Otherwise, if one tactic doesn't work, the interrogator won't know which tactic is best to use next.

In addition, it is important for interrogators to be able to look beyond their own value systems and attempt instead to see things from the suspect's value system. What may seem important to interrogators can often mean little or nothing to a suspect and vice versa. But by seeing things through a suspect's value system, good interrogators will be able to determine what it may take before a suspect will confess. For example, while an interrogator might assume that the suspect would fear going to jail or prison and consequently losing his or her job and contact with family members, the suspect may not be concerned at all about this and actually fear most a loss of status among his or her peers. While many people may have a hard time understanding how something so vitally important to them could be so very unimportant to others, good interrogators use this knowledge about a suspect's value system, along with the rapport they have built, to persuade the suspect to give admissions or make a confession by showing the suspect some way that what he or she fears most can be mitigated.

For any interrogation to be successful, however, homicide detectives must always be cordial and polite to a suspect no matter what the suspect's attitude and demeanor, even in the face of angry and hostile insults. In addition, good interrogators must never show shock, disgust, or any type of judgment, no matter what the suspect tells them. Also, experienced interrogators must be even-tempered and objective, and must always appear interested in and sympathetic to the suspects, as most suspects will try to portray themselves not as evil, but rather as good people who have done something bad. Along with all of the above, good interrogators, while the questioning is going on, are always looking for some way that will allow the suspects to save face while still confessing to the crime or giving relevant information about their involvement in it. Many suspects want to confess, but they want to do it in a way that paints them as victims themselves: victims of circumstance, victims of unbearable stress, and so on. Very, very few people want to be seen as someone with evil intentions. Good interrogators, therefore, are always looking for and suggesting scenarios and themes surrounding the crime that will paint the suspects in this light.

However, in spite of all the preparation and rapport building, before the police can question a suspect in custody about a murder, there are certain legal barriers that must first be overcome. The U.S. Supreme Court requires police officers, before a custodial interrogation, to advise suspects of their Miranda rights against self-incrimination. These rights warnings come from the famous 1966 *Miranda v. Arizona* case.[13] Although attempts have been made through legislation to override the necessity of giving these warnings, the U.S. Supreme Court in the recent *Dickerson v. United States* case recognized the Miranda rights as having reached "Constitutional proportions."[14] What this means is that the Supreme Court has ruled that Congress cannot legally pass a law that would restrict the necessity of giving these rights warnings, as they are now considered an integral part of the U.S. Constitution. The Miranda rights warnings are the following:

1. You have the right to remain silent.
2. Any statements made can be used against you.
3. You have the right to have an attorney present during questioning.
4. An attorney will be appointed for you if you cannot afford one.

If the police do not advise a suspect of these rights before a custodial interrogation, usually any statements given by the suspect cannot be used in a trial. There are exceptions to this rule, however. For example, in emergency situations involving the public's safety, the police can question suspects before advising them of their Miranda rights. In *New York v. Quarles*, for example, the court ruled that a person captured after a chase, during which a gun was discarded that could have been found and picked up by children, could be immediately asked by the police where the gun was, and that any statements given could be used against the suspect.[15] Also, in *Illinois v. Perkins*, the court ruled that an undercover police officer who is pretending not to be a police officer, naturally, does not have to give the Miranda warnings before talking to criminals.[16]

The Miranda warnings, however, apply specifically to the interrogation of individuals in police custody. Therefore, they do not apply if suspects are being questioned voluntarily and are free to call off the questioning and leave whenever they want. However, being in police custody is often a matter of a person's perception, and most police officers, if they think they might elicit incriminating information, will usually give the Miranda warnings even if the person came in for questioning voluntarily.

However, they don't have to. For example, in 2000, the Supreme Court of New Mexico refused to throw out the conviction of Lawrence Nieto for four counts of felony murder, even though the police didn't give Nieto the Miranda warnings before he confessed to the murders during questioning at the police station. The court held that Nieto had voluntarily accompanied the officers to the police station and had agreed to be interviewed. Even though the interrogation during which Nieto gave incriminating statements occurred in a closed office at the police station, in which Nieto claimed he felt the police were holding him in custody—since a police detective stood in front of the door—the court said that he in fact was not in custody and could have left at any time.

In addition to giving the Miranda warnings, the interrogations of juveniles involved in a murder case have traditionally required other special handling. Before conducting the questioning of a juvenile suspected of murder, interrogators in the past, along with giving the Miranda warnings, have also had to obtain the permission of a parent or guardian. In addition, the parent or guardian had a right to be present during the interview or interrogation if he or she wished. However, on June 1, 2004, the U.S. Supreme Court ruled in the case of a seventeen-year-old murder suspect, whom the police interrogated while making the parents wait outside, that the police do not have to give any special treatment to juvenile murder suspects.[17]

In any murder interrogation, once the Miranda rights have been given, the questions, particularly at first, should be simple, open-ended, and non-threatening. Suspects are under tremendous stress, and asking complex or threatening questions right away will likely only confuse or scare them into silence. Therefore, one of an interrogator's greatest attributes is patience. Trying to rush an interrogation will almost certainly doom it to failure. It takes time to break down a suspect, get little admissions, and then finally a confession.

"An interview is more of a marathon than a sprint," said former FBI agent Charles L. Yeschke.[18]

If interrogators, though, feel that a suspect is very likely guilty, they may state early in the interrogation that they believe the suspect is involved in the incident in some manner, and then will look for ways to help the suspect make the small admissions that will eventually lead to a confession. Also, interrogators note what response came from the initial accusation of involvement in the murder. Anything but an instant and emphatic denial, which is delivered without signs of deception, means that the interrogators should start to work looking for admissions.

As talked about above, almost all murderers know that what they did was wrong, but few want to think of themselves as evil people. Most murderers therefore rationalize why they killed a person, usually in a manner that makes them seem like not such a bad person. A good interrogator facilitates this. A good interrogator tries to find rationalizations for why a person committed a murder, but does it in a way that allows the murderer to save face.

Many times this rationalization by murder suspects will involve projection and minimization. In projection, even though the suspect admits committing the act, the blame for it is projected onto someone else, sometimes even onto the victim. For example, suspects may claim that the victims antagonized them until they snapped, or that another person would have harmed them or a loved one if they didn't commit the murder, and that person therefore deserves the blame. In minimization, again suspects admit their involvement, but minimize their own blame, or see their part in the incident as minor, even though they may have pulled the trigger. For example, they may claim that the person they killed had done something bad and deserved to die, or that the person unnecessarily resisted during a robbery or other crime. Therefore, their blame is minimal. Often also, murderers are willing to confess, but only if they can do it in a way that doesn't cast them in the role of an evil person, but rather as a person under tremendous stress who was simply pushed too far, or perhaps as a person who went along with a plan developed by others, such as a robbery, but who certainly didn't know that the robbery would end in a murder. Many suspects will listen eagerly to any theme presented by the interrogator that will cast them in a good or sometimes even neutral light.

However, as occasionally happens, if the crime is seen by the suspects as being so heinous that they simply can't talk about it, interrogators can often get a discussion started by using a third-person narrative about some other individual who was involved in very similar circumstances. Suspects will often feel more comfortable discussing what might have occurred to this other person the interrogator is talking about.

Many times, after an interrogator offers a third-person narrative such as this and discusses it with a suspect, or after an interrogator has obtained several admissions from a suspect that change the original story given, the suspect will occasionally still not admit anything significant or offer a confession, but will instead become very passive. The body may slump, the suspect may not be able to meet the detective's eye, and he or she may even begin crying. Suspects realize that the detective knows for certain that they committed the crime, but still they aren't certain whether they should make a full confession or not. The suspects also realize that lying and denials are no longer working. The suspects may want very much to confess but just can't quite make themselves do it.

A skilled interrogator, seeing this change, uses the rapport already established and gently guides the suspects into a confession, allowing the suspects to use whatever rationalizations or face-saving excuses will make their confessions easier. It is at this point that a touch on the shoulder or hand may be appropriate. The interrogator tells the suspects in a soft, soothing voice that all of the lying and deception are what has caused the pain and turmoil they are experiencing, and that just by telling the truth the suspects can rid themselves of the tremendous crushing pressure they're under. The interrogator might even suggest that, since the murder, the suspect's life has probably become a nightmare. Only by coming clean will this change.

At the moment just before confession, interrogators have been known to pray with suspects or ask suspects to visualize what their mother or father or someone who is in heaven would want them to do. This is also the proper time for such phrases from the interrogator as, "I know you didn't mean this to happen" or "I know you never really meant to hurt anyone."

Once a suspect begins a confession, however, an experienced interrogator never interrupts, but allows the suspect to completely finish before asking follow-up and clarification questions. Interrupting will break the suspect's train of thought and narrative flow, and can cause important details to be left out. If a suspect does need prodding during a confession, good interrogators always use open-ended questions such as, "Then what happened?" or "What did you do next?" These types of questions encourage the suspects to talk and expound on what happened during the commission of the murder.

Experienced homicide detectives also realize that few suspects ever confess to murder without a lot of work by the interrogator, and that few confessions come full-blown by themselves, but usually only follow a series of small admissions. Consequently, experienced interrogators attempt to get suspects to make these small admissions, such as being in the area of the crime. Following this admission, the interrogator will then attempt to get an admission that places the suspect even closer to the crime, and so forth until eventually the suspect is involved in the crime. Admissions also come when the interrogator catches the suspect in a lie or discrepancy.

To explain these, the suspect must often make a small admission. Enough of these small admissions will eventually lead to a confession. And yet, because no one wants to be cast in the role of an evil person, most confessions don't contain all of the details, particularly details that would put the suspect in an unfavorable light. These details must often be obtained from witnesses, physical evidence, or even from the confessions of other suspects.

Often though, before obtaining a confession, or when questioning a witness, the police may believe that some of the statements given are not true. There are a number of ways during an interview or interrogation for a homicide detective to tell whether a subject is telling the truth or not, none of them, though, 100 percent accurate. As a matter of fact, an article in the *FBI Law Enforcement Bulletin* stated, "Repeated studies have shown that traditional methods of detecting deception during interviews succeed only 50 percent of the time, even for experienced law enforcement officers."[19] What this means is that homicide detectives can never depend on any one sign to mean that a person is lying, but rather they must watch for clusters of signs that denote deception.

What are some of these signs of deception during an interview or interrogation? There are many. For example, lying usually makes people very uncomfortable and nervous, and they will often fidget in their seats, cross and uncross their legs, drum their fingers, preen by picking real or imagined lint off of their clothing, or constantly look at the clock. Other signs of discomfort and nervousness caused by lying include closing the eyes for long periods of time, rubbing the face or head, and blinking. According to the article in the *FBI Law Enforcement Bulletin* quoted above, "Research also has shown that when people are nervous or troubled, their blink rate increases, a phenomenon often seen with liars under stress."[20]

Along with looking for deception, interrogators also look for signs that subjects are telling the truth. "Truthfulness is signaled by an acute memory, a perceptive recanting of facts, and flowing narration," said former FBI agent Charles L. Yeschke. "Truthful interviewees display a consistent recollection of details and attempt to dig up related specifics, often offering more information than they were asked for." However, Mr. Yeschke also adds, "When interviewees express themselves in a calculated, disassociated, or awkward manner rather than a smooth, flowing way, something, somewhere, is not altogether right."[21]

Also, a number of studies have found that people who are telling the truth use nonverbal gestures to emphasize their words. Liars have usually planned out what they are going to say, but have not planned out a presentation, and if they do use a lot of nonverbal gestures these gestures will be out of rhythm with, and don't seem to fit, what they are saying, as would gestures that come naturally when a person is telling the truth. Interrogators always look for gestures that appear to be inappropriate for what is being said, such as nodding the head when denying a crime, or a shaking of the head that isn't consistent with the words.

In particular, though, interrogators question any statement beginning with, "To tell you the truth" or "To be honest" or "I swear to God that," and so on. Individuals use these preambles to impress the interrogator, and such things often precede deception.

Eye contact, on the other hand, is many times not a good indicator of deception or honesty. Practiced liars know that many people judge the truthfulness of statements through the amount of eye contact, and so they practice maintaining it. Also, in some cultures it is considered disrespectful for individuals to look at someone of superior status in the eye if that person is accusing them of wrongdoing.

Some individuals who study deceit claim, "Truthful people tend to lean forward as they converse; liars tend to move away."[22] Also, some experts claim that liars rarely point a finger when talking. "Finger pointing or hand movements," these experts claim, "exude confidence—a quality liars usually lack."[23] In addition, some experts claim that if a right-handed person gazes to the left, that person is attempting to recall truthful information, and vice versa for left-handed people. It has been found, however, that liars, rather than trying to recall information, often stall for time when being questioned. They do this by asking to have a question repeated or by trying to misdirect the interrogator through asking him or her a question. Along with the above, according to an article in FBI Law Enforcement Bulletin, "Research shows that guilty people often avoid using contractions. Instead of saying, 'It wasn't me,' liars will say, 'It was not me,' to ensure the listener clearly hears the denial."[24]

Although there are always exceptions, people who are telling the truth will tell their stories with a smooth, even flow, and with very little break time to think about what they are going to say. They will want to cooperate with the investigation and, though perhaps nervous at being questioned, will not be overly so. Individuals telling the truth will respond immediately to questions and will refute instantly and clearly any accusations of guilt. Innocent people will usually express surprise or shock at being accused of something they didn't do.

On the other hand, individuals lying during an interrogation will often appear extremely nervous and anxious. When accused of being involved in a murder, they will feign either anger or resignation that they are going to be a scapegoat. Also, they will often pause several seconds before each response, and will many times respond to accusations of guilt with evasive answers rather than denials, such as saying, "What could make you think that I would want to kill him?" rather than simply saying, "I didn't kill him." Deceptive individuals, it has been found, tend to talk around questions, will challenge any information given by the interrogator, and will often offer far-fetched scenarios about what might have happened during a murder.

To detect deception, homicide detectives will also sometimes ask suspects what they feel should be done to someone who committed a crime similar to the one being investigated. Innocent people usually describe some type of punishment, while guilty people often want to mitigate the consequences. Guilty people will also many times question whether a crime was really even committed at all, and, even if so, they will try to mitigate its seriousness and suggest a degree of punishment usually much less than that suggested by innocent people.

While many people might not think it is fair for interrogators who are attempting to detect deception during the questioning of suspects to use deception themselves, interrogators often do this because it so often works. Interrogators will many times suggest to suspects that they have more evidence connecting them to the crime than they really do, that they have witnesses they really don't have who can place the suspects at the crime scene, or that the suspects' partners are at this moment spilling their guts and likely implicating the suspects as the key players in the murder. Also, interrogators might tell suspects that they are getting ready to have an imaginary piece of evidence analyzed by the crime lab, and that they and the suspects both know that the results will implicate the suspects. Some detectives will even bring to the interrogation a large file or a videotape with the suspect's name on it. It is simply laid somewhere and not spoken about.

Although many readers might believe that this type of deception and staging is unethical and would void any confession brought about through it, the courts have supported this type of interrogation, apparently on the premise that it will only make guilty people confess. Of course, this tactic has to be used carefully by interrogators and only at a time in the interrogation when it appears that the suspect is on the verge of confessing. If used too early in an interrogation, a suspect may call the interrogator's bluff, and, once it has been established that the interrogator is lying, little will be accomplished after this.

In those cases in which homicide detectives believe, either through the signs discussed above or through other evidence gathered, that witnesses or suspects are lying to them, often they will offer the witnesses or suspects an opportunity to take some type of mechanical lie detection test. There are two types of lie detection devices used by the majority of police departments in the United States: the polygraph and the voice stress analyzer.

The polygraph, which has been around and in use by the police for decades, utilizes various measuring devices attached to the person being questioned to record physiological changes that occur when a person lies. A polygraph measures changes in the heart rate, electrodermal activity of the skin, blood pressure, and breathing of the person being questioned.

During a polygraph examination, the polygraph operator fastens two tubes around the chest and abdomen of the test subject. The examiner uses these to measure the test subject's respiratory rate, which changes when lying. The polygraph operator also places a blood pressure cuff around the test subject's upper arm to measure heart rate and blood pressure, which also change when lying. Finally, the examiner attaches devices called galvanometers to two of the test subject's fingers. The human fingers are some of the most porous spots on the body, and these galvanometers check for increased sweatiness caused by deception. They do this by measuring changes in electrical conductivity caused by increased perspiration. Most polygraph operators also use a countermeasures cushion. This is a device the test subject sits on that detects any movement the test subject makes, no matter how slight. Some subjects, when answering the examiner's questions, attempt to thwart a polygraph test by clenching their buttocks or pressing one of their toes against a tack or rock placed in their shoe. This has been known to confuse the results of a polygraph test. A countermeasures cushion will detect this.

While in the movies, polygraphs are shown as machines with long needles that scribble jagged lines onto graph paper, polygraph operators seldom use these types of polygraphs any longer. Today, rather than the old analog polygraph described above, polygraph operators use digital polygraphs that display the results on a computer screen, which can be printed out if necessary.

Examiners usually conduct polygraph tests in several segments. There will be a pretest time during which the polygraph examiner will talk with the test subject, who is hooked up as described above, and explain to the subject what is going to occur. The examiner will also discuss the questions so that the test subject knows exactly what will be asked. The only stress of the test should be answering the questions, not wondering what the questions will be. During this pretest the examiner will profile how the test subject is responding. Following this will be the actual polygraph test, during which the examiner will ask a dozen or so questions. However, only three or four of the questions actually relate to the incident being investigated. The rest will be control questions used to gauge how the subject is responding to the test. Following this, the examiner will often review the test with the subject and allow him or her a chance to offer an explanation for any signs of deception.

Various analytical inquiries into the validity of polygraph tests show their success rate at between 70 and 90 percent. From my experience, I believe it is somewhere in the middle of this range. As part of my research for another book, I took a polygraph test. I was amazed at how dependent an accurate test is on the phrasing of the questions. This is why the examiner must discuss the questions in great detail with the person being examined before the actual test.

In my own case, during my investigation for another book I stumbled onto the number 1917. While this turned out to be part of a date, I didn't know at the time whether it was a date, an address, or simply the number 1917. When the polygraph operator asked me during my test, "Did you know the significance of the *date* 1917 when you found it?" I answered no. The polygraph showed a "significant physiological reaction." I suggested changing the question to "Did you know the significance of the *number* 1917 when you found it?" When I answered this question no, the polygraph showed a truthful response.

In addition to being certain of the exact phrasing of the questions, several polygraph operators have told me that the questions must also be phrased so that the test subject doesn't have to think about them, but simply answer yes or no. Thinking about a question will also often bring about a "significant physiological reaction." Therefore, much of a polygraph's success rests in the ability of the polygraph operator. He or she must be able to properly phrase the questions, to interpret what the polygraph records, and then be able to use this information to either clear the test subject or document deception.

However, regardless of its limitations, the polygraph can be a powerful tool for a homicide detective. While using it can often bring about a confession, it can also assist homicide detectives in narrowing down the number of suspects.

"Over the years, polygraph testing has markedly improved the effectiveness of criminal investigations worldwide, most notably in its unique ability to exclude individuals from the 'suspect pool,'" said R. Michael Martin, PhD, owner of the Global Polygraph Network. "The recent advent of computerized polygraphs with advanced scoring algorithms and countermeasures detection equipment has only improved this time-tested technique for discovering the truth. Thousands of cases have been solved—and hundreds of wrongly convicted persons have been cleared— through the use of the polygraph, which continues to evolve and gain acceptance in the scientific community."[25]

The voice stress analyzer, unlike the polygraph, doesn't have to be attached to the subject of the inquiry in order for it to work. This device, instead of measuring physiological changes, measures changes in the frequency modulations of a person's voice. These changes reportedly occur because of the stress brought on when a person lies as compared to the ordinary frequency modulation of a person telling the truth. Voice stress analyzers can be used with or without the subject's cooperation, and can be used with tape recordings. This device, when in use, records frequency modulations graphically onto a computer screen. These can also be printed out on a strip of graph paper. A person trained in the use of the voice stress analyzer examines the graphs for changes in the frequency modulation when a subject makes certain statements or answers certain specific questions. Like the polygraph test, the success rate of the voice stress analyzer falls short of 100 percent. However, both of these devices can be extremely useful tools for a homicide investigator who doesn't base his or her whole case on them, but instead uses them as just one aspect of the case.

In addition to the two devices above, modern science has stepped in recently and greatly expanded the field of lie detection. For example, research using an fMRI (functional magnetic resonance imaging) machine shows that when a person lies, certain areas of the brain, specifically the anterior cinglate and right superior frontal gyrus, become more active than they do when a person tells the truth.

"The fact that deception requires extra work in a number of brain regions may indicate that the deception involves inhibition of the 'default' response—truth," said Professor Daniel Langleben of the University of Pennsylvania.[26]

Along with the above findings, researchers Drew C. Richardson and Lawrence Farwell have discovered that the ability to detect activity in parts of the brain used in memory recovery can also be useful in criminal investigation. They have shown that stored memories will excite certain areas of the brain when recovered. They have found that when criminals are shown pictures of a crime they committed, their brains will exhibit a specific electrical brain wave called P300, which individuals not involved in the crime will not exhibit if shown the same pictures. For example, if a murderer is shown pictures of random individuals, nothing will happen. However, if the murderer is shown a picture of the murder victim, a P300 brain wave activates because the murderer's brain is accessing memory of the crime. This is a totally involuntary response that cannot be stopped or controlled by the test subject.

Dr. Richardson and Farwell's device for detecting P300 brain waves, which they call "brain fingerprinting," consists of a headband with attached electrodes that are hooked to a computer. They used this device recently to assist attorneys in freeing a man who had served almost twenty-five years for a murder he apparently didn't commit.

Terry Harrington had been convicted of the 1978 murder of a Council Bluffs, Iowa, night watchman. However, when shown pictures of the murder a jury had convicted him of, Harrington's brain showed no signs of P300 brain waves, but did when shown pictures of his alibi, which the jury had rejected. When Dr. Richardson confronted Harrington's chief accuser with the results of the brain fingerprinting, the accuser recanted and admitted falsely accusing Harrington in order to throw suspicion off of himself. In 2003, the Iowa Supreme Court overturned Harrington's conviction. He is now a free man.

In an opposite outcome, a man suspected of being a serial murderer offered to be tested through brain fingerprinting in order to prove his innocence. However, the tests showed that the man's brain held memories of several of the killings. He subsequently pled guilty and confessed to the murders.

In other experiments, Dr. Richardson and Farwell's invention has been able to identify, with 100 percent accuracy, which out of a group of men were FBI agents by showing them photographs only FBI agents would recognize. Because of its success, the FBI and CIA are now injecting major funding into more research into brain fingerprinting, seeing the possibility of it being used not only to find criminals but also in other ways, for example, using it in instances in which they need to confirm whether or not a person is lying about being a terrorist.

Interestingly, while police investigators are concerned about criminals lying during interrogations, they are also just as concerned about innocent people lying when they falsely confess to crimes. Often, when murder cases receive large amounts of media attention, innocent people will, for various reasons, attempt to confess to them. While many of these people have obvious mental problems, occasionally seemingly normal people will falsely confess to crimes. For example, in 1991, Laverne Pavlinac found herself involved in an abusive relationship with her boyfriend, John Sosnovske, and wanted out. She thought she saw a way.

When Pavlinac heard that the police were searching for the person who had raped and murdered Taunja Bennett, she came up with a plan. After thoroughly researching all of the media information about the case, Pavlinac called the police and told them that Sosnovske had forced her to help him rape and then murder Bennett. She told the story so convincingly, and with enough facts, that the police eventually believed her and turned the case over to the prosecutor. The prosecutor, also thinking it a good case, filed charges, and a court found both Pavlinac and Sosnovske guilty. Sosnovske received a life sentence and Pavlinac received a sentence of ten years in prison.

Apparently, however, going to prison herself hadn't been part of Pavlinac's plan for escaping abuse by Sosnovske, and so she immediately began recanting. However, no one believed her. It finally took the confession of the real killer of Bennett, serial murderer Keith Jesperson, who had to take the police to where he had hidden Bennett's purse, before they believed Pavlinac. A court finally freed Pavlinac and Sosnovske, after almost five years in prison.

"The evidence they had at the time was ample evidence to convict," said Multnomah County District Attorney Michael Schrunk, who filed the paperwork to have Pavlinac and Sosnovske released.[27]

It is to prevent cases such as this that homicide detectives often try not to release all of the information they have about a murder case to the news media. They many times try to keep secret several facts that only the murderer would know, and thereby prevent being taken in by false confessions.

While the brain fingerprinting and fMRI talked about earlier are tools of the future, homicide detectives are usually able to obtain a considerable amount of reliable information about a murder by using the tools available today. However, once homicide detectives have gathered all of the physical evidence and have taken all of the witness statements, they must then focus their energies on deciding who the most likely suspect in the murder is. While sometimes this is both easy and apparent, often it isn't. Consequently, as we shall see in the next chapter, homicide detectives can many times spend weeks or months sifting through all of the physical evidence and witness statements in an attempt to find the key that points them toward a likely suspect.

CHAPTER 6

Developing Suspects

In 1982, Homicide Detective David Reichert became the first detective assigned to investigate what would eventually become known as the Green River murders. Named after the river south of Seattle, where the first of forty-eight victims of this murderer would be found, this investigation eventually became, because of the number of victims, one of the worst serial murder cases in U.S. history.

Twenty years after being assigned to the case, Reichert would still be involved in trying to solve it. By then, having been elected the sheriff of King County, Washington, Reichert revived the police interest in the murders, which had waned and then been rekindled several times since 1982. Over these years, a large number of detectives had worked on one of the various Green River task forces that had unsuccessfully looked into the ever-increasing number of murders.

Reichert would at last, however, also become involved in finally developing a viable suspect in the case. This suspect would eventually, because of the mounting, and finally conclusive, evidence amassed by the police, plead guilty to the forty-eight Green River murders.

On July 15, 1982, two fifteen-year-old boys out riding their bicycles stumbled onto the body of sixteen-year-old Wendy Coffield. They found her floating just below the surface of the Green River near Kent, Washington, south of Seattle. "When we discovered it was a body, with the hair underwater, to this day, I don't like seeing hair underwater," said Galen Hirschi, one of the boys who found Coffield's body. "There's a connection there."[1]

Within six months, five more bodies turned up near the Green River. The police discovered that all of the victims had been young prostitutes, and all had been strangled to death. In the following years, more bodies of strangled women, ranging in age from fifteen to thirty-eight, all attributed to the work of the same murderer, began turning up around the Seattle area. Some, the police found, had been slipped into the river, some buried, some covered with brush, and some simply dumped. All had been prostitutes. The different ways in how the killer disposed of the bodies led an FBI profiler to erroneously conclude that more than one killer was involved. Eventually, however, the killer branched out, and new victims of the Green River murderer would turn up as far away as Oregon.

When it became clear early on in the case that Seattle had a serial murderer at work, the police formed a task force and began amassing clues, witness statements, and any other information that might prove valuable in developing a suspect. Unfortunately, this was before the advent of personal computers, and the paperwork became so voluminous that much of it, even though valuable, was never reviewed or used to develop a suspect.

Over the years, however, the Green River task forces did use an FBI profiler, who unfortunately missed the mark entirely several times. They also used a psychic named Barbara Kubik-Paitern, who successfully predicted where one of the victims would be found. One time, in order to search a large area for remains, one of the Green River task forces employed a group of explorer scouts. These youngsters discovered a victim of the Green River murderer in a vacant lot near the Seattle airport. One of the Green River task forces even received an offer of help from convicted serial killer Ted Bundy, then on death row in Florida. In 1984, he contacted the Green River task force and offered them his assistance.

"Don't ask me why I believe I'm an expert in this area," Bundy wrote the task force, "just accept that I am and we'll start from there."[2] Bundy soon became a consultant to the task force, giving them valuable insight into the mind of a sexual serial murderer.

While the tips and clues kept coming in, and the police initially identified several suspects, they eventually cleared most of these individuals of any involvement in the case. But not all of them. In 1983, one of the suspects, Gary Leon Ridgway, had been identified as the last person the boyfriend of a murdered prostitute, Marie Malvar, had seen her with. In 1980, the task force discovered, Ridgway had also been accused of trying to choke a Seattle prostitute. In 1982, he had been stopped by the police and questioned because he had a known prostitute in his truck. This prostitute would later become a Green River murder victim. In 1984, the police arrested Ridgway when he tried to solicit sex from an undercover policewoman. Naturally, all of this activity involving area prostitutes made Ridgway a prime suspect in the Green River murders. However, when the police brought Ridgway in and administered a polygraph test, asking him about the Green River murders, he passed it and so they released him.

In April 1987, however, still listing Ridgway as one of their key suspects despite the polygraph test, which, as mentioned earlier, is only 70 to 90 percent effective, the police served a search warrant at his home and also took saliva samples from him. At this time though, the Green River task force didn't have enough evidence to arrest Ridgway, and so they simply kept him on their suspect list.

In April 2001, David Reichert began his first term as the sheriff of King County, Washington. The Green River murders had been an obsession with Reichert for nearly twenty years, and he had never given up hope that they might be solved. Even though the various Green River task forces instituted and then dissolved over the years had spent in excess of $15 million in their fruitless pursuit of the Green River killer, Reichert decided to institute a new task force.

Reichert began with six members, including several forensics experts, whose job it would be to take a look at all the physical evidence accumulated over the years. Before long, though, because of the mountain of evidence and statements to examine, the task force grew to over thirty members. Fortunately for the newly revived task force, a huge development in scientific crime detection was now available that hadn't been available before: DNA testing. The task force sent semen samples taken from several of the earliest victims of the Green River killer to a laboratory for DNA analysis.

On September 10, 2001, Detective Tom Jensen told Sheriff Reichert, "Dave, we've got the guy."[3] A match had come back from the semen to the saliva samples taken from Gary Leon Ridgway.

The police then began an in-depth investigation into the now fifty-four-year-old Ridgway. Reportedly, they found, he had always had a huge sexual appetite. According to his ex-wives and girlfriends, he routinely demanded sex several times a day. He also had an obsession with prostitutes, frequently complaining about them being in his neighborhood, and yet at the same time frequently partaking of their services. As an FBI profiler had predicted, Ridgway was fanatically religious, often carrying a Bible around with him.

On November 30, 2001, the police arrested Ridgway, who for thirty years had worked for the same company as a truck painter. Along with matching Ridgway's DNA, the police also matched paint flakes found on several of the victims with the type of paint used by Ridgway's employer. Faced with mounting evidence and wanting to avoid the death penalty, Ridgway struck a deal with King County prosecutor Norm Maleng, who had once vowed never to bargain away the death penalty. In exchange for not getting the death penalty, Ridgway agreed to plead guilty to forty-eight murders, tell the police about all of the murders he had been involved in, and assist them in locating the remains of any victims not known to the police or yet found.

Attempting to justify the plea bargain after his earlier statements, Maleng said, "The mercy provided by today's resolution is directed not at Ridgway, but toward the families who have suffered so much, and to the larger community. The justice we could achieve was to uncover the truth."[4] As might be expected, some of the victims' families opposed the plea bargain, while others applauded the closure it brought.

Ridgway stuck to the deal he had made with the prosecutor. Not only did he tell the police about all of the killings he could remember, but he even led the police to the bodies of four victims whose murders and identities had been unknown to them. The last killing, the police found, apparently occurred in 1998.

"I killed most of them in my house near Military Road," Ridgway told investigators, "and I killed a lot of them in my truck not far from where I picked them up." He also told the police, "I picked prostitutes as my victims because I hate most prostitutes.... I knew they would not be reported missing right away and might never be reported missing. I picked prostitutes because I thought I could kill as many of them as I wanted without getting caught."[5]

Ridgway went on to relate that he would often drive by the areas where he had disposed of the bodies because it excited him, and occasionally he would want to stop and have sex with the corpses. "That's when I had to start burying them," he told detectives. "I was keeping away from an urge of doing that."[6]

During the police questioning of Ridgway, he also told them that he liked to leave some of the jewelry he had taken from his victims in the women's restroom where he worked. He said it excited him to think of the women he worked with wearing the jewelry of his dead victims.

He also told the police that he had purposely tried to develop and maintain a very meek and mild-mannered look so that prostitutes wouldn't be afraid to go with him. Ridgway said that several prostitutes, upon being picked up by him, had asked whether he was the Green River killer, and he had told them of course not, the killer would have to be a big, powerful man.

"Choking is what I did," Ridgway boasted, however, "and I was pretty good at it."[7]

After gaining Ridgway's cooperation, the police learned that he had enjoyed matching wits with them, and had often left false clues behind. For example, he told them that he would occasionally drop cigarette butts and chewing gum wrappers at the spots where he left the bodies. Ridgway neither smoked nor chewed gum. One time he even sent a letter to the Green River task force, which one of the FBI profilers the task force was using erroneously decided wasn't from the actual killer. Instead, the profiler dismissed the letter as the work of "someone inside the task force seeking undue attention."[8]

In the letter, Ridgway attempted to mislead the police by saying that the killer smoked cigarettes and chewed gum. But he told the truth when he said in the letter that the killer cut off his victims' fingernails in order to prevent the police from gaining any evidence from them. Apparently, several of his victims had scratched him while he was choking them to death.

As we discussed in the previous chapter, even the most heinous of criminals like to see themselves in a positive light. Ridgway was no exception. He told the police, "I thought I was doing you guys a favor, killing, killing prostitutes. Here you guys can't control them, but I can." He also told detectives that he wasn't an evil killer. "I killed 'em," he said. "I didn't torture 'em. They went fast."[9]

Explaining why he killed so many women, Ridgway again tried to paint himself in a positive light. "I had control when I killed the women. I got my rage out for a time. I did cry, yes I did, and that was the good part of me."[10]

On December 18, 2003, King County Superior Court Judge Richard Jones sentenced Ridgway to forty-eight consecutive life sentences. He also fined him $480,000. At the sentencing hearing, the judge ordered forty-eight seconds of silence to remember the victims of Ridgway.

"I'm sorry for the scare I put into the community," Ridgway told the court. "I have tried for a long time to keep from killing any ladies."[11]

While in many murder cases a suspect is immediately apparent, in many others all the police have are a victim and a certain amount of physical evidence and witness statements, but no obvious suspects. Naturally, in these cases the next step, after the physical evidence and witness statements have been analyzed and reviewed, is the development of a suspect or suspects. At times this can flow smoothly to an arrest, but at other times it can end in frustration and the necessity to start over.

As demonstrated in the Green River murders, homicide detectives involved in attempting to develop and identify a suspect often expend a great deal of time and effort trying to do so. In their attempts to identify the Green River killer, the police used a criminal profiler, which we will discuss below, a psychic, and even another sexual serial killer. Eventually, however, it became the physical evidence left at the crime scenes that actually identified the suspect.

There are numerous types of physical evidence left at murder scenes that can assist homicide detectives in developing and identifying a suspect. These can range from things as small and innocuous as a single strand of hair to as large and obvious as a dropped wallet (this has actually happened in several cases I know of in which a physical struggle preceded the murder). Anything left at a crime scene can be used to develop a suspect.

As shown in the Green River murders, DNA analysis has become a major force in modern criminal investigation. DNA, or deoxyribonucleic acid, is the blueprint for our bodies that all of us carry in most of our cells, and is as unique as a fingerprint (except in identical twins). DNA can be recovered from bodily fluids, skin cells, hair, and almost any other bodily trace left behind. This is important because many murders involve a violent struggle, during which the murderer will almost certainly leave DNA traces behind.

"DNA is to the twenty-first century what the smoking gun was to the twentieth," Greensboro, North Carolina Homicide Detective Leslie A. Lejeune told me. "Crime scenes can be contaminated, witnesses make mistakes, and suspects lie, but DNA can't be disputed."[12]

To assist in making suspect identifications, most states have now established DNA banks in which they store samples of the DNA taken from individuals convicted in their states of violent crimes. Because of the success of DNA identification, in 1998 the FBI set up the Combined DNA Index System, or CODIS, which links the information stored in the various state DNA banks. With CODIS, the DNA recovered from a murder scene in California can be matched to a criminal arrested for a violent crime in New York. As of April 2004, the FBI had over 1.6 million convicted offender profiles stored in CODIS, and the system had produced over 11,000 "hits," or DNA matches between crime scene DNA and a suspect.

"This basically is the fingerprint technology of this century," said Joseph M. Polisar, president of the International Association of Chiefs of Police. "The potential for us in the criminal justice field to solve crimes with this technology is boundless."[13]

We had a case recently here in Indianapolis that demonstrates the power and value of CODIS. On April 13, 1985, Sergeant Mike Crooke of the Indianapolis Police Department Homicide Branch received a new assignment. Earlier that day, police officers had been called to a creek bed on the north side of the city. There they found the body of fifteen-year-old Tracey Poindexter, who an autopsy would show had been raped and murdered. Relatively new as a homicide detective, Sergeant Crooke nevertheless thoroughly investigated this case. However, no arrests resulted. Although he sent the semen recovered from Poindexter's body to the police department's property room, in 1985 it held little evidentiary value without a suspect. The Tracey Poindexter murder became Sergeant Crooke's first unsolved case, and he never forgot it.

In 2001, Sergeant Crooke attended a conference where he listened to a speaker who talked about the FBI's new CODIS system. Immediately upon returning to Indianapolis, Sergeant Crooke recovered the semen sample taken from Poindexter and sent it in for a DNA analysis. Several weeks later, Sergeant Crooke received the news he had hoped for.

A DNA match had come back to a man named Sterling Riggs, who, Sergeant Crooke discovered, had just been released from prison after serving fifteen years for a kidnapping and rape very similar to the Poindexter case. In November 2001, after a jury convicted Riggs for Poindexter's rape and murder, a judge sentenced him to 130 years in prison. Under Indiana law, this means that, with good behavior, Riggs will have his first parole hearing in 2066.

How the police obtain DNA samples from individuals suspected of murder, but who (unlike Riggs) are not in the state's DNA bank, depends on the case. If there is a considerable amount of evidence connecting a suspect to a murder, the police can usually persuade a judge to issue a limited search warrant that will allow them to obtain a DNA sample, often a simple swab of the mouth. In other cases the police have to be ingenious and occasionally even a little sneaky. The police have often been known to invite a suspect to headquarters for a not-in-custody talk and then recover cigarette butts or a water glass the suspect drank from for DNA. But sometimes they have to go even farther than this.

In 1982, Seattle police officers found the body of thirteen-year-old Kristen Sumstad, who had been raped and strangled. While they suspected neighbor John Athan of the crime, they had little physical evidence; and in 1982 the semen recovered during the autopsy held little value. By 2003 though, when the police reviewed the case, this evidence had become extremely valuable. They knew they could compare it to Athan's DNA. However, they found that Athan had since moved to New Jersey and had apparently stayed out of serious trouble, so the police didn't have a sample of Athan's DNA to compare it with, and not enough evidence to obtain a limited search warrant. So the police came up with a plan.

Officers printed up stationary from a fictitious law firm and sent Athan a letter saying that he was eligible for money as part of a class-action lawsuit concerning the city overcharging for parking tickets. All he had to do was fill out an enclosed form and mail it back, which he did. Homicide detectives then had a sample of Athan's DNA from his saliva where he had licked the envelope to seal it. The police sent this sample in for analysis, and a positive match to the semen came back. The police then had enough evidence to arrest Athan.

Naturally, Athan's lawyer argued that the police had obtained their DNA evidence, if not illegally, then certainly unethically, and that it should be thrown out. The judge, however, disagreed, citing other examples where the police regularly use ruses to obtain evidence, such as prostitution stings, acting as drug dealers, and setting up phony fencing operations. The DNA evidence was legal. On January 21, 2004, a jury in Seattle convicted Athan in the murder and rape of Kristen Sumstad; and on March 5, 2004, the judge sentenced Athan to ten to twenty years in prison.

While DNA analysis is relatively new, the use of fingerprints to identify murder suspects has been around for nearly a century, as everyone's fingerprints, like DNA, are unique to them. However, until the last few decades the recovery of a fingerprint at a murder scene had little value if the police didn't have a known suspect to compare it with. For many years there was no realistic way to compare a fingerprint recovered at a murder scene against the millions of individual fingerprints police departments routinely had on file. However, that was before the advent of the Automated Fingerprint Identification System (AFIS). This is a complex computer system that analyzes fingerprints digitally and stores these digital images in its memory. Then, when a fingerprint recovered at a murder scene is inserted into AFIS, the computer analyzes the fingerprint digitally and compares it against the millions stored in its memory. Usually in just a few minutes, the computer brings up the closest matches to the analyzed fingerprint, a task that would take years if done by hand. A fingerprint technician then manually examines the ten or so fingerprints given by the computer against the evidentiary fingerprint to find the correct match.

In 2004, the Indianapolis Police Department became the first police department in the United States to use an AFIS computer system for the comparison of not only fingerprints, but also palm prints. Homicide detectives find that nearly as often as recovering fingerprints, they recover palm prints at murder scenes. These, like fingerprints, are unique to each individual. It is expected that within the next few years most other major cities in the United States will follow Indianapolis' example.

As with CODIS, the FBI maintains a link of the various AFIS computers in local police departments across the United States. This can be a tremendous help in apprehending criminals who routinely move from state to state. For example, we had a man arrested several years ago at Indianapolis International Airport for having a stolen gun in his luggage. Since we knew he was giving us a false name, we sent him down to Identification and then ran his fingerprints through the FBI AFIS hookup. Before he could be transported up to our office, we received a hit from Birmingham, Alabama, giving us his real name and informing us that he was wanted there on bank robbery charges.

"The introduction of AFIS has meant to law enforcement in the last of the twentieth century and on into the twenty-first what the two-way radio meant to police agencies in the early twentieth century," Royce Taylor, a former police officer and now AFIS consultant, told me. "Its positive impact on criminal investigations has been immeasurable."[14]

Along with DNA and fingerprints, the evidence left behind by murderers who kill with firearms can also be used to identify possible suspects. As talked about earlier, it has been found that the rifling, or grooves cut into the inside of a gun barrel, makes distinctive and unique marks on the bullets fired through the barrel. This same uniqueness holds true for the imprint put on a primer casing by a gun's firing pin, and also for the markings made on a semi-automatic bullet casing when it is ejected from a gun.

Using the Integrated Ballistics Identification System (IBIS), police departments can now digitally scan bullets and bullet casings recovered from various sources and enter this data into their firearms computer databank. Then, bullets or bullet casings recovered at murder scenes can be analyzed and compared against the bullets or casings in the police department's databank. This can often link them to a specific gun and gun owner. Much as the FBI does with CODIS and AFIS, the Bureau of Alcohol, Tobacco, Firearms and Explosives (ATF) maintains the National Integrated Ballistics Information Network (NIBIN), which links the firearms computer databanks in local police departments across the United States.

According to an article about NIBIN, "Through its National Integrated Ballistics Information Network (NIBIN) Program, the Bureau of Alcohol, Tobacco, Firearms and Explosives (ATF) deploys Integrated Ballistic Identification System (IBIS) equipment into state and local law enforcement agencies for their use in imaging and comparing gun crime evidence."[15] Presently, ATF has 228 law enforcement agencies hooked into NIBIN, and the system has made over 7,500 "hits," or positive comparisons, since the program's inception in 2000.

Often, the police find, when they send a bullet or bullet casing in for comparison, it will be determined through NIBIN that not only was the gun the bullet came from used in the case under investigation, but often also used in other, older murder cases, too. For example, on June 2, 2000, the police in Houston, Texas, found a security guard murdered, and they subsequently recovered a .40-caliber bullet casing at the crime scene. When homicide detectives entered the bullet casing into NIBIN they discovered that the .40-caliber gun used in the murder had also been used in a robbery with shots fired on May 20, 2000. On the same day, the police found, another robbery occurred in Houston, but in this case the robber had murdered two store clerks, also with a .40-caliber weapon. A NIBIN comparison showed that the same weapon had been used in all of these crimes. In looking at other robberies with shots fired, the Houston Police Department discovered that the same gun had been used in a robbery on February 11, 2000. In this robbery, a credit card had been taken, and soon afterward someone had unsuccessfully attempted to use it. In talking with the clerk at the store where the unsuccessful attempt to use the credit card had occurred, the police finally got her to admit that she knew the man who had presented the card. Subsequently, the police arrested two men and found the .40-caliber gun that had been used in the murders and robberies. In a similar case, the Boston Police Department used NIBIN to connect one 9-mm firearm to fifteen different shootings between June 2, 1999, and July 20, 2000.

A further way the federal government assists local police departments in developing suspects in murder cases is through the Violent Criminal Apprehension Program (VICAP). The FBI manages this program through its National Center for the Analysis of Violent Crime. VICAP works by comparing information submitted by local police departments about unsolved murders with murder cases submitted by other jurisdictions. According to a booklet from the FBI about VICAP, "The information is accepted at VICAP, checked for accuracy, and becomes part of an increasingly comprehensive data bank of homicides that will always be available for comparing and tracking serial offenders. The case information is then compared to other cases in the data bank for similarities in physical, informational, and behavioral characteristics."[16]

As I have shown in several of the instances so far involving serial killers, these murderers often move around through many jurisdictions when committing their crimes. But by utilizing VICAP, two or more police agencies can determine whether it is likely that they are working on separate murders committed by the same individual. Often, one jurisdiction will have the key piece of evidence needed by another jurisdiction to link the cases and identify a suspect.

"Linkage blindness is basically a communication problem," said University of Houston criminologist Steven Egger. "It's an Achilles heel in the nation's strongly decentralized police departments, which can range from one-man departments to thousands."[17]

Homicide detectives who are looking to develop and identify a murder suspect may also occasionally, as was demonstrated in the Green River murders, use the services of a criminal profiler. These are forensics specialists who, using the physical evidence left at the crime scene, the composition and layout of the crime scene itself, victim characteristics, witness statements, and any other information relevant to the case, draw a picture of the probable characteristics and lifestyle of the criminal who committed the murder.

Brent E. Turvey, in his book *Criminal Profiling*, describes his occupation this way: "Criminal profiling is the inference of offender traits from physical and/or behavioral evidence."[18]

However, criminal profiling is only a tool like the polygraph; and, like the polygraph, though quite often accurate, can also occasionally be totally wrong, as it was several times in the Green River murders. Profilers base a criminal profile on the belief that certain types of people commit certain types of crimes. While this is often true, a homicide detective must remember that not everyone is alike, and not everyone fits a certain pattern. Consequently, criminal profiles should be considered only as probabilities.

"Any discipline that involves interpreting the multidetermined nature of human behavior cannot be referred to as a hard science with a straight face," says Brent E. Turvey. He goes on to add about criminal profiling, "It cannot typically point to a specific person, or individuate one suspect from all others. It can, however, give insight into *general* personality and characteristics of the person responsible."[19]

As the Green River murder cases demonstrated, the criminal profilers they used were partly right and partly wrong about the profile they developed for the Green River murderer. Therefore, while a criminal profile can be a useful tool to assist a homicide detective in knowing where to look for a suspect, depending on it as if it were infallible can be a serious mistake that can cause a homicide detective to waste hundreds of hours talking to the wrong people. Readers have only to recall the Washington, DC, area sniper case in October 2002. Several criminal profilers had publicly declared that the sniper was a white male working alone. Of course, the snipers turned out to be two black males.

In addition to criminal profiling, there are also many scientific studies available that claim to delineate the most common characteristics of various types of killers. These, too, must be used cautiously. Although they may point a homicide detective in a general direction, every human being is different from every other one, and a suspect may or may not actually fall into one of these scientific classifications.

Scientific studies and computerized identification systems aside, as I discussed in the first anecdote in this book, the Tahnesia Towner murder, we partially developed a suspect in this case by reconstructing the crime (though other events also contributed to the identification of the suspect). We decided that since Towner had been killed during a busy time in her apartment complex, her body must have been hidden somewhere in the apartment building until dark. This led us to believe, rightly so, that the killer lived in Towner's apartment building. While we reconstructed this crime in the office simply by discussing it, reconstructing a murder can often require homicide detectives to seek the assistance and services of many other specialists, such as forensic anthropologists, criminal profilers, pathologists, psychologists, crime lab technicians, and others.

Along with all we have discussed so far, homicide detectives, when looking to develop a suspect, always search for a motive. Although there are murderers who seemingly kill at random, even these murderers have a motive, usually involving the satisfaction of some sexual or psychological need or fantasy. Most murderers, though, have a much clearer motive. Most murderers kill their victims for very concrete reasons. For example, whenever we have an adult female murdered, we first look to a relationship motive because so many female murder victims are killed by husbands, ex-husbands, boyfriends, and ex-boyfriends. Whenever we have a young child murdered, we again suspect a relationship motive and look first at the parents or caretakers as the murderers because, as an FBI report states, "The number of infanticides (victims under age 5) has grown roughly in proportion to the number of young children in the population, with most perpetrators being a parent."[20] This is not to say that a stranger or non-family member never kills a very young child, only that it is rare.

Even in cases not as clearcut as relationship murders, the police can often establish a motive by looking extensively into the background of the victim, a discipline called victimology. An article on victimology concerning the murder of a young, single female stated, "The gathering of information about the victim is of such importance that it should begin upon the investigator's arrival at the crime scene with the questioning of witnesses and neighbors." The article goes on to state, "Such information will include: what were the characteristics and traits of [the victim]? What were her hobbies, her habits, her sexual interests, her lifestyle, her reputation, and her pastimes? Who were her associates? Did she habitually place herself in situations and/or locations which put her at risk of becoming the victim of a violent crime?"[21]

In my experience working with homicides, I have found that answering the questions above about a victim's background can also occasionally answer the question of why a person was murdered and by whom. For example, recently in Indianapolis we had a young man who worked in the ministry shot and killed while in a high-crime area of Indianapolis. Those who knew him insisted that he was a fine young man who, besides working in the ministry, also held two jobs. They claimed that he must have been killed when he stopped to help someone in distress, which they said he was known to do quite often. However, a little checking into his background showed that, along with being in the ministry, he was also heavily involved in narcotics. Narcotics detectives found us an informant who told us that he was present when the young man had stopped to buy some dope. Apparently, the young man didn't have enough money to pay for it, and so he grabbed the dope out of the pusher's hand and tried to drive away. The pusher shot him through the rear window of his car and killed him.

In determining a motive, as in the case above, we always look for risk factors in a person's life. What did this person do, or with whom did this person associate, that would put him or her at risk of being murdered? Often, in order to develop a murder suspect we must first understand the victim. We all have sides of us that we don't want others to know about; and many times, the police find, these can figure into the motive for murder, as in the case of the young minister above. Of course, in trying to determine a motive, homicide detectives always check to see who benefits most from the death of the victim. Sometimes the benefit is life insurance money, sometimes it's a new love, and occasionally it's just an attempt to escape a loveless or violent relationship.

Occasionally in a murder investigation, all a homicide detective has to go on when looking to identify a suspect is a nickname given by witnesses to the murder. It's amazing but true that in some neighborhoods individuals are known only by their nicknames, and that if you ask for or about a person using his or her real name, no one knows to whom you are referring. Fortunately, most large police departments keep searchable nickname files on the police departments' computer systems. While there will often be several people with the same nickname, this can still narrow down considerably the hunt for suspects. In those cases in which witnesses describe suspects by tattoos, noticeable scars, or some other unusual physical trait, again most major police departments store this information in searchable computer files.

However, when all of the trails leading to the development of a murder suspect hit dead ends, homicide detectives may turn to their or other detectives' informants. All good police officers who have been on the job for any length of time have developed informants. These individuals are often petty criminals or people who have a lifestyle that places them in frequent contact with criminals, and who, for various reasons, will pass on information they receive to the police. Some want to be paid for the information, some want to work off criminal charges they are facing, and some want to do it just because they like the thrill of working with the police.

The police find that using informants often works because a very common, though self-destructive, trait of criminals is the desire to brag about their crimes. While a rational person might suppose that murderers would know better than to ever tell anyone about their crimes, this telling happens regularly. We had a case here in Indianapolis in which a murderer wanted to boast so badly about his crime that he even brought a friend back to the murder scene to show him the body. The friend, immediately upon getting away from the murderer, called the police. Homicide detectives, therefore, often will go to their informants and ask whether they have heard anything about a murder, and, if not, tell the informants to check around and see if anyone is talking about it.

But what a lot of readers probably don't realize is that, using all of the scientific advances and just plain police work I have talked about so far in this chapter, homicide detectives are not looking just to develop a suspect. They are also looking to eliminate suspects. This can save a tremendous amount of work. Eliminating suspects can save weeks or months of running down leads that actually lead nowhere since the person being investigated is not the murderer.

Sometimes, though, no matter how hard a detective works on a murder case, there is simply not enough evidence to develop and identify a suspect. Sometimes all a homicide detective encounters during an investigation are dead ends. Since most large municipalities experience murders on a regular basis, homicide branch supervisors must regularly check on the status of their detectives' cases. When a murder case has been worked for some time and no leads have developed, often the supervisors will deactivate the case so that the detective can give more attention to new cases and to any older cases that do have leads.

However, over time things change. Witnesses unknown at the time of the murder may surface, intimate relationships may sour, new evidence may appear. For this reason, as we will see in the next chapter, many large police departments have formed cold case squads. These are squads of homicide detectives who look into old murder cases and reactivate them if there appears to be any possibility of now solving them.

CHAPTER 7

Cold Case Investigation

For teenagers who lived during the 1970s in Belle Haven, a gated community near Greenwich, Connecticut, the night before Halloween had become known as "Mischief Night." It was the night when the teenagers, armed with shaving cream and toilet paper, played pranks on their neighbors. In 1975, however, it became the last night in the short life of fifteen-year-old Martha Moxley.

The pretty blond teenager, whose family had moved to Connecticut from California a little over a year before, had almost immediately upon moving in attracted the attention of most of the teenage boys in Belle Haven, including Thomas and Michael Skakel, who lived across the street from the Moxleys. The Skakels were close relatives of the Kennedy family. However, Thomas and Michael Skakel were known around Belle Haven as rude and unruly. Most people who knew them felt that the boys had become this way because they saw very little discipline meted out from their widowed father, who, according to neighbors, spent most of his time traveling and drinking.

"Both boys [Thomas and Michael] had reputations among critics as unruly, out of control and violent boozers," said an article in *Insight Magazine*. "And both had their sights set on the new girl in the neighborhood, Martha Moxley, the recent blond arrival from California."[1]

On Mischief Night 1975, Martha's mother, Dorothy Moxley, had set a curfew for her daughter and waited in the living room for her to return, but fell asleep. Awaking at 3:00 a.m. and not finding Martha at home, the concerned mother called the police, who assured her that teenagers often stayed out late on this night, and that Martha would almost certainly return home soon. However, at the mother's insistence, the police conducted a search, but didn't locate Martha.

The next morning, a friend crossing the three-acre Moxley estate found the body of Martha Moxley under a pine tree near the house. Her bloody corpse showed graphic evidence of being bludgeoned to death with a six-iron golf club. Reportedly, a broken piece of the golf club still protruded from Martha's neck, where it had been plunged by the murderer, though this piece of evidence would later disappear. Other pieces of the broken club lay nearby. Martha's slacks and panties, the police found, had been pulled down around her knees, though an autopsy would show no evidence of a sexual assault. Several witnesses in the neighborhood reported last seeing Martha alive on Mischief Night talking to Thomas Skakel.

The golf club used to kill Martha, police called to the scene discovered, turned out to be a Toney Penna golf club, an expensive brand. The police quickly found out that the deceased mother of Thomas and Michael Skakel had owned a set of Toney Penna clubs. Upon learning this, the police naturally went to the Skakel house. At first, Rushton Skakel, the father of Thomas and Michael, cooperated with the police, allowing them to look around the house, where they found a set of golf clubs matching the one that killed Martha. For some reason the police didn't take the clubs as evidence at that time, but did come back later and get them.

The Skakel family, however, soon stopped its cooperation with the police, and eventually the family would not allow any more interviews with Thomas or Michael. For some reason, the police never attempted to obtain a search warrant for the Skakel house, which should have been standard procedure in such a case. Some critics of the case say that the police were intimidated by the Skakels' close relationship to the Kennedys, while others point to the fact that the town of Greenwich had never had a murder of this sort and consequently the police had no experience in dealing with this kind of crime. Interestingly, the handle of the golf club, the one that witnesses said had been seen poking out of Martha's neck, and which later disappeared, would have had Thomas and Michael's deceased mother's name on it.

According to an article in the *New York Times*, "Chief of Police Stephen N. Baran Jr. said that in his thirty years with the Greenwich

Police Department there had only been 'one or two' homicides and 'nothing of this nature at all.'"[2]

Regardless of their inexperience, the Greenwich Police Department conducted an investigation and a number of people, along with Thomas and Michael Skakel, became suspects, including the tutor of Thomas and Michael, a man named Ken Littleton. While the Skakel family had still been cooperating with the police, Michael told them that he and Thomas had left Belle Haven at a little after 8:00 p.m. on the night of the murder. He said that they went to a cousin's house across town, where they watched television, smoked pot, and drank alcohol. Other witnesses, however, including Skakel family members, disputed this account. Regardless, though, of having several suspects, the police made no arrests following their investigation, and so the case eventually went into the department's inactive file. Consequently, the case stayed unsolved through the 1970s, '80s and '90s.

Interestingly, it was the 1991 rape trial of another Kennedy relative, William Kennedy Smith, that brought renewed attention to the Moxley murder case. Rumors spread during the trial that William Kennedy Smith had been visiting the Skakels on the night someone murdered Martha. While these rumors proved false, they nevertheless started investigative reporters looking again into the Moxley murder case.

Finally, Rushton Skakel, the father of Thomas and Michael, apparently tiring of all the speculation about his sons' involvement in Martha's murder, hired a private investigative firm, Sutton Associates, to look into the case and clear his sons' names once and for all. However, when investigators from the firm talked to Thomas and Michael, they found that the brothers had changed the stories they had been telling since 1975. While both Skakel brothers had claimed in 1975 to have been across town at the time of Martha's murder, both now told the private investigators that they had instead been at home, Thomas even claiming to have had a session of mutual masturbation with Martha that night. Enough other discrepancies turned up in the private investigation that Rushton eventually fired the firm he had hired to clear his sons from suspicion.

However, copies of the private investigative firm's file somehow got into the hands of writer Dominick Dunne, who wrote a novel based on the Martha Moxley murder, titled *A Season in Purgatory*. A copy of the report also reached the hands of ex-Los Angeles Police Department Detective Mark Fuhrman, of O. J. Simpson trial fame. Using it, he wrote a non-fiction book about the case, titled *Murder in Greenwich*, and in his book Fuhrman named Michael Skakel as the most likely suspect.

"Martha died because of wealthy people, because wealthy people intimidate the police not to assert themselves," Fuhrman said.[3]

Because of all the attention brought to the case through the books and the William Kennedy Smith trial, a special grand jury began looking into the murder and eventually, in January 2000, issued an arrest warrant for Michael Skakel, charging him with killing Martha Moxley. A trial for the 1975 murder would finally take place.

At the beginning of Michael Skakel's trial, his attorney felt extremely confident of an acquittal because of the scarcity of physical evidence connecting Michael to the murder. Most legal experts who watched the trial agreed. The prosecution, however, brought forth a dozen witnesses who all said that Michael had confessed to them that he murdered Martha. Michael apparently had problems keeping the family secrets secret. According to an article in *Insight Magazine*, "He [Michael Skakel] was the source of tales that led to the late Michael Kennedy's trouble over an affair with a baby-sitter, having blurted out the story at an Alcoholics Anonymous meeting."[4]

Skakel family tutor Ken Littleton told the audience during a television interview that Michael had confessed Martha's murder to him, and that he believed it was the drugs that made Michael do it. "Michael Skakel wasn't Michael Skakel at the time of the murder," Littleton said. "It was the drug dealers who caused his mind to be altered and polluted."[5]

At the trial of Michael Skakel, which began in April 2002, one of the witnesses whom jurors heard from was John Higgins, who had been a student with Michael at the Élan School in Maine. The Élan School is a facility for youngsters with behavioral and substance abuse problems. Higgins told the court that Michael had confessed to him about the Moxley murder while they were sitting on a porch at the school.

"There was a party of some kind or another," Higgins said Michael had told him, "and he related that he later was in his garage and he was going through some golf clubs, and he related that he was running through some woods, he had a golf club in his hands, he looked up, he saw some pine trees."[6]

When asked by the prosecutor if Michael admitted the crime to him, Higgins said, "Yeah, through a progression of statements he said that he didn't know whether he did it, he said that he may have done it, he didn't know what happened, eventually he came to the point that he did do it, he must have done it; 'I did it.'"[7] As a side note, people who knew Michael as a youth said that he used to amuse himself by killing cats and squirrels with a golf club.

The prosecution during the murder trial also played the tape of a 1997 interview Michael had had with a writer who proposed to write an exposé on the Kennedy family, titled *Dead Man Talking: A Kennedy Cousin Comes Clean*. In the interview, Michael admitted being a window peeper in his youth and how on the night of the Moxley murder he had climbed a tree near what he believed to be Martha's bedroom window. Michael told the writer that while up in the tree he masturbated. In the interview, Michael also talked of his jealousy over Thomas' relationship with Martha and how Thomas had always been his "nemesis" when he was growing up.

In addition to the tape recording of the interview, Andrea Renna, a childhood friend of Michael's, testified that Michael's alibi about being across town during the murder was a lie, that he never got into the car that went to his cousin's house, as he had claimed he had for years. Also used as evidence at the trial was testimony from Julie Skakel, Michael's sister, who had told the police in 1975 that near the time of the murder she saw Michael run across the front lawn.

Along with all of this testimony, the prosecution also put Martha's diary into evidence. In it she wrote how she liked Thomas, not Michael, who had complained to several people that Thomas had stolen his girlfriend.

During the trial, Michael Skakel didn't take the stand in his own defense. His attorney claimed that he didn't need to because he had already given his testimony in the tape-recorded interview with the writer that the jury had already heard.

On June 7, 2002, after four days of deliberations, the jury returned a guilty verdict against Michael Skakel for the murder of Martha Moxley. On August 29, 2002, the judge in the case sentenced Michael to twenty years to life.

"I didn't believe his alibi," said Kevin Cambra, foreman of the jury. "There were several holes in that story. He put himself at the scene of the crime on the night of the murder."[8]

Apparently none of the jury believed totally in Michael's innocence when they began deliberations, though four started off undecided. "When we initially took the first poll, there were eight guiltys and four undecideds," Cambra said. "There was not one not guilty."[9]

At the end of the deliberations, however, all twelve jurors finally agreed that Michael was guilty. The jurors found the changes that Michael made to the story he told the police in 1975 very damning. They felt the switch in his story from not being at the scene to being there and masturbating was just his way of hopefully explaining away any of his DNA the police might find at the scene.

"It's nice to say, once in a while, that justice delayed doesn't have to be justice denied," said State's Attorney Jonathon Benedict of the verdict.[10]

While there is an axiom in murder investigation that states that if a murder isn't solved within seventy-two hours the chances of it ever being solved decrease dramatically, the above case demonstrates that there are certainly exceptions. Although it's true that the difficulty of solving murder cases increases as the cases age, there is also always the possibility that as time passes new evidence will surface or that witnesses unknown about when the case was first investigated will suddenly appear. And of course, as technology advances, previously unusable evidence can suddenly become crucial evidence that points to a specific suspect. For this reason, many homicide units in major police departments across the United States have formed cold case squads, whose job it is to look into old unsolved murder cases with the hope of finding any investigations that might now have a better chance of being solved.

"A lot of these cases, we believe, are solvable," said Cincinnati Police Captain Vince Demasi of the department's look at its old murder cases. "So we feel compelled to do this. We just need some time to take a hard look at them."[11]

Sometimes in murder investigation, no matter how competent or how thorough a homicide detective is, a case will come along that may at first appear promising but then lead to nowhere but dead ends. Witnesses can be reluctant to talk to the police, or lie to the police, or have disappeared when the police go to talk to them. In some murder cases, even though there may have been important evidence recovered during the investigation, including even suspect fingerprints or DNA, nothing in either national database matches the evidence. Unfortunately for homicide units, the above problems are not that uncommon as, according to national statistics, 200,000 murders have gone unsolved in the United

States since 1960, and this number grows by 6,000 unsolved murder cases every year.[12]

After seeing their detectives spend several weeks or even months working unsuccessfully on these types of cases, homicide branch supervisors will often have the detectives deactivate them. This means that the murders are no longer being actively investigated, but can be re-opened if new evidence or new witness testimony suddenly becomes available. Homicide branch supervisors must do this so that their detectives can give their full energies to the new murder cases that appear regularly and to the old murder cases that do have substantial leads worth pursuing.

"We had made great strides initially but then got bombarded with other cases," said Charlotte, North Carolina Homicide Detective Valerie Gordon, talking about one of her old unsolved murder cases that was recently solved by Charlotte's cold case squad. "When another murder takes place, the one you are working on takes the back burner."[13]

As we saw in the last chapter with Detective Sergeant Michael Crooke and the Tracy Poindexter murder case, some detectives simply can't forget certain cases, and eventually this pays off. However, in most major cities, homicide detectives are constantly being given new cases, and so most don't think much about the majority of their old, unsolved cases.

However, these unsolved murder cases can pile up until there can be hundreds or even thousands of them in a police department's files. Consequently, in the last decade many major police departments have formed cold case squads. These are squads of homicide detectives whose job it is to look into the police department's old murder cases, pick out the ones that for various reasons now appear to have a chance of being solved, and then to give these cases a preliminary look. If, after this preliminary look, a case appears to have definite promise of being solved, the cold case squad will then reactivate the case.

However, not every homicide detective will make a good cold case investigator, because the work can be much more frustrating than ordinary homicide investigation. "Only the most experienced, innovative, and persistent investigators should work cold cases," said FBI agent Charles L. Regini, "because these cases, by their very nature, represent some of the most perplexing and frustrating investigations that detectives face."[14]

Retired Miami Detective Sergeant David Rivers, who led that department's homicide cold case squad, told me, "We discussed who would come into the squad and we all agreed not all homicide detectives would make good cold case detectives. The reasons for this are varied. Action doesn't come fast and furious. These cases are old and were originally worked by others. There has to be a pragmatic approach. You cannot undo what was done wrong nor can you do what was not done. In other words, you have to get over the 'Why didn't they do this?' syndrome."[15]

Of course, since some police departments can have hundreds or even thousands of unsolved murder cases in their files, reviewing all of these murders and deciding which ones merit a further look can be very manpower-intensive. To meet this challenge, a number of police departments have been hiring back retired former homicide detectives. For example, in 2000, the Los Angeles County Sheriff's Department found that it had over 3,000 unsolved murders in its files; and so, to address this problem, it hired back six former homicide detectives to staff its newly formed cold case squad. How have they done? So far they have reviewed nearly 2,000 of the cases, have solved twenty-nine of them, and have eighty-eight of the cases awaiting evidence testing that wasn't available when the original murders occurred.

The oldest case solved so far by the Los Angeles County Sheriff's Department's cold case squad dates back to 1957 when a man known as the Lover's Lane Bandit killed two police officers who attempted to stop him. Fingerprints that were of no value in 1957, since the police didn't have a specific suspect to match them against, were submitted by the cold case squad to the FBI's national fingerprint databank. The fingerprints came back with a match to Gerald F. Mason, a retired gas station owner in Columbia, South Carolina. In 2003, Mason pled guilty in the case and received a life sentence.

"It's worth the time and effort," said Captain Frank Merriman, head of the Los Angeles County Sheriff's Department's Homicide Branch. "It's going to take a long time to finish this, but at the conclusion of it we will be satisfied that we have done all that we can do for these cases."[16]

Other police departments, not being able to afford to hire back retired homicide investigators, are asking for volunteers to man their cold case squads. Douglas County, Oregon, for example, has four retired police officers who volunteer to work cold cases several days a week, and who started off by solving a 1975 murder. Following this, they solved a 1988 murder.

"Law enforcement has been good to me," said Thomas Schultz, a retired detective who now volunteers his time in the Douglas County cold case squad. "I don't mind donating some time back to the community."[17]

In Nebraska, a grant of $200,000 to the Omaha Police Department and the Nebraska State Patrol is being used to reanalyze evidence from old murder and sexual assault cases. Using this grant money, the police are searching for cases with a likelihood now of solution, and have already solved a twenty-five-year-old double murder.

The Chicago Police Department's cold case squad is made up of a lieutenant, two sergeants, and eighteen detectives. So far, the unit has solved 101 old murder cases. They operate under a five-year grant from the Illinois Criminal Justice Information Authority, totaling almost $100,000 a year, which helps to pay for many of the cold case unit's expenses.

It must be remembered, however, that many old unsolved murder cases are simply not good candidates for a cold case squad. Some cases are no better today than they were when they were deactivated, and in some cases special circumstances prevent any chance of ever solving them.

"There are cases that you'd love to solve, but the evidence is gone and the witnesses are dead," said Lieutenant Thomas Keane, commander of Chicago's cold case squad. "You would just be spinning your wheels."[18]

What positive changes are cold case squads looking for in murder cases that were previously deemed unsolvable? What changes improve the chances of solving an old murder? "Over time people's relationships with each other change," said Detective Gary Smith of the Miami-Dade cold case squad. "Friends are no longer friends. People divorce. They might find religion. So those people who didn't give information before might now be willing."[19] Detective Sergeant Maurice Allcron of the Indiana State Police cold case squad adds, "Ex-husbands and ex-wives make good witnesses. So do jilted girlfriends and boyfriends."[20]

Homicide detectives find that in a new murder investigation, one of the major reasons the investigation can become stalled is because a major witness is in a romantic relationship with the suspect and is therefore un-cooperative with the police. Over time, though, relationships can sour, and witnesses who once felt only love for a murder suspect can now feel only contempt. In other cases, occasionally a person who was stopping a suspect from confessing to a murder will die. For example, we had a case here in Indianapolis in which the murderer of a little girl couldn't bring himself to confess while his mother was alive because he didn't want her to know what kind of person he really was. After she died, however, homicide detectives talked to him, and he eventually confessed to the murder.

In other cold cases, witnesses to a murder might have originally been frightened to testify against a suspect, but now aren't any longer because of a change in their circumstances or in those of the suspect, such as the suspect now being in jail on other charges or being incapacitated in some other way. For example, in Martinsville, Indiana, in 1968, a seven-year-old girl witnessed her father kill a twenty-one-year-old encyclopedia saleswoman, reportedly because she was a black person who had dared to enter a white neighborhood. Although warned by her father to be quiet about what happened, in 2002, with her father now in a nursing home, the woman went to the police and told them what she had witnessed. The police arrested her seventy-year-old father.

Occasionally, witnesses to a murder are just not able to live with themselves being silent any longer. For example, in 1963 Bruce January witnessed the murder of his brother. The murderer threatened that Bruce would receive the same if he ever told what he saw. For forty years the memories of what had happened and how he'd lied to the police about the events of that night tortured January. Finally, when he couldn't stand it any longer, he went to the police and told them what had really happened. Baltimore police arrested a sixty-three-year-old suspect in the forty-year-old murder case.

However, along with reluctant witnesses, another serious problem homicide detectives often encounter while working cold cases is trying to locate witnesses or suspects who may have changed their names or jobs, or who may have moved a half-dozen times in the intervening years. Fortunately, advances in computer science now lessen this problem. In Indianapolis we use a computer program called Accurint, which has access to over 3 billion records and makes locating people, even those who have changed their names or jobs, or who have moved many times, much easier. There are several other computer search programs available that provide similar information services.

In an innovative approach in their search for information about cold cases, a number of police departments now list data about these murders on their Web sites. By putting this information out to the public, police departments hope that perhaps it will jog someone's memory or conscience. In Indianapolis, along with using the police department's Web site, we have also displayed pictures of the victims of unsolved murders on outdoor billboards in neighborhoods where the residents might have information about them.

Finally, scientific advances in forensics technology can often make what was once useless evidence in an old murder case now very valuable. Also, cold case detectives many times find that evidence that was once worthless because it didn't match anyone in the various national databases may now match someone who has been entered into the database since the police department deactivated the case.

One of these national databases, which we talked about in a previous chapter, is the FBI's Automated Fingerprint Identification Systems (AFIS) link. Cold case detectives, as the Los Angeles County Sheriff's Department's detectives did in the incident related above, find that many cold cases for which recovered fingerprints were originally useless can now be solved through the use of the FBI's national AFIS link.

Along with AFIS, another huge scientific advance in forensic technology, also talked about in a previous chapter, is the use of DNA for criminal identification. Much as leaving a fingerprint at a crime scene can positively place a suspect there, so can leaving a DNA trace.

Also, newer DNA testing now requires only very minute samples. "In the '80s, to analyze blood we needed a stain the size of a quarter," said Carl Sobieralski, DNA supervisor for the Indiana State Police. "Now we're working with DNA samples we can't even see."[21]

"DNA technology has changed so much in the last ten, even five years," said Captain Merriman. "It is so much better now. The more advanced it gets the more cases we solve."[22]

As proof of what Captain Merriman above said, cold case units across the United States are now using DNA identification regularly to solve old murder cases. For example, on December 11, 2003, a jury in Houston, Texas, sentenced thirty-seven-year-old William Irvan to death for the February 14, 1987, murder of Michelle Shadbolt. A DNA match to semen taken from the victim convinced jurors that Irvan was the murderer. Homicide detectives in Washington County, Pennsylvania, used DNA evidence in October 2003 to charge forty-eight-year-old David Robert Kennedy with the 1977 rape and murder of Deborah Jeannette Capiola. However, at the same time, they used Kennedy's DNA to eliminate him as a suspect in other rape/murders that the police had originally thought were committed by the same man who had raped and murdered Capiola. In September 2003, Bryan Gelenaw pled guilty in a Seattle court to the 1981 murder of Angela Axelson. A DNA match from evidence at the crime scene convinced Gelenaw that his guilt was obvious and that a trial would be futile. On July 31, 2003, detectives in Houston, Texas charged Charles Ray Bailey with the March 5, 1986, murder of Debra Oliver. DNA taken from a sock used to gag Oliver matched Bailey's.

In one of the oldest cold cases to date solved by DNA identification, on December 10, 2003, police in Wauwatosa, Wisconsin, arrested John Watson, eighty-two, for the 1958 rape and murder of Edna Mauch. Homicide detectives found Mauch's pajamas and other evidence still stored in their property room, and so they sent all of it in for a DNA analysis. Semen on several hairs found on the evidence matched Watson's DNA.

"It was kind of eerie to see all that," said Homicide Detective Lisa Hudson. "I opened the box and there were her bloody pajamas and the bedding, preserved."[23]

Since the case had happened over forty-five years earlier, the suspect likely thought that he'd never be caught for it. "Granted, he may be eighty-two now, but our concern is what he did in 1958," said Detective Keith Warner, who worked the case along with Detective Hudson.[24] As might be supposed, Watson was no stranger to the police, but had a lengthy criminal history, which included a number of cases involving attacks on women.

Reportedly, DNA has provided leads now in more than 8,000 cold cases nationally. "This is one of the wonderful things about DNA," said Paul Morrison, a county district attorney. "We never say never, now. As long as we've got evidence preserved, we're able to go back."[25]

Along with fingerprints and DNA now becoming valuable evidence in cold case investigations, so can bullets and bullet casings that may also have been of limited evidentiary value when the murder case was new. As discussed in a previous chapter, the Bureau of Alcohol, Tobacco, Firearms and Explosives (ATF) maintains a national link among the various local police department firearms computer databases. Consequently, bullets and bullet casings from old murder cases can now be compared for a match in the ATF's national firearms computer database.

Interestingly, while homicide detectives investigating cold cases find that they can get help in their investigations from many governmental agencies, such as the FBI and ATF talked about above, there are also several private groups that have been formed solely for the purpose of assisting in the investigation of cold cases. These groups usually include forensics specialists from many areas.

Max Houck, a forensic anthropologist who once worked at the FBI's crime lab and who assisted in identifying victims of the 9/11 attack on the Pentagon, recently formed the non-profit Institute for Cold Case Evaluation (ICCE). His idea was to make a staff of experienced forensics experts available to police departments wanting help with cold cases.

"They're not publicly known names," Houck said of the forensics experts to whom ICCE will refer police departments' cold case units. "They spend more time in the lab than in front of the camera, but these are people who really do the work."[26] His staff includes pathologists, entomologists, DNA analysts, trace evidence analysts, forensic anthropologists, chemists, and biologists. "We have a very broad stable of experts to choose from," Houck said, "with expertise in everything from firearms and pathology to entomology."[27]

Houck recently attended the International Homicide Investigators Association conference in Las Vegas, where he met with many homicide detectives in order to let them know about ICCE. "The law enforcement agencies are overburdened," Houck said. "They don't have the resources, manpower or funds. We want to give them an edge, a little jump start and help them over that obstacle they may need to solve the case."[28]

According to ICCE's mission statement, "ICCE employs subject matter experts that consist of highly skilled forensic professionals, prosecutors and investigators that have been selected for their operational expertise and reputation within their respective fields. ICCE will establish and maintain a knowledge center of cold case related information to assist in the solution of unsolved cases across the United States, providing closure to state and local law enforcement agencies, victims, and their families."[29]

A similar organization, which has been around since 1990, is the Vidocq Society, named after Eugene Francois Vidocq, a criminal-turned-cop who in 1811 helped form and then become the first chief of the French Surete. The society is made up of lawyers, former prosecutors, former homicide detectives, and forensics scientists. Every month the society meets and its members discuss old murder cases that have been brought to the Society's attention, attempting to give stalled police investigations new directions that may help solve the case.

According to the society's Web site, "All work is done at no cost to victims' families or law enforcement, pro bono as part of the Society's commitment to public service."[30] The Web site also lists over seventy-five areas of forensics science in which the members have expertise.

Since 1990, the Vidocq Society has been consulted several hundred times by police departments and others about cold cases, and it has been credited with solving a number of them. For example, in 1992, Philadelphia police detectives consulted the society about the murder of Deborah Lynn Wilson, a Drexel University student found beaten to death. After reviewing the murder file and discussing the case at their monthly meeting, the members of the Society suggested that the police check for a suspect with a foot fetish. The police did this and it led to an arrest and conviction in the case.

All homicide investigations, fresh or cold, initially aim toward one thing: arresting the person who committed the murder. However, this is often just the beginning for much of the homicide detective's work, because then he or she must prepare for the trial. The trial is the end result of most murder investigations; and while, as we will see in the next chapter, much of what happens during a murder trial is beyond the control of the homicide detective, at the same time, much of the input into a trial that can decide which way the jury will vote relies directly on the work of the homicide detective.

CHAPTER 8

The Trial

Twenty-three-year-old Craig Elias, a former national honor student and standout high school football player, reportedly operated a very profitable drug-dealing business out of a house he rented with twenty-one-year-old Jared Henkel in the Mt. Washington area of Pittsburgh. In this rowhouse, to protect the proceeds of their illegal business, the two men kept several safes that allegedly contained not only drugs but also thousands of dollars in cash. However, upon returning home one evening in March 2002, they discovered that someone had broken into their home and stolen the safes. After checking around to determine who might have committed the burglary, Elias and Henkel then set out to get their stolen property back. With the help of a friend, twenty-one-year-old Jared Lischner, Elias and Henkel abducted two men whom they had worked with several times selling drugs and whom they thought were the most likely ones to have committed the burglary: twenty-two-year-old Anthony Brownlee and nineteen-year-old Andrew Jones.

After six hours of beating and torturing Brownlee and Jones, the three men holding them captive decided to free Brownlee on his promise to bring them at least $3,000 of his own drug money and to never tell anyone about what had happened to Jones and him. Brownlee, seeing the chance to escape with his life, immediately agreed to the terms. The three men figured that Brownlee, being a drug dealer, couldn't go to the police. They also felt certain that he didn't have the courage to retaliate against them for the kidnapping and beating.

The three men did fear that Jones, on the other hand, would retaliate, and so Elias allegedly suffocated him to death and then stuffed his body into a trash bag. Finding that they needed help in disposing of Jones' body, Jared Henkel called his brother, Matthew, and gave him a shopping list of items he needed him to bring to the Mt. Washington home, including duct tape, a fifty-pound weight, and a four-wheel-drive vehicle. Matthew, however, unable to locate a four-wheel-drive vehicle, instead borrowed a white Nissan pickup truck from a friend.

Once at the Mt. Washington house, Matthew helped Elias load Jones' body into the bed of the pickup truck. Although they had originally planned to dump the body in nearby Cheat Lake, West Virginia, and actually started out for there, after a couple hours of driving around, the lost Elias and Matthew eventually ended up in Steubenville, Ohio, about forty miles west of Pittsburgh. On the Market Street Bridge over the Ohio River, they waited until the traffic cleared, and then Elias threw Jones' body off the bridge and into the water. The two men had earlier stopped at a Lowe's store and purchased a chain and padlock, which they used to fasten the fifty-pound weight to Jones. For Matthew's part in helping to dispose of Jones' body, Elias reportedly paid him $1,000.

However, soon afterward, Matthew went to the police and told them what he had witnessed and where Elias had dumped the body. On April 12, 2002, the police pulled Jones' body from the forty-two-degree water of the Ohio River, which had preserved the corpse well enough that it could be easily identified. Soon afterward, the police arrested Craig Elias, Jared Lischner, and Jared Henkel, charging them all with the murder of Andrew Jones. The prosecutor granted immunity to Matthew Henkel in exchange for his testimony about what he had witnessed.

With Matthew's cooperation, the homicide detectives' trial preparation became very straightforward. The detectives attended the autopsy and collected the coroner's report, they searched the Mt. Washington home, they recovered a security videotape from the Lowe's store showing Matthew purchasing the padlock and chain found on Jones, they took a statement from a man who had been called the night of the murder for advice about where to dispose of a body, and they took the statements of both Matthew and Brownlee.

In October 2003, the trial for the three accused men began in Pittsburgh, with jurors brought in from Eire County because of extensive pretrial publicity. The testimony and evidence presented were straightforward and damning. The prosecution had Jones' body bound with the chains and a padlock from the Lowe's store; and, more importantly, they had two eyewitnesses to the crime: Matthew and Brownlee.

Although the defense attorneys for the three accused men did the best job they could, even having Matthew Henkel's father testify that Matthew had confessed to him that he actually murdered Jones, the jury didn't buy it. It appeared transparent to them that the father could blame Matthew without endangering him, because Matthew had received a grant of immunity from the prosecutor.

"We were all under the impression that that was enough to raise some reasonable doubt," said defense attorney Duke George about the testimony of Matthew's father. "But obviously the jury didn't feel there was enough doubt...."[1]

Along with Matthew's testimony about the disposal of Jones' body, the prosecution also presented the eyewitness testimony of Brownlee, who told the court that Elias was the one who had beaten and choked him several times. The coroner supplemented this testimony by telling the jury that Jones had also been beaten and had died from suffocation.

While throughout the trial the three defendants had many times laughed and joked among themselves, the humor disappeared and the three men appeared somber when, on October 21, 2003, the jury convicted Craig Elias of first-degree murder, and Jared Henkel and Jared Lischner of second-degree murder. They did this because they believed that Elias was the one who had actually killed Jones, but that the other two were in on the plot.

"It's very difficult listening to all the evidence and facts," said juror Richard Knaver, who also said there was "no doubt" among his fellow jurors that the three men were guilty of murder. Instead, he said, jurors debated only on which degree of murder.[2]

On January 22, 2004, a judge sentenced all three men to life imprisonment. Although the jury also found the men guilty of the kidnapping and assault on Brownlee, the judge let the sentences for these crimes run concurrently with the murder sentences.

While the above case can certainly serve as an example of a typical murder trial, with the expected outcome, not all murder trials, even those with considerable evidence, end this way. Because juries are made up of people, no one can ever predict with 100 percent accuracy how they will view the evidence, what testimony they will give the most weight to, what exactly they will do when deliberating, or what decisions they will come to, no matter what type of case the prosecution presents them with. In the case talked about in chapter one, for example, involving the murders of Reverend and Mrs. Mathias, the jury, even though presented with what prosecutors thought was damning evidence, still didn't convict suspect Sean Rich of the murders, only of lesser, related crimes. Another demonstration of how jurors can view evidence much differently than prosecutors believe they will is the 2003 trial of accused murderer Robert Durst.

A thirteen-year-old boy fishing in Galveston Bay, Texas, on September 30, 2001, spotted something unusual floating in the water. When he pointed it out to his father, the father at first thought it must be a dead pig. He soon discovered to his horror, however, that it was instead a male human torso minus the arms, legs, and head.

The arms and legs of the dismembered body turned up floating in trash bags in Galveston Bay several days later. Following this, a trash bag that contained a .22-caliber automatic pistol washed up. Besides the gun and the human remains—minus the head, which the police never recovered—authorities also discovered a receipt inside one of the trash bags from a local hardware store and a newspaper with a mailing label for 2213 Avenue K in Galveston.

Fingerprints from the dismembered corpse identified it as that of seventy-one-year-old Morris Black, who lived in a four-unit apartment building at 2213 Avenue K in Galveston. Across the hall from Black, the police discovered during the investigation, lived a woman by the name of Dorothy Ciner. The landlord said that Ciner was mute and communicated only by written messages.

The woman, however, turned out actually to be a man named Robert Durst. Durst was at that time a quarter owner of a multi-billion-dollar company, the Durst Organization, which owns major properties in midtown Manhattan. He had allegedly fled to Galveston after the police reopened the nearly twenty-year-old investigation into the disappearance of his wife, Kathleen. He also quickly became a suspect in the murder of Morris Black.

According to news accounts, the Durst marriage, before Kathleen's disappearance, had fallen onto hard times, and Kathleen had reportedly told a friend, "If something happens to me, check it out. I'm afraid of what Bobby will do."[3]

Something did happen to Kathleen, and detectives who in early 1982 took the missing person report from Robert Durst immediately became suspicious because they found that he had waited four days to report her as missing and he seemed very calm about it. However, police efforts to locate Kathleen were unsuccessful and they never charged anyone in the case. Consequently, Kathleen Durst's disappearance remained as a missing person case for almost twenty years. However, in 2000, the murder of Susan Berman, a friend of the Durst family, renewed the police interest in the Kathleen Durst disappearance. The police had been scheduled to meet with Berman, whom they believed had information about Kathleen's disappearance, but someone killed her before she could talk to them. Durst headed for Galveston and into his disguise as Dorothy Ciner soon afterward.

After Morris Black had been killed and dumped into Galveston Bay in September 2001, Robert Durst fled to New Orleans, but eventually returned to Galveston, where the police arrested him for Black's murder. After posting a $300,000 bond, Durst fled again, but the police arrested him six weeks later for shoplifting a $5.49 chicken salad sandwich in Hanover Township, Pennsylvania. Interestingly, when the police took him into custody for shoplifting they found that Durst carried over $500 in cash in his pockets. The police also discovered that Durst had used Black's identification while on the run. A court soon extradited him back to Texas.

At his trial, Durst pled not guilty and claimed that he had come home and found Black in his apartment. He said that he had once given Black a key, but had taken it back, and figured that Black must have had a copy made. Durst testified in court that, after he ordered Black out of his apartment and Black refused, they struggled over a gun and it went off accidentally, striking Black in the face and killing him. Durst went on to tell the court that he feared the police wouldn't believe him about what had happened and so he used a saw to dismember Black and then dump his body into Galveston Bay.

Looking at the facts of the case, I'm certain that the prosecutor and the homicide detectives assigned to it must have thought that it would be an easy guilty verdict. After all, who could believe that an innocent person would dismember someone they had accidentally killed? In addition, the prosecutor had a blood spatter expert testify that the blood spatter pattern showed that Durst was standing over Black when the shot was fired, and not in a struggle as Durst had claimed. Also, while Durst told the court that he hadn't cleaned the firearm and that the shooting had taken place at close range, the crime lab found no blood spatter or fingerprints on the gun, which they should have if Durst were telling the truth. On top of this, Durst originally told the court that he had no recollection of dismembering Black, but then later described his horror at all the blood that ran out as he sawed Black into pieces.

Cutting up Black's body was like a "nightmare with blood everywhere," Durst told the court. "I remember like I was looking down on something and I was swimming in blood and I kept spitting up and spitting up and I don't know what is real and I don't know what is not real."[4]

However, on November 11, 2003, the jury acquitted Durst. Interestingly, several of the jurors said that they discounted most of Durst's testimony on the stand because of "inconsistencies and past lies." Durst, for example, claimed that he didn't wipe the gun clean, but one of the jurors said, "We know Morris Black (the victim) didn't wipe those fingerprints off that gun."[5] One juror even stated that he found Durst's testimony too unbelievable to consider. "Durst had holes in his story," the juror said.[6] However, all of the jurors said that they did believe his story when Durst claimed that he had killed Black by accident and then panicked, and that it was this panic that made him hack the body into pieces and throw it into Galveston Bay.

When asked whether he was surprised by the verdict, Gerald Shargel, a defense attorney who had followed the Durst trial, said, "Everyone, including Durst, was surprised." He added, "I think the prosecutors put on a good case, but this was just a matter of being outlawyered."[7] Wendy Murphy, a law professor and former prosecutor, said, "Sometimes common sense gets trumped by other things."[8]

The court did not free Durst, however, following the jury's not guilty verdict. He remained in jail under a $3 billion bond on new charges of bond jumping and evidence tampering. Even Durst with his huge fortune couldn't afford this bail.

Reportedly, Durst's attorney, Dick DeGuerin, said that he thought the new indictment for evidence tampering amounted to "sour grapes" on the part of prosecutors who lost a case that many thought would be a sure thing.[9]

While many people might be stunned at the jury's verdict in the Durst case, my experience with juries has led me to never be surprised by what they do or decide. Juries, I've found, often see things differently than the prosecutor thinks they will. In addition, many times things other than the facts presented during the trial will also enter into their decisions. For example, some experts who followed the Durst trial suspect that the jury likely came back with its verdict not because they didn't believe the facts and think that Durst was guilty, but because the way prosecutors charged Durst left the jurors unable to find him guilty of anything that didn't involve the death penalty. What many homicide detectives have found over the years is that, while many jurors have no difficulty in believing that someone committed a murder, they do have a problem in returning a conviction if they believe it will lead to the death penalty.

A recent article about murder cases and the death penalty stated, "Even when defendants seem truly evil, it is difficult to accept the judge's strict instructions, to dole out punishment, to take at least partial responsibility for a human being's life or death. No philosophy class, no religious training, no school of hard knocks prepares anyone for pressure like that."[10] This is the reason why, even though the evidence may be overwhelming, juries will often find murder defendants guilty of something less than first-degree murder, guilty of something that doesn't involve the death penalty, as we saw likely occurred in the Mathias case in chapter one.

However, sometimes jurors can reach their decisions in more unusual ways than just that of worrying about the possible penalty. For example, in Indianapolis we had a murder case similar to the Durst case in that we thought we had more than enough evidence to support a guilty verdict. However, the jury came back with a not guilty finding. When we spoke with the jury afterward, one of the jurors stated very matter-of-factly, "Well, we knew the officer was wrong because that's not the way they do it on *NYPD Blue*."

While this was so ludicrous as to be almost humorous, unfortunately much of the background information that juries use to make their decisions comes from television and movies. Retired Miami Homicide Detective Sergeant David Rivers told me this about the effect of television and movies on juries: "They come to expect us to be able to do all the things they see on *CSI* and like shows. We actually need to watch (sometimes this can be painful) these shows to know what a witness or family member is talking about. During a trial the prosecutor has to educate the jury to the TV phenomena."[11]

A recent magazine article on evidence recovery also reflects on the effect that television programs such as *CSI* have on the public's perception: "As we keep going forward, the public scrutiny is going to be even five times harder because they believe the shows, what they see and how quick they think that you can turn around crime scene evidence and get the bad guy."[12]

Homicide detectives find that juries do often wonder, as expressed in the article quoted above, why it sometimes takes the police months before they finally arrest the guilty party in a murder case. This is particularly true for those jurors who every week watch homicide detectives routinely arrest the bad guy before the end of their favorite television police show. Consequently, juries many times may give credence to a defense attorney's claim that his or her client is just a fall guy because the police investigation had stalled with no real suspect. After all, nobody on television or in the movies ever takes that long to catch the bad guy.

But what other factors, beyond those already discussed, can cause juries to come to these sometimes odd decisions? What other factors can cause them to side with a defendant when all of the evidence points toward his or her guilt? Some of the reason for this has to do with how defense attorneys present the case for their clients and how juries decide on the value and believability of the testimony given by both sides. However, the main reason for odd jury decisions is that good defense attorneys can have a strong hand in deciding who get on a jury. They do this through careful and studied jury selection.

The legal process of *voir dire*, which literally means "to speak the truth," is meant to be a mechanism by which the court can find a pool of jurors from the community who will impartially judge the case at hand. This process involves allowing both the prosecution and the defense to question prospective jurors about issues that they believe will affect the person's objectivity. As a part of *voir dire*, both sides have a limited number of "peremptory" challenges, through which they can remove a certain number of prospective jurors without having to give any reason. After these peremptory challenges are exhausted, however, attorneys must then show cause for eliminating a prospective juror.

While *voir dire* may be intended to bring about an impartial jury, actually both sides use it for just the opposite reason. Both sides hope to be able to pack the jury with individuals who will be sympathetic to their proposed presentation.

"Attorneys select jurors whom they will be able to persuade, not jurors who will be 'fair and impartial' to both sides," said attorney Marni Becker-Avin in a recent article about jury selection.[13]

As an example of this desire to find jurors who will be favorable to the defendant's case, in the 2004 trial of Scott Peterson in California, in which Peterson was accused of killing his wife and unborn child because he was involved in an extramarital affair, defense attorneys asked prospective jurors some very personal questions that related directly to the facts of the case. They asked prospective jurors whether they had ever lost a child, what their opinion was about extramarital affairs, and how they stood on the death penalty. Along with these questions, the actual questionnaire the court required prospective jurors to fill out (which was twenty-three pages long) also asked them such things as whether they read *Field & Stream* magazine and what bumper stickers they had on their cars.

While readers can likely see the rationale behind the first three questions, most will probably wonder why anyone would care about *Field & Stream* magazine and bumper stickers. The reason is that jury selection in the United States has risen to the level where high-priced attorneys now regularly employ "jury consultants." These are individuals or firms that, using various psychological principles, can supposedly tell defense attorneys generally what kind of jurors, and even specifically which of the prospective jurors, will most likely be sympathetic to their clients. Apparently, in the Scott Peterson case these psychological principles can somehow relate magazine readership and belief in certain causes, which bumper stickers would seemingly foretell, to the type of jurors who would be most sympathetic to Peterson. However, since the jury eventually convicted and sentenced Peterson to death, this demonstrates that professional jury selection is not yet an exact science.

Yet still, sometimes carefully picking a jury can pay big dividends. In a news article about why the jury returned a not guilty verdict in the Durst case, writer Heber Taylor said, "[T]he defense team did a remarkable job of picking a jury. Initial polls showed 88 out of 100 people thought Durst was guilty, while 12 thought he was not. Defense attorneys found those 12."[14]

Of course, the Durst case aside, there have been many other murder trials, such as the Scott Peterson case, in which carefully picked juries have not come back with the verdict defense attorneys had hoped for. This is usually a direct result of the type of case the homicide detectives have put together. To be successful, the homicide detectives and prosecutor must be able to anticipate what the accused murderer's attorney will use as a defense and be ready to counter it. This can often lead to much more investigative work for the homicide detectives. It is not uncommon for prosecutors to give homicide detectives long shopping lists of additional items they want investigated before they will be ready to charge a defendant with murder or to try the case in court. While my detectives often grumble that some of the items are nitpicking, a good prosecutor doesn't want to be caught unprepared during a trial.

"Any prosecutor who has tried murder cases will attest: there's no such thing as a 'simple homicide case,'" Johnson County, Indiana Prosecutor Lance Hamner told me. "Witnesses must be meticulously interviewed, evidence must be protected both physically and legally, and arguments must be crafted so that they are as persuasive to the unsophisticated juror as to the highly educated one. The grueling process ends only when the verdict is read. And the verdict must be unanimous, or it's not a verdict at all."[15]

Defense attorneys, however, even those who feel they have successfully countered the extensive work talked about by Mr. Hamner above—and contrary to what happened every week on the *Perry Mason* television program—really don't expect anyone in the audience or on the witness stand to suddenly break down and admit that they, rather than the accused, actually committed the murder. Rather, in many murder cases, defense attorneys know or highly suspect that their clients are guilty. Their hope is not to be able to prove beyond a reasonable doubt that their client didn't commit the murder, but only to raise even small doubts in the jurors' minds. The prosecution, not the defense, is the one who has to prove the case beyond a reasonable doubt. The defense doesn't need nearly that level of proof.

Defense attorneys attempt to raise these small doubts by bringing in their own "experts" to counter what the prosecution witnesses have stated and to give their own interpretation or analysis of evidence. Defense attorneys also try to raise doubt in jurors' minds by getting witnesses on the stand to change their testimony, even in very minor ways, from the statements they gave to the police. This, defense attorneys hope, will then raise questions in the jurors' minds about the credibility of the witnesses.

Attorneys for accused murderers also attempt to raise small doubts in the jurors' minds by employing a tactic called "You can't unring the bell." What this involves is defense attorneys suggesting things to the jury, such as a conspiracy by the police to railroad their client, which the prosecutor will immediately object to. While the judge may sustain the objection and instruct the jury to disregard the statement, defense attorneys know that they have planted the idea in the jurors' minds.

What else can homicide detectives expect from defense attorneys during a murder trial? There are many tactics taught in law schools about how to defend against criminal charges. One of these is a three-pronged tactic that states, first, attack the evidence. If this doesn't work or isn't possible, attack the witnesses. If this doesn't work or isn't possible, attack the police.

How does this three-pronged line of attack come into play during a murder trial? First, defense attorneys attack the evidence by attempting to have any incriminating items collected by homicide detectives excluded from the trial, usually by claims that they were obtained illegally or improperly. They may also attack the chain of custody, implying that the evidence has been tampered with, or they may simply attack the validity or relevance of the evidence.

If this attack on the evidence fails, defense attorneys will often move on to attacking the state's witnesses. Defense attorneys will question the witnesses' credibility and the reliability of what they saw or heard, and they may even accuse them of lying against the defendant for various reasons.

Last, when other efforts have failed, defense attorneys attack the police in a variety of ways. They may accuse homicide detectives of having a vendetta against their client, particularly if their client has a long arrest record, something often common with murderers. Defense attorneys may also accuse homicide detectives of doing a sloppy job of investigation and attempting to cover it up by railroading their client. Finally, defense attorneys may claim that mistakes were made in the police investigation that led to the "erroneous" arrest and prosecution of their client.

A homicide detective testifying on the stand, therefore, must understand the subtleties of what the defense attorney is trying to do. The defense attorney doesn't really expect the homicide detective to admit a vendetta or to making a mistake, but only wants to plant the idea in the jurors' minds. Defense attorneys also want to raise doubts in the jurors' minds about a homicide detective's credibility. They do this by attempting to get homicide detectives to contradict themselves. In many murder trials, defense attorneys take depositions before the actual trial. Depositions are sworn statements about the case taken by the defense attorney in the presence of a prosecutor. These not only allow defense attorneys to get a pretrial look at what testimony will be given at the trial, but defense attorneys often study these statements intensely in the hope that a homicide detective will say something on the stand that contradicts, even in some small way, what he or she said in the deposition. If this occurs, the defense attorney will usually instantly attack the detective's credibility, again in the hope of planting a small seed of doubt in the minds of the jurors.

Consequently, there are a number of rules homicide detectives have developed over the years that guide them in preparing for a murder trial and for their courtroom testimony:

1. While the lead homicide detective will be the person most intimately acquainted with the facts of the murder case being tried, all of the homicide detectives who have worked on the case in any capacity may be called to testify, and therefore should also be intimately acquainted with all the facts of their part of the case. However, a few minutes before being called to testify is not the time to review the case. Because murder trials are often complex and time-consuming, they many times do not take place until a year or so after the actual crime, and sometimes even longer than this. Between the time the detective investigated the murder and the actual trial, he or she may have worked a dozen other murder cases. Because of this, relevant facts can become confused or forgotten. Homicide detectives, therefore, should give themselves time to completely review the case, or at least their part in it, and should particularly review any depositions they have given in the case because the defense attorney has most certainly studied them and will jump on any changes in testimony. When jurors see a police officer on the witness stand who seems unsure of the facts of the case, they will often tend to lean toward the defense attorney's argument

of reasonable doubt. Testimony that flows smoothly and naturally will be given more credence than will testimony from someone who fumbles through notes or who simply reads the information to the jury.

2. A strict rule for homicide detectives is, "If it's not in the report, it didn't happen." Homicide detectives can be certain that defense attorneys have obtained and read copies of all of the police reports in any murder case. Talking about something on the witness stand that is not included in the official police reports will almost certainly be immediately attacked by defense attorneys as proof of a cover-up and plot to wrongly convict their clients. In addition, this information will likely be stricken from the trial anyway because it wasn't given to the defense during the "discovery" process, which is a legal procedure by which defense attorneys receive access to all of the evidence the prosecution has.

3. Homicide detectives on the witness stand should answer only the questions asked, and never elaborate. Defense attorneys are always looking for information not given to them during the discovery process and will attempt to get police officers, and witnesses, to provide them with this information by having them elaborate on the questions asked. They many times do this by pausing for lengthy periods after the officer or witness has finished answering a question. Many people find long periods of silence like this uncomfortable and will often attempt to fill them. Experienced homicide detectives know better and simply patiently wait for the next question.

4. Homicide detectives on the witness stand should *never* lose their temper, no matter what a defense attorney says or implies. Homicide detectives who lose their temper play very badly in front of juries. It says that perhaps, as the defense attorney has suggested, they are hotheads who are trying to railroad an innocent person after all. Besides, experienced homicide detectives know that the defense attorney usually doesn't really mean it when he or she accuses them of wrongdoing or sloppy police work, but is simply doing it in the hope of influencing the jury. But even more important than not losing their temper, homicide detectives should never attempt to engage in a battle of wits with a defense attorney. This will also often play badly to the jury, making the detectives appear smug and patronizing.

5. The dress and demeanor of a detective can greatly affect the amount of credibility a jury gives his or her testimony. Experienced homicide detectives know to dress conservatively and neatly, and to always be polite and attentive on the stand. How a witness looks and acts affects the jury's perception of the value of that person's testimony. Homicide detectives should always strive to appear as professionals simply doing a job, and doing it well.

But one of the hardest things for many police officers to do when testifying in court is to speak without using police jargon, which the jury may not understand. Homicide detectives must learn to tell about the incident in simple, ordinary language that jurors cannot misinterpret.

6. Homicide detectives are usually the ones responsible for bringing the physical evidence of a murder case to court. Experienced homicide detectives know that they must check on this evidence several days before the trial. Property rooms of large police departments can be huge, with thousands of items stored there, and things do get lost or misplaced. The morning of the trial is not the time to begin a search for missing evidence.

7. Since a lengthy period of time can often pass between the arrest of a murder suspect and the trial, important witnesses can often move residences or simply disappear during this time. It is the responsibility of the homicide detective to locate these witnesses and to be certain they appear to testify. Again, this is not something to begin doing the day of the trial. As talked about in a previous chapter, the use of computer search programs such as Accurint has greatly assisted homicide detectives in finding these missing witnesses.

As I have spoken about several times in this chapter, the ultimate end of every homicide investigation is not the arrest of the murderer, but rather the trial that uses the evidence gathered by homicide detectives. However, as can be seen by the two cases at the beginning of this chapter, evidence presented to a court, even what appears to be very damning evidence, can be viewed in different ways by different juries. After enough years on the job, though, homicide detectives seldom worry or concern themselves about what juries do with the evidence they have uncovered. Experienced homicide detectives simply do the best job they can based on what information and evidence they recover. Second-guessing or trying to figure out a jury's logic would lead them to become so cynical and bitter they would likely no longer be effective detectives.

While this chapter so far has been about murder trials from a homicide detective's point of view, our Constitution guarantees everyone accused of a crime the chance to be heard in court, to cross-examine witnesses, and to present evidence in their favor. Therefore, as might be expected, preparing for a murder trial is not just hard work for homicide detectives and the prosecutor, but also for defense attorneys. As defense attorney Hilary Bowe Ricks told me,

Representing clients charged with murder is difficult for several reasons. First, you usually have individuals who are scared about the possibility of spending a large part of the rest of their life in prison, with a family who is also scared of losing their loved one to the prison system. Most clients are not cold, unfeeling monsters, and, depending on the circumstances, they may feel great sadness at what occurred, even if they don't feel criminally responsible.

Second, the evidence in a murder case is often circumstantial, which in some ways is harder to defend against than direct evidence, which can be proved or disproved more easily. Even if there are eyewitnesses, each may have a different version of what happened, making sorting through to find the evidence favorable to the client time-consuming. And while investigating officers are generally diligent in trying to gather all the evidence, they are human too and may have missed something, so defense counsel should conduct a complete independent investigation.

Third, regardless of the outcome of the trial, no one involved is ever "OK." The deceased's family continues to suffer the loss and the client is either imprisoned or released with the stigma of a murder charge on his or her criminal history.[16]

As Mrs. Ricks so aptly points out, even in those cases where the trial ends, the jury returns a guilty verdict, and the judge sentences the murderer, the case is still not over for everyone. For some people the case will never end. While the person murdered is usually seen as the victim in homicide cases, few people realize that there are also secondary victims of murder: the family and friends of the murder victim. As we will see in the next chapter, dealing with and recovering from the effects of the murder of a family member or friend can many times take years. While there is often closure for homicide detectives at the conclusion of a murder trial, this closure may never come, or at best can still be years away, for the secondary victims of murder.

CHAPTER 9

Secondary Victims of Murder

Starting in 1979, a serial murderer began a killing spree in the Detroit and Ann Arbor areas of Michigan. Because most of the early murders took place on Sunday mornings, the news media dubbed the killer "The Sunday Morning Slasher." Homicide detectives investigating these murders soon began suspecting a man named Coral Eugene Watts of being the culprit. In order to gather evidence against Watts, detectives began an around-the-clock surveillance of him, even going so far as to attach a tracking device to his vehicle. Watts, however, apparently suspecting that the police were on to him, soon moved to Houston, Texas, where he quickly continued his killing spree.

Unfortunately, at this time the Houston Police Department was extremely understaffed and had little money for overtime; therefore, the police department couldn't keep tabs on Watts as well as it should have, and it is believed that he killed at least a dozen women in Texas. Finally, however, on May 23, 1982, the police arrested Watts when they caught him soon after he had broken into an apartment and attempted to drown the woman who lived there.

Watts had already killed one woman on the morning of May 23, 1982, but later told the police that he just didn't feel satisfied yet. Looking for more prey, he spotted a woman as she pulled her car into an apartment area parking lot. He sat and watched her as she got out of her car and then walked to a nearby apartment building. Seeing his next victim, Watts followed the woman inside the building, grabbed and choked her to near unconsciousness, and then dragged her upstairs to her apartment. Using the victim's key to get inside, Watts yanked the woman into the apartment, but quickly discovered that she had a roommate.

Watts, unperturbed, bound the roommate using metal clothes hangers and then filled the bathtub with water and attempted to drown the semi-conscious woman he had dragged up the stairs. The roommate, naturally fearing for her own life, made her way out onto the balcony, still bound, just as the police arrived, alerted by a neighbor who had seen Watts grab and choke the woman in the hallway. Hearing the police, Watts attempted to escape before he could finish drowning the woman. The police, however, soon took Watts into custody and now had a good case against him as they had three terrified, but live, witnesses who could identify him.

Watts' victims, however, weren't the only ones to experience a fear of him. The defense attorney who handled Watts' case, even though used to dealing with criminals, felt something different with Watts. "There's something evil in the man," said Zinetta Burney. "He never threatened me. He was always quiet and polite to me, but he scared me more than anyone I've ever dealt with."[1]

Unfortunately however, because the prosecutor didn't feel that the state had enough evidence to convict Watts in any of the other numerous attacks the police suspected him of, he allowed Watts in 1982 to enter into a plea bargain under which he would plead guilty to Burglary of a Habitation with Intent to Commit Murder. Upon entering this plea, Watts agreed to accept a sixty-year sentence. This, the prosecutor thought, would keep Watts confined in prison for the rest of his life. As an additional part of this plea bargain, Watts would receive immunity from prosecution for any murders in Texas he wanted to confess to. He reportedly confessed to thirteen of them, but didn't want to talk about most of his murders in Michigan, as they weren't covered under the Texas prosecutor's grant of immunity.

A detective who had investigated Watts for several murders in Michigan, and who came to Texas to question Watts about these murders, believed that Watts had killed many more than just thirteen people. Homicide Detective Paul Bunten recalls, "At one point, I said, 'Coral, I haven't got enough fingers and toes to count the number of people you've killed, have I?' And he looked around the room and he said, 'There's not enough fingers and toes in the room.' How many people were in the room? Four of us, including him."[2]

Interestingly, unlike most serial murderers, Watts displayed no patterns or rituals in his many killings. He appears to have simply picked his victims indiscriminately and at random, and then killed them the same way. "Most serial killers have an MO (mode of operating)," said Donna Pendergrass, a Michigan state assistant attorney general. "This guy didn't have one. He drowns, chokes, hangs and does whatever violence he can do whenever he can do it."[3]

Circumstances have changed, however, since Watts' incarceration that may have disastrous results. While the prosecutor believed in 1982 that the sixty-year sentence Watts agreed to would effectively imprison him for the rest of his life, changes to Texas' prison sentencing statutes since Watts' incarceration mean that he is now scheduled to be released, without any supervision, in May 2006. While Texas' very lenient mandatory release program, which was meant to help ease prison overcrowding, has been rescinded, Watts, because he began his incarceration in 1982, still falls under it. He would be the first serial killer in the history of the United States to be released from prison for serving a completed sentence. Unbelievably, Watts will have to be released without supervision, even though he has said that as soon as he is set free he will kill again.

"Since Watts received a 60-year sentence, we figured Watts would die in prison," said Lieutenant George Van Tiem of the Grosse Pointe Farms (Michigan) Police Department.[4]

Naturally, the possibility that a serial killer who has devastated the lives of at least thirteen families, and likely many more, will be released soon from prison has been like a punch in the face to these families, who have already had to deal with the enormous grief of having a family member murdered. While Watts has been incarcerated now for a little over twenty years, giving time for these families to work through their grief and attempt to reconstruct their lives, his imminent release reopens the old wounds.

"I used to spend nights in a closet when my husband was away," said the woman for whose attempted drowning Watts received the sixty-year sentence. "I'd try different closets in the house. Sometimes one would seem safer than another. I'd sit there in the heat, sweating, holding a pistol ... all night."[5]

"Coral Watts has never got what's intended for him," said Judy Krueger, whose sister was believed to have been killed by Watts. "His life continues, his needs are taken care of on a daily basis while he sits back waiting for his freedom."[6]

Fortunately, however, Watts' reluctance to confess to all of the murders he has committed may be the key to keeping him incarcerated. Homicide detectives in Michigan have been reviewing old murder cases in which they suspect Watts to be the killer, looking for evidence that in the 1970s and 80s was of little value, but which now can be analyzed and used to implicate Watts. Apparently, they recently struck pay dirt.

On March 3, 2004, Michigan Attorney General Mike Cox authorized charging Watts in the 1979 murder of Helen Dutcher. The thirty-six-year-old woman died from multiple stab wounds. It is speculated that DNA from the case can be matched to Watts.

"This man is a confessed killing machine who has admitted he will kill again," said Attorney General Cox. "The specter of Watts' release has haunted Michigan families, the nation, and untold victims and their families for too long."[7]

Many of the loved ones of Watts' victims, naturally, are bitter because they had been told that he would never be released from prison in Texas. Yet now he will be, and consequently they will have to deal with a very long trial with all of its legal wrangling and the almost certain resurgence of the sorrow and sadness of losing their loved one. "Until we actually have a conviction of murder and someone can come up to our doorstep and say, 'He's gonna be put up for life,' that's when you'll see the biggest smile on my face," said the sister of one of Watts' believed victims.[8]

"No one understands the magnitude of this," said the loved one of a murder victim. "You end up a body with no life in it."[9]

While I have titled this chapter "Secondary Victims of Murder," these individuals, who can include spouses, parents, children, lovers, friends, and co-workers of murder victims, are also often referred to in the literature as co-victims. This is because, while the murder victim may have suffered the most direct effect of the crime, these individuals also suffer from the effects of a murder. And while the actual murder victim may have only suffered for a few seconds, secondary victims of murder can often suffer for years.

As anyone who has experienced such an incident knows, the unexpected and sudden death of a loved one can be traumatic and difficult for the survivors to deal with. Even deaths from unavoidable accidents still require the family, friends, and loved ones of the victim to go through a period of grieving and questioning why it happened. With these types of deaths, though, usually the survivors are able to recover within a year or two and move on with their lives.

With a murder, however, many other factors enter into the situation that complicate and aggravate the healing and recovery process. A murder isn't just an unfortunate accident. It is an intentional, often evil, act, and the loved ones of a murder victim can many times never understand why a person would want to kill their loved one. People in general, it has been found, like to believe in the philosophy of a just world, yet the murder of a loved one seems to say that this may not be so. Consequently, a murder can cause emotional and psychological problems for the survivors because, since they want to believe in a just world, they also believe that there must be some explanation within the framework of their belief system that will explain the murder. But there isn't.

"The perception that one's situation is not fair diminishes personal control; the perception that the world is unfair diminishes one's belief in a just world," said social psychologist Melvin Lerner. "Neither perception is good for psychological well-being."[10]

In addition to causing problems with one's belief system, a murder also forces the loved ones of the murder victim to undergo the additional stress of having to deal with the criminal justice system during the investigation, apprehension, and trial of the murderer. Unfortunately, this can often take years and, like the case involving Coral Watts, may never seem to be over. Just as unfortunate, many of the loved ones of murder victims find that the criminal justice system is not structured around concern or compassion for their well-being, or even for the victim, but rather around protecting the rights of the accused murderer.

"While the criminal justice process grinds along slowly, surviving family members must take the initiative to be kept in the communication loop," police chaplain Philip Bacon told me. "In a sense, survivors become outsiders to the system, merely looking on. They often feel victimized by the process. Although crime victim families have legal rights, many are not versed in these and must rely upon someone in the system to be their advocate."[11]

"There are rights in some states, but if a prosecutor doesn't follow [them], there's nothing to fall back on," said Nancy Ruhe-Munch, executive director of Parents of Murdered Children. "With a constitutional amendment, there would be repercussions if victims don't have these rights observed."[12]

U.S. Senators Dianne Feinstein and Jon Kyle have introduced a proposal for just such a Constitutional amendment that would guarantee victims' rights. These rights would include keeping victims up to date on whatever is happening in their case, making sure the court hears from them, and giving victims a say in decisions made about their case.

However, not everyone agrees with this idea. "The Constitution exists to protect the accused from the government," said defense attorney Robert Hammerle, "not to give protection to those who are already paid attention to."[13]

When dealing with the criminal justice system, often the first interaction the loved ones of a murder victim have is in their dealings with the police. While most people report very positive feelings about the police and their interaction with them during a murder investigation, some don't.

One of the first, and often potentially most negative, interactions that the loved ones of a murder victim have with the police is when one of them comes to the actual murder scene. They naturally want to go into the inner crime scene and see the deceased. However, the police won't allow them to do this because at that moment the most important priority of the police is protection of the crime scene. Loved ones of murder victims don't realize that sometimes it's trace evidence, something as small as a single hair or drop of bodily fluid, that will solve the crime. If the police allowed individuals to enter the crime scene and/or have contact with the body before the crime scene was processed, this trace evidence could be destroyed.

The mother of a murder victim, however, expressed it this way: "It's my daughter, not yours.... They took possession of my daughter.... It was very, very upsetting to me that their criminal investigation took precedence over just letting me see her."[14]

While I, as a parent, can certainly sympathize with this woman and her disbelief that the police wouldn't let her see her daughter, I have also been at a number of murder scenes in which the police have had to physically restrain family members from rushing up and grabbing their loved ones' bodies. Many people want to hug or kiss the murdered person, which is certainly understandable, but allowing them to do so could negate the criminal investigation. Fortunately, we and most other large police departments usually have a chaplain on call or at the murder scene to handle such events.

Another problem that secondary victims of murder have when dealing with the police is that, since most watch countless television cop shows and movies, they seem amazed when the police don't solve their loved ones' cases right away, and they become particularly disgruntled if the police don't solve the case at all. After all, they've seen it done quickly a thousand times on television and at the movies. And no one on television or in the movies ever fails to solve a murder, no matter how difficult the case appears to be. Sadly, however, every year one third of the murders in the United States do go unsolved, and this leaves the loved ones of some murder victims feeling less than gracious about the police. But along with this, having a loved one's murder go unsolved can also affect secondary victims of murder emotionally and psychologically.

"Sometimes it still feels like his death is not real," said Bruce Stewart, the brother of a murder victim. "Not knowing who did it, you don't have a way to put it out of your mind. You don't even start to have closure."[15]

However, the emotional stress and ungracious feelings about the police really begin when the police have no apparent suspect in a murder and, still trying to pinpoint one, begin questioning family members and loved ones about their relationship with the deceased, their location at the time of the murder, and so on. Murder is a unique crime in that the victims cannot talk to the police about their victimization. Therefore, when there are no apparent suspects, the police must suspect everyone; and statistically people are much more likely to be killed by someone they know than by a stranger. Consequently, in a murder with no apparent suspects, the loved ones of the murder victim are suspects. Depending on how the police handle this, for the loved ones of a murder victim this questioning and suspicion by the police can range from being uncomfortable to upsetting to devastating.

An article in *Texas Monthly* magazine tells about the initial contact the loved one of a murder victim had with the police: "They took me downtown and fingerprinted me. A bald detective called Curly led me to a tiny room and told me to write down everything I had done in the past two days."[16]

The loved one goes on to express how shocked he was when it dawned on him that the police actually suspected him of being the murderer, and how deeply offended he was when he heard detectives in a nearby office laughing about the murder. Within the next day or so, the police arrested the real murderer, but I'm certain this man will never forget his experience with the police, nor will he ever again be able to look at them positively.

A very interesting aspect of human nature I've discovered during the last thirty-six years is that for some reason, people who call the police expect them to know the truth immediately about whatever incident it is they've been called to investigate, and particularly to know who's guilty and who's not. Many people, I've found, become very insulted if the police don't instantly and totally accept their version over someone else's about what happened, and the people become particularly offended if the police question any of the facts they have given them. People who are innocent know it and believe the police should know it, too. Unfortunately, though, we often don't.

What the man experienced in the incident described in *Texas Monthly* magazine unfortunately occurs often in murder investigations. In cases with no apparent suspects, homicide detectives almost always suspect loved ones as the murderers because they so often are. Many times, the police find that the person who appears most shaken by the murder is actually the killer. Readers have only to recall the October 1994 drowning murder by Susan Smith of her two small children in South Carolina. Smith, before being arrested, had told the police that her automobile had been carjacked and her two children taken with it. She then went on national television and tearfully pled with the supposed kidnapper to return her children unharmed. At that time, few people other than the police would have believed that she was actually a cold-blooded killer. Few people other than the police would have believed that the mother of two tiny children could kill them simply because they had become an inconvenience to her. In any murder investigation without apparent suspects, the police have to suspect everyone, including family members and loved ones; and this, we find, often highly offends innocent people. Naturally, this suspicion only adds to the stress the loved ones of a murder victim undergo.

The shock that the person in the *Texas Monthly* article felt when overhearing police officers in a nearby room laughing about the murder is also certainly understandable, and shouldn't have occurred. To think that a person could laugh about another's death is so astounding as to be almost unbelievable to many people. However, it's not as bad as it sounds. As a police officer who has been involved in homicide investigation for a number of years, I can confidently state that, while these police officers may have been laughing, they really didn't see anything funny in the incident. Almost every day, homicide detectives see the horrible things that human beings do to each other. They see people cut down needlessly in their youth, they see people mutilated, they see people who no longer look human. Laughing, or graveyard humor, is the way police officers attempt to deal psychologically with what they experience; and the more horrible the incident, the more likely it is that they will laugh about it. If they didn't, and instead became very emotionally caught up in these types of investigations, they would burn out as homicide investigators in no time.

"[T]hese emergency response professionals laugh at things most of us would consider to be in bad taste," said Professor Paul McGhee, talking about the police use of dark humor. "But they have all learned that they need to laugh, because it helps them adapt to the terrible things they are exposed to."[17]

However, should the officers have joked or laughed within earshot of a loved one of the murder victim? Absolutely not.

Many people, unfortunately, may come away from a murder investigation believing that the police are totally unsympathetic and unfeeling. This is not true. However, police officers cannot allow themselves to become too emotionally involved in their cases, because if they did they would become emotional and psychological wrecks in no time. Police officers learn various coping measures, including humor, to avoid and distance themselves from the emotional side of their investigations.

"Professionals, particularly detectives, use the avoidance strategy because they are not comfortable seeing the pain of bereaveds' loss, and they recognize that there is not much that brings them comfort," said the authors of a report on homicide and bereavement. "Detectives along with prosecutors use counselors as organizational shields to create a buffer between them and the bereaved."[18]

The police, however, are usually just the beginning of the negative exposure to the criminal justice system that the loved ones of a murder victim will have. In those cases (about two thirds) in which an arrest in a murder is made, secondary victims of murder must then wait through all of the legal wrangling that takes place before the actual trial begins, which can often span a year or two, during which time old wounds keep being reopened.

The trial itself, however, even when it finally comes, rather than acting to finally give closure to the loved ones of murder victims, instead often simply exacerbates the emotional turmoil. Secondary victims of murder who attend the trial experience a system under which all of the concern seems to be centered on protecting the rights of the accused rather than the victim. During the trial, loved ones of a murder victim can often hear disturbing details of the murder that they may not have heard before, and they often have to listen to defense attorneys as they attempt to mitigate the murder by speaking well of the defendant and ill of the victim.

"Many families and friends think that the court proceedings will somehow take care of their pain," said Reverend Wanda Henry-Jenkins, whose mother was murdered, "only to find after the trial that the grief has only just begun."[19]

A mother who had to live through the initial trial of the murderer of her son, and then a second trial when a court overturned the first verdict, said, "It was hard for me for them to try it again and I wonder if there will be another trial. Having to relive it during the first trial was bad and now I've had to relive it again."[20]

Interestingly, a study by Professors Sarah G. Goodrum and Mark C. Stafford concerning depression among the loved ones of murder victims found it highest among those who had experienced a trial and its resolution as opposed to those whose loved one's murder had not been solved. "The unsolved bereaved have the lowest mean depression score and solved-resolved bereaved have the highest mean depression score," Drs. Goodrum and Stafford said in their report. They go on to add, "There are two possible explanations: hope and answers. Bereaved whose loved one's murder case remains unsolved may hold out hope that there will be some resolution to the case, and this hope may keep the depression at bay."[21] The study also found that the more contact a bereaved has with the criminal justice system, the worse the depression.

Another study of secondary victims of murder, this one by Professor J. Scott Kenney, concluded, "Generally, those survivors who had, or chose, *extensive* involvements with the Criminal Justice System, Coroner's inquests, civil lawsuits, and Criminal Injuries Compensation tribunals reported faring *worse* than those who did not. This was chiefly due to their institutionalized powerlessness, the intensive *reliving* of what happened in these contexts, added to by negative outcomes, and frustrating bureaucratic delays such that survivors had to 'put their grief on hold' and 'live from hearing to hearing.'"[22]

Convicted serial murderer Keith Jesperson apparently understands the results of the two studies above. "People talk about closure," he said, "but in my opinion, it just doesn't exist. It's almost better for someone to believe their loved one is going to come home, rather than them knowing they're dead and dumped somewhere."[23]

Having dealt with many murder survivors, I certainly have to agree with the above studies' findings and conclusions. People at first really do expect that a trial and a guilty verdict, followed by a proper sentence, will bring closure and an end to the worst part of the grieving process. But instead, few people find themselves satisfied at the end of a murder trial. Most find themselves frustrated at how impersonal and unsatisfying it is. Many secondary victims of murder feel that few people in the criminal justice system have treated them or the deceased with enough respect and compassion, and one can only imagine how emotionally upsetting and frustrating it must be for the loved ones of murder victims when a jury, for totally unknown reasons, finds the defendant not guilty or guilty of a lesser offense than murder.

According to a study on homicide survivor bereavement, "For bereaved, the jury's inconceivable ruling in a case distorts the bereaved's view of the system as legitimate. The inability of the system to bring justice for some bereaved may inhibit their ability to restore order to their view of the loss and the world."[24]

In addition to the criminal justice system, though, another particularly stressful situation for many loved ones of a murder victim is the media coverage of the murder, followed by their coverage of the ensuing police investigation, and the trial. Because the news media are in the business of making money, and to do this they must have as many viewers or readers as possible, some media outlets will often try to sensationalize a murder case, particularly if it is newsworthy or particularly gruesome. Unfortunately, this can cause the news media to print things about the crime and the victim that they probably shouldn't, and will often cause members of the news media to hound the loved ones of a murder victim, looking for interviews or new information.

An article about murder co-victim grief stated, "Co-victims are quickly thrust into public view and become fair game for public consumption."[25] At a time when the loved ones of a murder victim are in shock and are grieving, this is an unwelcome intrusion they could certainly do without. This is why many families of murder victims will select a spokesperson, such as the family attorney, to give a statement to the press.

A study of the loved ones of victims of the 1995 Oklahoma City bombing said, "Since the nature of news is what is 'new,' the pace in which the media intrudes in the victims' families is uncanny and often quite ruthless. The press often try to sensationalize tragedy when the truth and facts alone are hard enough for the families to cope with."[26]

With all of this said, I'm not trying to imply that everyone who works in the news media is heartless and unfeeling. Many experience deep sympathy for the secondary victims of murder. As Bonnie Druker, a reporter for the CBS affiliate station in Indianapolis, told me, "When I cover a murder story I feel like I walk a fine line. My heart hurts when I see family members in shock, in pain, and in tears. But I always wonder—what do they know? Sometimes I get the opportunity to ask them, sometimes I don't. My mission is always this: get the story, meet the deadline, show compassion. I always ask myself: what would I do if this were my family?"[27]

As we have seen in this chapter, the murder of a loved one can often leave family members, friends, and co-workers devastated; and this sudden, inexplicable loss can many times manifest itself in various emotional and psychological maladies, including posttraumatic stress disorder. This is a psychological disorder that affects those who have experienced a tragic event outside the usual human experience. Its symptoms can include such things as a loss of appetite, inability to sleep, lack of concentration, loss of self-esteem, thoughts of suicide, and panic attacks.

Fortunately, there is help. The cities of Seattle and Philadelphia, for example, both have programs designed to assist the loved ones of murder victims. These programs consist of two ten-week segments. The first half involves acquainting the loved ones of murder victims with the realities of the criminal justice system and what they can expect. The second half addresses responding to and coping with the emotional and psychological difficulties they can expect when trying to deal with the reality of the murder of a loved one.

Other cities have developed other ways to assist the secondary victims of murder in dealing with their grief and loss. For example, in Indianapolis, the prosecutor's office published a book titled *Food for Our Souls: Cooking Up Memories*. This is a cookbook of the favorite recipes of murder victims, supplied by their loved ones.

"There are names and faces attached to each recipe," said former Marion County Prosecutor Scott Newman. "The people we honor in this cookbook will be remembered as long as someone prepares Brian's chicken and noodles or sloppy tacos or any of the other dishes."[28]

"This book comes at the right time for me," said Judy Black, the mother of a murder victim. "It lets me know that the City of Indianapolis never forgot about my daughter. She's more than a number."[29]

Luckily, in those cities without organized recovery programs like the ones in Seattle and Philadelphia, there still exist a number of local organizations that the loved ones of a murder victim can turn to for support. These organizations are usually made up of and run by others who have had loved ones murdered. Being able to talk to other people who have experienced something similar to what the loved ones of a murder victim are experiencing can often help tremendously in reducing these loved ones' anxiety and depression.

Most of these organizations can be located through the local victims' advocate group or the local prosecutor's office. Ask about them.

In addition to all of the above, there are also a number of national organizations that can assist secondary victims of murder. Three are listed here:

1. The National Coalition of Homicide Survivors, Inc.
   32 North Stone, 11th floor
   Tucson, AZ 85701
   (520) 740-5729
   www.mivictims.org/nchs/
2. National Organization of Parents of Murdered Children, Inc.
   100 East Eighth Street, Suite B-41
   Cincinnati, OH 45202
   (800) 818-7662
   www.pomc.com
3. Survivors of Homicide
   www.geocities.com/Heartland/Plains/6857/survivemain.html

Some Final Thoughts

Police chaplain Philip Bacon has consoled the family members of murder victims for many years. When I asked him about the effect of murder on a family, he told me,

> Murder not only ends a life prematurely, it devastates the surviving family members. There is no time to say "goodbye," thus shattering any sense of peace between family and victim.
>
> Surviving family members are suddenly thrust into a new and frightening world. They must now deal face-to-face with the police and the criminal justice system. Additionally, survivors often question their spiritual and theological framework. Where was God in this violent, senseless act?
>
> Even after the funeral, the trial, and sentencing, for the survivors, it isn't over. From the moment they receive the horrible news of the murder of their loved one, their lives are permanently altered. The wounds to the soul never quite heal.[1]

As chaplain Bacon points out, while the family members of a murder victim will almost certainly find their lives altered forever, fortunately they can seek assistance through individuals such as chaplain Bacon or through the various programs talked about in the previous chapter. However, the murder victims themselves don't have this opportunity.

They will never have the chance to try to heal. Yet still, they need an advocate. They need someone to stand up for them and see that the crime committed against them is dealt with. This is where the homicide detective steps in. But only those individuals who are willing to go far beyond the typical eight-hour day and five-day week, only those individuals who are willing to totally commit themselves to their jobs, can truly become advocates for murder victims.

I have been fortunate to work the last six years with just such a group of totally committed men and women, individuals who have made it their lives' work to step up and right a wrong for those who can no longer stand up for themselves. The victims whom homicide detectives represent have been wrongly denied the right to ever see their children grow up, to ever again go to a family gathering, or to ever again even stop in at a friend's house for a cup of coffee. Because of a murderer's actions, these people can no longer speak up for themselves and demand that the crime committed against them be dealt with. That is the work of the homicide detective.

Notes

Chapter 1

1. Interview by author, June 28, 2000.

2. Ibid.

3. Ibid.

4. U.S. Department of Justice, *Crime in the United States* (Washington, DC: U.S. Government Printing Office, 2003), p. 19.

5. U.S. Department of Justice, *Capital Punishment, 2002* (Washington, DC: U.S. Government Printing Office, 2003), pp. 1–8.

6. U.S. Department of Justice, *Crime in the United States*, p. 20.

7. Judi Villa, "Phoenix Sets Record for Homicides," *Arizona Republic* (December 12, 2003), p. A1.

8. "Detroit's Child Murder Rate Doubles," CBSNEWS.com (December 26, 2002), available at http://cbsnews.com/stories/2002/12/26/national/main534324.shtml.

9. Jane Prendergast, "Three-Year Homicide Rate Rises," *Cincinnati Enquirer* (December 14, 2003), p. A1.

10. Andrew Blankstein and Richard Winton, "Homicides in L.A. up 5% in First 3 Months of 2004," *Los Angeles Times* (April 1, 2004), p. B1.

11. U.S. Department of Justice, *Homicide Trends in the United States: 2000 Update* (Washington, DC: U.S. Government Printing Office, 2002).

12. Ibid.

13. U.S. Department of Health and Human Services, Centers for Disease Control, *National Vital Statistics Report—Deaths: Leading Causes for 2001* (Washington, DC: U.S. Government Printing Office, November 7, 2003).

14. U.S. Department of Justice, *Homicides of Children and Youth* (Washington, DC: U.S. Government Printing Office, 2002), p. 6.

15. Ibid., p. 9.

16. Ibid., p. 5.

17. U.S. Department of Justice, *Homicide Trends in the United States: 2000 Update*.

18. U.S. Department of Justice, *Crime in the United States*, p. 21.

19. U.S. Department of Justice, *Homicide Trends in the United States: 2000 Update*.

20. Ibid.

21. Ibid.

22. U.S. Department of Justice, *Crime in the United States*, p. 24.

23. Ibid., p. 20.

24. Ibid., p. 27.

25. U.S. Department of Justice, *Drugs and Crime Facts* (Washington, DC: U.S. Government Printing Office, 2003), p. 3.

26. Interview by author, May 18, 2004.

27. Kevin O'Neal, "A Nightmare before Christmas," *Indianapolis Star* (December 17, 1996), p. A1.

28. Ibid.

29. John R. O'Neill, "Minister's N.Y. Church Mourns Couple's Slaying," *Indianapolis Star* (December 18, 1996), p. C1.

30. Richard D. Walton, "The Mathias Murders," *Indianapolis Star* (June 17, 1997), p. A1.

31. Ibid.

32. Interview by author, June 30, 2000.

33. George McLaren, "Teens Give Differing Accounts of Ax Slayings," *Indianapolis Star* (January 28, 1998), p. A1.

34. William J. Booher, "Friend Blamed in Ax Slayings," *Indianapolis Star* (February 25, 1999), p. B1.

35. Ibid.

36. Walton, p. A6.

37. Interview by author, June 30, 2000.

38. David Karp, "Man Convicted of Drug Counselor's Murder," *St. Petersburg Times* (September 25, 2001), p. A1.

39. Ibid.

40. Logan D. Mabe, "Tip Leads to Suspect in Drug Center Slaying," *St. Petersburg Times* (April 3, 2001), p. B3.

41. Ibid.

42. Ron Sylvester, "Nathaniel Bell Is Convicted of First-Degree Murder for Stabbing a 22-Year-Old Man in April," *Wichita Eagle* (September 27, 2003), p. B1.

43. "Wife Convicted of Mercedes Murder," CNN.com/U.S. (February 13, 2003), available at http://www.cnn.com/2003/US/02/13/mercedes.murder.ap/.

44. Ibid.

45. See, U.S. Department of Justice, *Homicide Trends in the United States*.

46. "Neighbors Say Family Had History of Domestic Violence," *Charlotte Observer* (December 15, 2003), p. A1.

47. Ford Fessenden, "They Threaten, Seethe and Unhinge, Then Kill in Quantity," *New York Times* (April 9, 2000), p. 1.

48. Paul H. Blackman et al., "The Varieties of Homicide and Its Research," Proceedings of the 1999 Meeting of the Homicide Research Working Group, FBI Academy, Quantico, VA.

49. Michael J. Rochon, "Alton Coleman, Guilty of 4 Murders, to Be Executed Friday," *Indianapolis Star* (April 25, 2002), p. A1.

50. Howard Wilkinson, "Alton Coleman Finally Faces Justice," *Cincinnati Enquirer* (April 24, 2002), p. A1.

51. Mike Barber, "Serial Killers—They're Not Always Who We Think," *Seattle Post-Intelligencer* (February 21, 2003), p. A1.

52. Ibid.

53. Lewis Kamb, "In Their Own Words: The Twisted Art of Murder," *Seattle Post-Intelligencer* (February 22, 2003), p. A1.

54. Ibid.

55. David Brin, "Names That Live in Infamy," Salon.com (August 13, 1999), available at http://www.salon.com/media/feature/1999/08/13/nameless/index.html.

56. "Claim of Serial Killings Called Bogus by Police," *Indianapolis Star* (January 2, 2004), p. B5.

57. "Inside a Killer's Mind," CBSNEWS.com (August 9, 2001), available at http://www.cbsnews.com/stories/2001/01/31/48hours/main268586.shtml.

58. Stephen G. Michaud, "To Have and to Kill," Salon.com (August 25, 1999), available at http://www.salon.com/health/feature/1999/08/25/serial_killer/print.html.

59. Ibid.

60. Alan C. Brantley and Frank M. Ochberg, MD, "Lethal Predators and Future Dangerousness," *FBI Law Enforcement Bulletin* (April 2003), p. 17.

61. U.S. Department of Health and Human Services, Centers for Disease Control, *Suicide in the United States* (December 11, 2003), available at http://www.cdc.gov/ncipc/factsheets/suifacts.htm.

62. National Institutes of Mental Health, *Suicide Facts* (December 23, 2003), available at http://www.nimh.nih.gov/research/suifact.cfm.

63. American College of Emergency Physicians, *Responding to a Suicide Emergency* (March 2002), available at http://www.acep.org/1,5215,0.html.

64. "Officer's Research Shows That 'Suicide by Cop' Incidents on the Rise in North America," Policemag.com (February 2004), p. 15.

65. U.S. Department of Justice, *Policing and Homicide, 1976-98: Justifiable Homicide by Police, Police Officers Murdered by Felons* (Washington, DC: U.S. Government Printing Office, March 2001).

66. Interview by author, May 18, 2004.

67. Jeff Grabmeier, "Study Finds Homicide Detectives Work Aggressively to Solve All Cases, Regardless of Victim Race," (June 6, 2003), available at http://www.acs.ohio-state.edu/researchnews/archive/homclear.htm.

Chapter 2

1. Caren Benjamin, "Rudin Indicted," *Las Vegas Review-Journal* (April 19, 1997), p. A1.

2. Glenn Puit, "Web of Deceit," *Las Vegas Review-Journal* (November 28, 1999), p. A1.

3. Peter O'Connell, "Rudin Verdict: Guilty of Murder," *Las Vegas Review-Journal* (May 3, 2001), p. A1.

4. Kimberly A. Crawford, "Crime Scene Searches," *FBI Law Enforcement Bulletin* (January 1999), p. 27.

5. David Rivers, "Crime Scene Investigation," Handout from Homicide and Forensic Death Investigation Conference, held at Public Agency Training Council, Indianapolis, IN, January 2004.

6. U.S. Department of Justice, *Death Investigation: A Guide for the Scene Investigator* (Washington, DC: U.S. Government Printing Office, November 1999), p. 1.

7. Interview by author, June 2, 2004.

8. U.S. Department of Justice, *Crime Scene Investigation: A Guide for Law Enforcement* (Washington, DC: U.S. Government Printing Office, January 2000), p. 16.

9. Interview by author, May 18, 2004.

10. David Rivers, "Crime Scene Investigation."

11. *Mincey v. Arizona*, 437 US 385 (1978).

12. *Katz v. United States*, 88 S. Ct. 507 (1967).

13. "Trooper Testimony Opens Jayson Williams Trial," SI.com (February 11, 2004), available at http://sportsillustrated.cnn.com/2004/basketball/nba/02/11/bc.bkn.williamstrial.ap/.

14. Jay Dix, MD, *Death Investigator's Manual* (Columbia, MO: Academic Information Systems, 2001), p. 53.

15. U.S. Department of Justice, *Without a Trace?* (Washington, DC: U.S. Government Printing Office, 2003), p. 8.

16. Interview by author, June 8, 2004.

17. Interview by author, June 3, 2004.

18. Rebecca Kanable, "Talk 'n' Trash," *Law Enforcement Technology* (November 2002), p. 32.

19. Interview by author, May 18, 2004.

Chapter 3

1. Glenn Puit, "Ted Binion, Troubled Gambling Figure, Dies," *Las Vegas Review-Journal* (September 18, 1998), p. A1.

2. Ibid.

3. Peter O'Connell, "Different Tales Spun at Trial," *Las Vegas Review-Journal* (April 1, 2000), p. A1.

4. Glenn Puit, "County Wants Binion Ruling Reconsidered," *Las Vegas Review-Journal* (July 17, 2003), p. A1.

5. Glenn Puit, "Expert Stands by Testimony in Binion Case," *Las Vegas Review-Journal* (July 24, 2003), p. A1.

6. Randy Hanzlick, MD et al., *A Guide for Manner of Death Classification* (Atlanta, GA: National Association of Medical Examiners, February 2002), p. 13.

7. Bernard Knight, *The Estimation of the Time since Death in the Early Postmortem Period* (Great Britain: Edward Arnold, 1995).

8. "New Version of C.S.I.; It's Crime Scene Insect," Associated Press (July 2, 2004), available at http://www.lineofduty.com/blotterstory.asp?StoryID= 65604.

9. Interview by author, June 9, 2004.

10. Ernest J. Tobin and Martin L. Fackler, MD, "Officer Reaction–Response Times in Firing a Handgun," *Wound Ballistics Review* (Spring 1999).

Chapter 4

1. J. M. Hirsch and Holly Ramer, "Dartmouth College Professors Found Dead in Home by Friend," *Portsmouth Herald* (January 29, 2001), p. A1.

2. Darren Thomas, "Half Zantop: 'He Was One I Admired,'" *Dartmouth Review* (January 29, 2001), available at http://www.dartreview.com/issues/1.29.01/half.html.

3. Stella Baer, "Susanne Zantop: 'Unfailingly Gentle.'" *Dartmouth Review* (January 29, 2001), available at http://www.dartreview.com/issues/1.29.01/susanne.html.

4. Nicole Neroulias, "Dartmouth Murder Suspects Apprehended," *Cornell Daily Sun* (February 20, 2001), p. 1.

5. "The Truth of the Slayings," *Crime Library* (February 7, 2004), available at http://www.crimelibrary.com/notorious_murders/young/dartmouth_murders/7.html?sect=10.

6. Mitchell Zuckoff and Marcella Bombardieri, "Youth Admits Role in Slayings," *Boston Globe* (December 8, 2001), p. A1.

7. Gordon Grice, "Crime Seen," *Popular Science* (August 5, 2004), available at http://www.popsci.com/popsci/crimeseen/article/0,20642,652674-2,00.html.

8. Alfred Allan Lewis and Herbert Leon MacDonell, *The Evidence Never Lies: The Case Book of a Modern Sherlock Holmes* (NY: Bantam Books, 1989).

9. Doug Hanson, "Bloodstain Pattern Analysis," *Law Enforcement Technology* (February 2004), p. 84.

10. Ibid.

11. Rebecca Kanable, "Do Sweat the Small Stuff," *Law Enforcement Technology* (March 2004), p. 54.

12. U.S. Department of Justice, *Crime in the United States* (Washington, DC: U.S. Government Printing Office, 2003), p. 23.

13. "The Shanabarger Murder Trial," INDYSTAR.com (2003), available at http://www.indystar.com/library/factfiles/crime/homicides/1999/shanabarger/shanabarger.html.

14. *Crime in the United States*, p. 23.

15. Paul L. Kirk, *Crime Investigation: Physical Evidence and the Police Laboratory* (NY: Interscience Publishers, 1953).

Chapter 5

1. Peter Serafin, "Puna Man Shot Pal Because 'I'd Given My Word,'" *Honolulu Star-Bulletin* (December 11, 2003), p. A1.

2. Chris Loos, "McGovern Led Police to Location of Bodies," *Hawaii Tribune Herald* (November 27, 2003), p. 1.

3. Ibid.

4. Rod Thompson, "Puna Shooter Awaits Jury's Decision," *Honolulu Star-Bulletin* (December 19, 2003), p. A1.

5. Ibid.

6. U.S. Department of Justice, *Eyewitness Evidence: A Trainer's Manual for Law Enforcement* (Washington, DC: U.S. Government Printing Office, September 2003), p. 16.

7. David Vessel, "Conducting Successful Interrogations," *FBI Law Enforcement Bulletin* (October 1998), p. 6.

8. Phuong Le, "Taping Interrogations Deters Coercion, Aids Investigations," *Associated Press* (July 28, 2003), available at http://www.lineofduty.com/blotterstory.asp?StoryID=52085.

9. Shannon Tan, "Confessions Rarely Questioned by Courts," *Indianapolis Star* (December 12, 2002), p. B1.

10. Charles L. Yeschke, *The Art of Investigative Interviewing* (NY: Butterworth-Heinemann, 2003), p. 36.

11. John E. Hess, *Interviewing and Interrogation for Law Enforcement* (Cincinnati, OH: Anderson Publishing, 1997), p. 6.

12. David E. Zulawski and Douglas E. Wicklander, "Special Report 1: Interrogations: Understanding the Process," *Law and Order* (July 1998), p. 87.

13. *Miranda v. Arizona*, 384 US 436 (1966).

14. *Dickerson v. United States*, 530 US 428 (2000).

15. *New York v. Quarles*, 467 US 649 (1984).

16. *Illinois v. Perkins*, 496 US 292 (1990).

17. *Yarborough v. Alvarado* (02-1684), 316 F.3d 841.

18. Yeschke, *Art of Investigative Interviewing*, p. 22.

19. Joe Navarro, "A Four-Domain Model for Detecting Deception," *FBI Law Enforcement Bulletin* (June 2003), p. 19.

20. Ibid.

21. Yeschke, *Art of Investigative Interviewing*, pp. 24–26.

22. David J. Lieberman, *Never Be Lied to Again* (NY: St. Martin's Press, 1988), p. 23.

23. Joe Navarro and John R. Schafer, "Detecting Deception," *FBI Law Enforcement Bulletin* (July 2001), p. 11.

24. Ibid., p. 12.

25. Interview by author, June 17, 2004.

26. Emma Young, "Brain Scans Can Reveal Liars," *New Scientist* (November 12, 2001), available at http://www.newscientist.com/news/news.jsp?id=ns99991543.

27. "Going Public," *Crime Library* (April 13, 2004), available at http://www.crimelibrary.com/serial_killers/predators/jesperson/public_7.html.

Chapter 6

1. April Zepeda, "Discoverer of First Green River Victim Looks for Closure," KOMO 1000 News (December 1, 2001), available at http://www.komotv.com/news/story_m.asp?ID=15645.

2. Sarah Kershaw, "20-Year Obsession Put Seattle Sheriff inside the Mind of a Serial Killer," *International Herald Tribune* (November 7, 2003), available at http://www.iht.com/articles/116798.html.

3. Tracy Johnson, "Sheriff's 21-Year Pursuit Is at an End," *Seattle Post-Intelligencer* (November 6, 2003), p. A1.

4. Vanessa Ho et al., "Ridgway Pleads Guilty to 48 Green River Killings," *Seattle Post-Intelligencer* (November 6, 2003), p. A1.

5. Marilyn Bardsley, "Reckoning," *Crime Library* (February 28, 2004), available at http://www.crimelibrary.com/serial_killers/predators/greenriver/8.html?sect=2.

6. "Tapes Show Ridgway's Horrifying Confession," KIRO TV (February 9, 2004), available at http://www.kirotv.com/print/2832250/detail.html? use=print.

7. Gene Johnson, "Suspect Pleads Guilty to Slaying 48 Women," *Indianapolis Star* (November 6, 2003), p. A3.

8. Mike Barber, "Letter from a Serial Killer," *Seattle Post-Intelligencer* (November 7, 2003), p. A1.

9. Tracy Johnson, "In Cruel Detail, a Monster Reveals Himself," *Seattle Post-Intelligencer* (November 6, 2003), p. A1.

10. "Tapes Show Ridgway's Horrifying Confession."

11. Gene Johnson, "Killer Says He's Sorry, Receives 48 Life Terms," *Indianapolis Star* (December 19, 2003), p. A8.

12. Interview by author, May 24, 2004.

13. John Solomon, "DNA Database Fingers 11,000 Suspects," *Detroit Free Press* (March 9, 2004), p. A1.

14. Interview by author, June 3, 2004.

15. Jennifer C. Budden, "Linking Crimes, Stopping Criminals," *Evidence Technology Magazine* (November–December 2003), p. 22.

16. U.S. Department of Justice, *The Victim's Voice* (Washington, DC: U.S. Government Printing Office, 2002), p. 2.

17. Mike Barber, "Serial Killers Prey on 'the Less Dead,'" *Seattle Post-Intelligencer* (February 20, 2003), available at http://seattlepi.nwsource.com/local/108705_predators20.shtml.

18. Brent E. Turvey, *Criminal Profiling* (NY: Academic Press, 2002), p. 34.

19. Ibid., pp. 44–45.

20. U.S. Department of Justice, *Homicide Trends in the United States: 2000 Update* (Washington, DC: U.S. Government Printing Office, 2003).

21. Michael R. Napier and Robert R. Hazelwood, "Homicide Investigation: The Significance of Victimology," *FBI NAA* (September–October 2003), p. 21.

Chapter 7

1. John Elvin, "The Rich and Powerful—Getting Away with Murder—Almost," *Insight Magazine* (May 31, 1999), available at http://www.insightmag.com/global_user_elements/printpage.cfm?storyid=209103.

2. Michael Knight, "Greenwich Girl, 15, Bludgeoned to Death," *New York Times* (November 1, 1975), p. 59.

3. Elizabeth Mehren, "Unsolved Murder Pushes Buttons of Celebrity, Notoriety, Wealth," *Los Angeles Times* (July 29, 1998), p. 5.

4. Elvin, "The Rich and Powerful."

5. "Tutor: Skakel Admits Moxley Murder," *1010 WINS* (December 11, 2002), available at http://www.1010wins.com/topstories/local_story_345074334. html.

6. Lindsay Faber, "Witness Says Skakel Confessed," *Greenwich Time* (May 17, 2002), available at http://www.marthamoxley.com/news/051702gt.htm.

7. Ibid.

8. John Springer, "Jurors Tell Court TV They Found Skakel's Alibi Hard to Believe," Court TV (June 11, 2002), available at http://www.courttv.com/trials/moxley/061102_ctv.html.

9. Ibid.

10. Lindsay Faber, "Skakel Convicted of Moxley Murder," *Greenwich Time* (June 8, 2002), available at http://www.marthamoxley.com/news/060802gt.htm.

11. Jane Prendergast, "Heat Turned Up in Slayings," *Cincinnati Enquirer* (November 25, 2003), p. A1.

12. Sanford Wexler, "Cold Cases Are Getting Hot," *Law Enforcement Technology* (June 2004), p. 19.

13. Melissa Manware, "Cold Case Unit Makes 1st Arrests," *Charlotte Observer* (May 22, 2003), p. 3B.

14. Charles L. Regini, "The Cold Case Concept," *FBI Law Enforcement Bulletin* (August 1997), p. 7.

15. Interview by author, June 3, 2004.

16. Christina S. N. Lewis, "Reviewing 3,000 Cold Cases, One by One," Court TV (March 25, 2003), available at http://www.courttv.com/news/feature/coldcasereview_ctv.html.

17. Joseph B. Frazier, "Retirees Warm to Cold Case Squad," *Los Angeles Times* (October 19, 2003), p. A35.

18. Frank Main, "Cold Case Detectives Scour Past for Fresh Leads," *Chicago Sun-Times* (May 16, 2004), p. 18.

19. Christina S. N. Lewis, "Solving the Cold Case: Time, Ingenuity and DNA Can Help," CNN.com (December 17, 2002), available at http://www.cnn.com/2002/LAW/12/17/ctv.cold.cases/.

20. Brian D. Smith, "Dead Men Talking," *Indy Men's Magazine* (November 2002), p. 61.

21. Ibid., p. 56.

22. Lewis, "Reviewing 3,000 Cold Cases."

23. Kristi Mayo, "DNA Technology Solves 1958 Homicide," *Evidence Technology Magazine* (February 2004), p. 14.

24. "Man Arrested for 1958 Wauwatosa Cold Case Murder, Rape," *The Milwaukee Channel* (December 11, 2003), available at http://209.157.64.200/focus/f-news/1038595/posts.

25. Dawn Bormann and Richard Espinoza, "Science Drives Crime-Fighting Forward," *The Kansas City Star* (August 10, 2003), p. A1.

26. Vicki Smith, "Forensic Scientist Forms Cold Case Consulting Group," *Burlington County Times* (March 6, 2004), p. 1.

27. Ibid.

28. Jen Lawson, "Warming Up Cold Murder Cases," *Las Vegas Sun* (September 12, 2003), p. A1.

29. "The Organization," *ICCE* (March 6, 2004), available at http://www.wvu.edu/~icce/Organization.html.

30. "Our Mission & Credo," The Vidocq Society (March 6, 2004), available at http://vidocq.org/what.html.

Chapter 8

1. Glenn May, "Jury Convicts Mt. Lebanon High Grads in Andrew Jones' Murder," *Pittsburgh Tribune-Review* (October 22, 2003), p. A1.

2. Ibid.

3. "What Happened to Kathleen Durst?" *Crime Library* (March 12, 2004), available at http://www.crimelibrary.com/notorious_murders/classics/robert_durst/2.html?sect=13.

4. "Prosecutors: Durst Wanted to Steal Victim's Identity," Click2Houston (October 28, 2003), available at http://www.click2houston.com/news/2589137/detail.html.

5. John Springer, "How Could a Jury Not Convict Durst?" Court TV (November 11, 2003), available at http://www.courttv.com/trials/durst/111103_analysis_ctv.html.

6. Scott E. Williams, "Durst Jurors Speak Out: 'It Just Wasn't There,'" *Galveston County Daily News* (November 12, 2003), p. 1.

7. "Mistrial of the Century?" *New York Magazine* (November 23, 2003), available at http://www.newyorkmetro.com/nymetro/news/people/columns/intelligencer/n_9528/.

8. Ibid.

9. John Springer, "New Indictment Means Durst Isn't Done," Court TV (February 12, 2004), available at http://www.courttv.com/trials/durst/021204_tamper_ctv.html.

10. Claudia Feldman, "Texas Jurors Say Capital Murder Cases Are Never Easy," *Houston Chronicle* (January 4, 2002), p. A1.

11. Interview by author, June 3, 2004.

12. Jennifer Mertens, "Lessons from the Body Farm," *Law Enforcement Technology* (June 2003), p. 37.

13. Marni Becker-Avin, "The Real Purpose of Voir Dire," *Trial Techniques Committee Newsletter—American Bar Association* (Fall 2001), p. 10.

14. Heber Taylor, "Lessons from a Sensational Case," *Galveston County Daily News* (November 19, 2003), p. 1.

15. Interview by author, August 5, 2004.

16. Interview by author, June 8, 2004.

Chapter 9

1. Evan Moore, "Dreams," *Houston Chronicle* (April 7, 1991), available at http://www.texansforequaljustice.org/protest/watts1.html.

2. Doug Miller, "Confessed Texas Serial Killer Faces Michigan Murder Charge," KHOU.com (March 4, 2004), available at http://www.khou.com/topstories/stories/khou040304_nh_coralwatts.532fe09c.html.

3. Joel Kurth, "Michigan Fights Serial Killer's Release," *Detroit News* (January 13, 2004), p. A1.

4. Tom Greenwood, "Confessed Killer Could Make Parole," *Detroit News* (March 12, 1989), available at http://www.detnews.com/2004/metro/0401/13/watts2.htm.

5. Moore, "Dreams."

6. Kurth, "Michigan Fights Release."

7. "Attorney General Mike Cox Charges Serial Killer Coral Watts," *Michigan Newswire* (March 4, 2004), available at http://www.michigan.gov/minewswire/0,1607,7-136-3452-87569--,00.html.

8. Miller, "Confessed Texas Serial Killer."

9. Connie Saindon, "Co-Victims of Homicide: Specialized Needs," *Selfhelp Magazine* (March 19, 2004), available at http://www.selfhelpmagazine.com/articles/trauma/covictims.html.

10. Melvin Lerner, *The Belief in a Just World Hypothesis: A Fundamental Delusion* (NY: Plenum Press, 1980).

11. Interview by author, June 4, 2004.

12. Mike Ellis, "Call for Legal Protection Highlights Victims' Plight," *Indianapolis Star* (April 26, 2002), available at http://www.starnews.com/article. php?victims26.html.

13. Ibid.

14. Sarah D. Goodrum, PhD, and Mark C. Stafford, PhD, *Homicide, Bereavement, and the Criminal Justice System, Final Report* (August 6, 2001), p. 65, available at http://www.ncjrs.org/pdffiles1/nij/grants/189566.pdf.

15. Jack Brown, "There Is Little Closure for the Mourners, but Now There is a Group That Offers Relatives Support," *Philadelphia Inquirer* (July 12, 1998), available at http://www.vidocq.org/inquirer/inq980712.html.

16. Jesse Sublett, "When a Loved One Is Murdered," *Texas Monthly* (July 1, 2002), p. 2.

17. Paul McGhee, PhD, *Humor and Health* (July 19, 2004), available at http:// www.corexcel.com/html/body.humor.htm.

18. Goodrum, p. 163.

19. Wanda Henry-Jenkins, "Homicide: A Brutal Bereavement," *Bereavement Magazine* (March 19, 2004), available at http://www.bereavementmag.com/ catalog/booklets/homicide.asp.

20. Don Lowery, "Former GA Deputy Convicted of Slaying Boyfriend, Encasing Body in Concrete," *Savannah Morning News* (March 26, 2004), available at http://www.lineofduty.com/blotterstory.asp?StoryID=62108.

21. Goodrum, p. 152.

22. J. Scott Kenney, PhD, "Survivors of Murder Victims," Paper presented to the X World Symposium on Victimology in Montreal, Quebec, August 6, 2000.

23. Lewis Kamb, "In Their Own Words: The Twisted Art of Murder," *Seattle Post-Intelligencer* (February 22, 2003), p. A1.

24. Goodrum, p. 110.

25. "Co-Victim Grief," *Ohio Crime Victim Services* (March 19, 2004), available at http://crimevictimservices.org/victimtypes/index/homicide/covictimgrief.html.

26. M. Victoria Cummock, "The Necessity of Denial in Grieving Murder: Observations of the Victims' Families Following the Bombing in Oklahoma City," *NCP Clinical Quarterly* (Winter 1995), available at http://www.ncptsd. org/publications/cq/v5/n2-3/cummock.html?printable=yes.

27. Interview by author, July 19, 2004.

28. Vic Ryckaert, "Cookbook Presents Recipes of Homicide Victims," *Indianapolis Star* (December 7, 2001), p. B3.

29. Ibid.

Some Final Thoughts

1. Interviewed by author, June 4, 2004.

Bibliography

American College of Emergency Physicians. "Responding to a Suicide Emergency," March 2002. Available at http://www.acep.org/1,5215,0.html.

"Attorney General Mike Cox Charges Serial Killer Coral Watts," *Michigan Newswire*, March 4, 2004. Available at http://www.michigan.gov/minewswire/0,1607,7-136-3452-87569--,00.html.

Bacon, Philip. Interviewed by Robert L. Snow, June 4, 2004.

Baer, Stella. "Susanne Zantop: 'Unfailingly Gentle,'" *Dartmouth Review*, January 29, 2001. Available at http://www.dartreview.com/issues/1.29.01/susanne.html.

Barber, Mike. "Letter from a Serial Killer," *Seattle Post-Intelligencer*, November 7, 2003, p. A1.

Barber, Mike. "Serial Killers Prey on 'the Less Dead,'" *Seattle Post-Intelligencer*, February 20, 2003. Available at http://seattlepi.nwsource.com/local/108705_predators20.shtml.

Barber, Mike. "Serial Killers—They're Not Always Who We Think," *Seattle Post-Intelligencer*, February 21, 2003, p. A1.

Bardsley, Marilyn. "Reckoning," *Crime Library*, February 28, 2004. Available at http://www.crimelibrary.com/serial_killers/predators/greenriver/8.html?sect=2.

Becker-Avin, Marni. "The Real Purpose of Voir Dire," *Trial Techniques Committee Newsletter—American Bar Association*, Fall 2001, p. 10.

Benjamin, Caren. "Rudin Indicted," *Las Vegas Review-Journal*, April 19, 1997, p. A1.

Blackman, Paul H. et al. "The Varieties of Homicide and Its Research." Proceedings of the 1999 Meeting of the Homicide Research Working Group, FBI Academy, Quantico, VA.

Blankstein, Andrew, and Winton, Richard. "Homicides in L.A. up 5% in First 3 Months of 2004," *Los Angeles Times*, April 1, 2004, p. B1.

Booher, William J. "Friend Blamed in Ax Slayings," *Indianapolis Star*, February 25, 1999, p. B1.

Bormann, Dawn, and Espinoza, Richard. "Science Drives Crime-Fighting Forward," *Kansas City Star*, August 10, 2003, p. A1.

Brantley, Alan C., and Ochberg, Frank M., MD. "Lethal Predators and Future Dangerousness," *FBI Law Enforcement Bulletin*, April 2003, p. 17.

Brin, David. "Names That Live in Infamy," Salon.com, August 13, 1999. Available at http://www.salon.com/media/feature/1999/08/13/nameless/index.html.

Brown, Jack. "There Is Little Closure for the Mourners, But Now There Is a Group That Offers Relatives Support," *Philadelphia Inquirer*, July 12, 1998. Available at http://www.vidocq.org/inquirer/inq980712.html.

Budden, Jennifer C. "Linking Crimes, Stopping Criminals," *Evidence Technology Magazine*, November–December 2003, p. 22.

"Claim of Serial Killings Called Bogus by Police," *Indianapolis Star*, January 2, 2004, p. B5.

"Co-Victim Grief," *Ohio Crime Victim Services*, March 19, 2004. Available at http://crimevictimservices.org/victimtypes/index/homicide/covictimgrief.html.

Crawford, Kimberly A. "Crime Scene Searches," *FBI Law Enforcement Bulletin*, January 1999, p. 27.

Cummock, M. Victoria. "The Necessity of Denial in Grieving Murder: Observations of the Victims' Families following the Bombing in Oklahoma City," *NCP Clinical Quarterly*, Winter 1995. Available at http://www.ncptsd.org/publications/cq/v5/n2-3/cummock.html?printable=yes.

"Detroit's Child Murder Rate Doubles," CBSNEWS.com, December 26, 2002. Available at http://cbsnews.com/stories/2002/12/26/national/main534324.shtml.

Dix, Jay, MD. *Death Investigator's Manual*. Columbia, MO: Academic Information Systems, 2001, p. 53.

Druker, Bonnie. Interviewed by Robert L. Snow, July 19, 2004.

Ellis, Mike. "Call for Legal Protection Highlights Victims' Plight," *Indianapolis Star*, April 26, 2002. Available at http://www.starnews.com/article.php?victims26.html.

Elvin, John. "The Rich and Powerful—Getting Away with Murder—Almost," *Insight Magazine*, May 31, 1999. Available at http://www.insightmag.com/global_user_elements/printpage.cfm?storyid=209103.

Faber, Lindsay. "Skakel Convicted of Moxley Murder," *Greenwich Time*, June 8, 2002. Available at http://www.marthamoxley.com/news/060802gt.htm.

Faber, Lindsay. "Witness Says Skakel Confessed," *Greenwich Time*, May 17, 2002. Available at http://www.marthamoxley.com/news/051702gt.htm.

Feldman, Claudia. "Texas Jurors Say Capital Murder Cases Are Never Easy," *Houston Chronicle*, January 4, 2002, p. A1.

Fessenden, Ford. "They Threaten, Seethe and Unhinge, Then Kill in Quantity," *New York Times*, April 9, 2001, p. 1.

Frazier, Joseph B. "Retirees Warm to Cold Case Squad," *Los Angeles Times*, October 19, 2003, p. A35.

"Going Public," *Crime Library*, April 13, 2004. Available at http://www.crimelibrary.com/serial_killers/predators/jesperson/public_7.html.

Goodman, Sarah D., PhD, and Stafford, Mark C., PhD. *Homicide, Bereavement, and the Criminal Justice System, Final Report*, August 6, 2001. Available at http://www.ncjrs.org/pdffiles1/nij/grants/189566.pdf.

Grabmeier, Jeff. "Study Finds Homicide Detectives Work Aggressively to Solve All Cases, Regardless of Victim Race," June 6, 2003. Available at http://www.acs.ohio-state.edu/researchnews/archive/homclear.htm.

Gray, John. Interviewed by Robert L. Snow, June 30, 2000.

Greenwood, Tom. "Confessed Killer Could Make Parole," *Detroit News*, March 12, 1989. Available at http://www.detnews.com/2004/metro/0401/13/watts2.htm.

Grice, Gordon. "Crime Seen," *Popular Science*, August 5, 2004. Available at http://www.popsci.com/popsci/crimeseen/article/0,20642,652674-2,00.html.

Hamner, Lance. Interviewed by Robert Snow, August 5, 2004.

Hanson, Doug. "Bloodstain Pattern Analysis," *Law Enforcement Technology*, February 2004, p. 84.

Hanzlick, Randy, MD et al. *A Guide for Manner of Death Classification*. Atlanta, GA: National Association of Medical Examiners, February 2002, p. 13.

Hatch, David. Interviewed by Robert L. Snow, May 18, 2004.

Henry-Jenkins, Wanda. "Homicide: A Brutal Bereavement," *Bereavement Magazine*, March 19, 2004. Available at http://www.bereavementmag.com/catalog/booklets/homicide.asp.

Hess, John E. *Interviewing and Interrogation for Law Enforcement*. Cincinnati, OH: Anderson Publishing, 1997, p. 6.

Hirsch, J. M., and Ramer, Holly. "Dartmouth College Professors Found Dead in Home by Friend," *Portsmouth Herald*, January 29, 2001, p. A1.

Ho, Vanessa et al. "Ridgway Pleads Guilty to 48 Green River Killings," *Seattle Post-Intelligencer*, November 6, 2003, p. A1.

Hobel, Mike. Interviewed by Robert L. Snow, May 18, 2004.

"Inside a Killer's Mind," CBSNEWS.com, August 9, 2001. Available at http://www.cbsnews.com/stories/2001/01/31/48hours/main268586.shtml.

Johnson, Gene. "Killer Says He's Sorry, Receives 48 Life Terms," *Indianapolis Star*, December 19, 2003, p. A8.

Johnson, Gene. "Suspect Pleads Guilty to Slaying 48 Women," *Indianapolis Star*, November 6, 2003, p. A3.

Johnson, Tracy. "In Cruel Detail, a Monster Reveals Himself," *Seattle Post-Intelligencer*, November 6, 2003, p. A1.

Johnson, Tracy. "Sheriff's 21-Year Pursuit Is at an End," *Seattle Post-Intelligencer*, November 6, 2003, p. A1.

Kamb, Lewis. "In Their Own Words: The Twisted Art of Murder," *Seattle Post-Intelligencer*, February 22, 2003, p. A1.

Kanable, Rebecca. "Do Sweat the Small Stuff," *Law Enforcement Technology*, March 2004, p. 54.

Kanable, Rebecca. "Talk 'n' Trash," *Law Enforcement Technology*, November 2002, p. 32.

Karp, David. "Man Convicted of Drug Counselor's Murder," *St. Petersburg Times*, September 25, 2001, p. A1.

Kelly, Frances. Interviewed by Robert L. Snow, June 9, 2004.

Kenney, J. Scott, PhD. "Survivors of Murder Victims." Paper presented to the X World Symposium on Victimology in Montreal, Quebec, August 6, 2000.

Kershaw, Sarah. "20-Year Obsession Puts Seattle Sheriff inside the Mind of a Serial Killer," *International Herald Tribune*, November 7, 2003. Available at http://www.iht.com/articles/116798.html.

Kirk, Paul L. *Crime Investigation: Physical Evidence and the Police Laboratory*. NY: Interscience Publishers, 1953.

Knight, Bernard. *The Estimation of the Time since Death in the Early Postmortem Period*. Great Britain: Edward Arnold, 1995.

Knight, Michael. "Greenwich Girl, 15, Bludgeoned to Death," *New York Times*, November 1, 1975, p. 59.

Kurth, Joel. "Michigan Fights Serial Killer's Release," *Detroit News*, January 13, 2004, p. A1.

Lawson, Jen. "Warming Up Cold Murder Cases," *Las Vegas Sun*, September 12, 2003, p. A1.

Le, Phuong. "Taping Interrogations Deters Coercion, Aids Investigations," *Associated Press*, July 28, 2003. Available at http://www.lineofduty.com/blotterstory.asp?StoryID=52085.

Lejeune, Leslie A. Interviewed by Robert L. Snow, May 24, 2004.

Lerner, Melvin. *The Belief in a Just World Hypothesis: A Fundamental Delusion.* NY: Plenum Press, 1980.

Lewis, Alfred Allan, and MacDonell, Herbert Leon. *The Evidence Never Lies: The Case Book of a Modern Sherlock Holmes.* NY: Bantam Books, 1989.

Lewis, Christina, S. N. "Reviewing 3,000 Cold Cases, One by One," Court TV, March 25, 2003. Available at http://www.courttv.com/news/feature/coldcasereview_ctv.html.

Lewis, Christina, S. N. "Solving the Cold Case: Time, Ingenuity and DNA Can Help," CNN.com, December 17, 2002. Available at http://www.cnn.com/2002/LAW/12/17/ctv.cold.cases/.

Lieberman, David J. *Never Be Lied to Again.* NY: St. Martin's Press, 1988, p. 23.

Loos, Chris. "McGovern Led Police to Location of Bodies," *Hawaii Tribune Herald*, November 27, 2003, p. 1.

Lowery, Don. "Former GA Deputy Convicted of Slaying Boyfriend, Encasing Body in Concrete," *Savannah Morning News*, March 26, 2004. Available at http://www.lineofduty.com/blotterstory.asp?StoryID=62108.

Mabe, Logan D. "Tip Leads to Suspect in Drug Center Slaying," *St. Petersburg Times*, April 3, 2001, p. B3.

Main, Frank. "Cold Case Detectives Scour Past for Fresh Leads," *Chicago Sun-Times*, May 16, 2004, p. 18.

"Man Arrested for 1958 Wauwatosa Cold Case Murder, Rape," *The Milwaukee Channel*, December 11, 2003. Available at http://209.157.64.200/focus/f-news/1038595/posts.

Manware, Melissa. "Cold Case Unit Makes 1st Arrests," *Charlotte Observer*, May 22, 2003, p. 3B.

Martin, R. Michael, PhD. Interviewed by Robert L. Snow, June 17, 2004.

May, Glenn. "Jury Convicts Mt. Lebanon High Grads in Andrew Jones' Murder," *Pittsburgh Tribune-Review*, October 22, 2003, p. A1.

Mayo, Kristi. "DNA Technology Solves 1958 Homicide," *Evidence Technology Magazine*, February 2004, p. 14.

McGhee, Paul, PhD. *Humor and Health*, July 19, 2004. Available at http://www.corexcel.com/html/body.humor.htm.

McGoff, John P., MD. Interviewed by Robert L. Snow, June 8, 2004.

McLaren, George. "Teens Give Differing Accounts of Ax Slayings," *Indianapolis Star*, January 28, 1998, p. A1.

Mehren, Elizabeth. "Unsolved Murder Pushes Buttons of Celebrity, Notoriety, Wealth," *Los Angeles Times*, July 29, 1998, p. 5.

Mertens, Jennifer. "Lessons from the Body Farm," *Law Enforcement Technology*, June 2003, p. 37.

Michaud, Stephen G. "To Have and to Kill," Salon.com, August 25, 1999. Available at http://www.salon.com/health/feature/1999/08/25/serial_killer/print.html.

Miller, Doug. "Confessed Texas Serial Killer Faces Michigan Murder Charge," KHOU.com, March 4, 2004. Available at http://www.khou.com/topstories/stories/khou040304_nh_coralwatts.532fe09c.html.

"Mistrial of the Century?" *New York Magazine*, November 23, 2003. Available at http://www.newyorkmetro.com/nymetro/news/people/columns/intelligencer/n_9528/.

Moore, Evan. "Dreams," *Houston Chronicle*, April 7, 1991. Available at http://www.texansforequaljustice.org/protest/watts1.html.

Napier, Michael R., and Hazelwood, Robert R. "Homicide Investigation: The Significance of Victimology," *FBI NAA*, September–October 2003, p. 21.

National Institutes of Mental Health. *Suicide Facts*, December 23, 2003. Available at http://www.nimh.nih.gov/research/suifact.cfm.

Navarro, Joe. "A Four-Domain Model for Detecting Deception," *FBI Law Enforcement Bulletin*, June 2003, p. 19.

Navarro, Joe, and Schafer, John R. "Detecting Deception," *FBI Law Enforcement Bulletin*, July 2001, p. 11.

"Neighbors Say Family Had History of Domestic Violence," *Charlotte Observer*, December 15, 2003, p. A1.

Neroulias, Nicole. "Dartmouth Murder Suspects Apprehended," *Cornell Daily Sun*, February 20, 2001, p. 1.

"New Version of C.S.I.; It's Crime Scene Insect," Associated Press, July 2, 2004. Available at http://www.lineofduty.com/blotterstory.asp?StoryID=65604.

O'Connell, Peter. "Different Tales Spun at Trial," *Las Vegas Review-Journal*, April 1, 2000, p. A1.

O'Connell, Peter. "Rudin Verdict: Guilty of Murder," *Las Vegas Review-Journal*, May 3, 2001, p. A1.

"Officer's Research Shows That 'Suicide by Cop' Incidents on the Rise in North America," Policemag.com, February 2004, p. 15.

O'Neal, Kevin. "A Nightmare before Christmas," *Indianapolis Star*, December 17, 1996, p. A1.

O'Neill, John R. "Minister's N.Y. Church Mourns Couple's Slaying," *Indianapolis Star*, December 18, 1996, p. C1.

"The Organization," *ICCE*, March 6, 2004. Available at http://www.wvu.edu/~icce/Organization.html.

"Our Mission & Credo," The Vidocq Society, March 6, 2004. Available at http://vidocq.org/what.html.

Prendergast, Jane. "Heat Turned Up in Slayings," *Cincinnati Enquirer*, November 25, 2003, p. A1.

Prendergast, Jane. "Three-Year Homicide Rate Rises," *Cincinnati Enquirer*, December 14, 2003, p. A1.

"Prosecutors: Durst Wanted to Steal Victim's Identity," Click2Houston, October 28, 2003. Available at http://www.click2houston.com/news/2589137/detail.html.

Puit, Glenn. "County Wants Binion Ruling Reconsidered," *Las Vegas Review-Journal*, July 17, 2003, p. A1.

Puit, Glenn. "Expert Stands by Testimony in Binion Case," *Las Vegas Review-Journal*, July 24, 2003, p. A1.

Puit, Glenn. "Ted Binion, Troubled Gambling Figure, Dies," *Las Vegas Review-Journal*, September 18, 1998, p. A1.

Puit, Glenn. "Web of Deceit," *Las Vegas Review-Journal*, November 28, 1999, p. A1.

Regini, Charles L. "The Cold Case Concept," *FBI Law Enforcement Bulletin*, August 1997, p. 7.

Ricks, Hilary Bowe. Interviewed by Robert L. Snow, June 8, 2004.

Rivers, David. "Crime Scene Investigation." Handout from Homicide and Forensic Death Investigation Conference, held at Public Agency Training Council, Indianapolis, IN, January 2004.

Rivers, David. Interviewed by Robert L. Snow, June 3, 2004.

Rochon, Michael J. "Alton Coleman, Guilty of 4 Murders, to Be Executed Friday," *Indianapolis Star*, April 25, 2002, p. A1.

Ryckaert, Vic. "Cookbook Presents Recipes of Homicide Victims," *Indianapolis Star*, December 7, 2001, p. B3.

Saindon, Connie. "Co-Victims of Homicide: Specialized Needs," *Selfhelp Magazine*, March 19, 2004. Available at http://www.selfhelpmagazine.com/articles/trauma/covictims.html.

Serafin, Peter. "Puna Man Shot Pal Because 'I'd Given My Word,'" *Honolulu Star-Bulletin*, December 11, 2003, p. A1.

"The Shanabarger Murder Trial," INDYSTAR.com, 2003. Available at http://www.indystar.com/library/factfiles/crime/homicides/1999/shanabarger/shanabarger.html.

Smith, Brian D. "Dead Men Talking," *Indy Men's Magazine*, November 2002, p. 61.

Smith, Vicki. "Forensic Scientist Forms Cold Case Consulting Group," *Burlington County Times*, March 6, 2004, p. 1.

Solomon, John. "DNA Database Fingers 11,000 Suspects," *Detroit Free Press*, March 9, 2004, p. A1.

Springer, John. "How Could a Jury Not Convict Durst?" Court TV, November 11, 2003. Available at http://www.courttv.com/trials/durst/111103_analysis_ctv.html.

Springer, John. "Jurors Tell Court TV They Found Skakel's Alibi Hard to Believe," Court TV, June 11, 2002. Available at http://www.courttv.com/trials/moxley/061102_ctv.html.

Springer, John. "New Indictment Means Durst Isn't Done," Court TV, February 12, 2004. Available at http://www.courttv.com/trials/durst/021204_tamper_ctv.html.

Sublett, Jesse. "When a Loved One Is Murdered," *Texas Monthly*, July 1, 2002, p. 2.

Sylvester, Ron. "Nathaniel Bell Is Convicted of First-Degree Murder for Stabbing a 22-Year-Old Man in April," *Wichita Eagle*, September 27, 2003, p. B1.

Tan, Shannon. "Confessions Rarely Questioned by Courts," *Indianapolis Star*, December 12, 2002, p. B1.

"Tapes Show Ridgway's Horrifying Confession," KIRO TV, February 9, 2004. Available at http://www.kirotv.com/print/2832250/detail.html?use=print.

Taylor, Heber. "Lessons from a Sensational Case," *Galveston County Daily News*, November 19, 2003, p. 1.

Taylor, Michael. Interviewed by Robert L. Snow, June 3, 2004.

Taylor, Royce. Interviewed by Robert L. Snow, June 3, 2004.

Thomas, Darren. "Half Zantop: 'He Was One I Admired,'" *Dartmouth Review*, January 29, 2001. Available at http://www.dartreview.com/issues/1.29.01/half.html.

Thompson, Rod. "Puna Shooter Awaits Jury's Decision," *Honolulu Star-Bulletin*, December 19, 2003, p. A1.

Tobin, Ernest J., and Fackler, Martin L., MD. "Officer Reaction—Response Times in Firing a Handgun," *Wound Ballistics Review*, Spring 1999, p. 8.

"Trooper Testimony Opens Jayson Williams Trial," SI.com, February 11, 2004. Available at http://sportsillustrated.cnn.com/2004/basketball/nba/02/11/bc.bkn.williamstrial.ap/.

"The Truth of the Slayings," *Crime Library*, February 7, 2004. Available at http://www.crimelibrary.com/notorious_murders/young/dartmouth_murders/7.html?sect=10.

Turvey, Brent E. *Criminal Profiling*. NY: Academic Press, 2002, p. 34.

"Tutor: Skakel Admits Moxley Murder," 1010 WINS, December 11, 2002. Available at http://www.1010wins.com/topstories/local_story_345074334.html.

U.S. Department of Health and Human Services, Centers for Disease Control. *National Vital Statistics Report—Deaths: Leading Causes for 2001*. Washington, DC: U.S. Government Printing Office, November 7, 2003.

U.S. Department of Health and Human Services, Centers for Disease Control. *Suicide in the United States*, December 11, 2003. Available at http://www.cdc.gov/ncipc/factsheets/suifacts.htm.

U.S. Department of Justice. *Capital Punishment, 2002*. Washington, DC: U.S. Government Printing Office, 2003, pp. 1–8.

U.S. Department of Justice. *Crime Scene Investigation: A Guide for Law Enforcement*. Washington, DC: U.S. Government Printing Office, January 2000, p. 16.

U.S. Department of Justice. *Crime in the United States*. Washington, DC: U.S. Government Printing Office, 2003, pp. 19–24.

U.S. Department of Justice. *Death Investigation: A Guide for the Scene Investigator*. Washington, DC: U.S. Government Printing Office, November 1999, p. 1.

U.S. Department of Justice. *Drugs and Crime Facts*. Washington, DC: U.S. Government Printing Office, 2003, p. 3.

U.S. Department of Justice. *Eyewitness Evidence: A Trainer's Manual for Law Enforcement*. Washington, DC: U.S. Government Printing Office, September 2003, p. 16.

U.S. Department of Justice. *Homicides of Children and Youth*. Washington, DC: U.S. Government Printing Office, 2002, p. 6.

U.S. Department of Justice. *Homicide Trends in the United States: 2000 Update*. Washington, DC: U.S. Government Printing Office, 2002.

U.S. Department of Justice. *Policing and Homicide, 1976-98: Justifiable Homicide by Police, Police Officers Murdered by Felons*. Washington, DC: U.S. Government Printing Office, March 2001.

U.S. Department of Justice. *The Victim's Voice*. Washington, DC: U.S. Government Printing Office, 2002, p. 2.

U.S. Department of Justice. *Without a Trace?* Washington, DC: U.S. Government Printing Office, 2003, p. 8.

Vessel, David. "Conducting Successful Interrogations," *FBI Law Enforcement Bulletin*, October 1998, p. 6.

Villa, Judi. "Phoenix Sets Record for Homicides," *Arizona Republic*, December 12, 2003, p. A1.

Walton, Richard D. "The Mathias Murders," *Indianapolis Star*, June 17, 1997, p. A1.

Wexler, Sanford. "Cold Cases Are Getting Hot." *Law Enforcement Technology*, June 2004, p. 19.

"What Happened to Kathleen Durst?" *Crime Library*, March 12, 2004. Available at http://www.crimelibrary. com/notorious_murders/classics/robert_durst/2. html?sect=13.

"Wife Convicted of Mercedes Murder," CNN.com/U.S., February 13, 2003. Available at http://www.cnn.com/2003/US/02/13/mercedes.murder.ap/.

Wilkinson, Howard. "Alton Coleman Finally Faces Justice," *Cincinnati Enquirer*, April 24, 2002, p. A1.

Williams, Scott E. "Durst Jurors Speak Out: 'It Just Wasn't There,'" *Galveston County Daily News*, November 12, 2003, p. 1.

Wright, John. Interviewed by Robert L. Snow, June 2, 2004.

Yeschke, Charles L. *The Art of Investigative Interviewing*. NY: Butterworth-Heinemann, 2003, pp. 22, 24–26, 36.

Young, Emma. "Brain Scans Can Reveal Liars," *New Scientist*, November 12, 2001. Available at http://www.newscientist.com/news/news.jsp?id=ns99991543.

Zepeda, April. "Discoverer of First Green River Victim Looks for Closure," KOMO 1000 News, December 1, 2001. Available at http://www.komotv. com/news/story_m.asp?ID=15645.

Zuckoff, Mitchell, and Bombardieri, Marcella. "Youth Admits Role in Slayings," *Boston Globe*, December 8, 2001, p. A1.

Zulawski, David E., and Wicklander, Douglas E. "Special Report 1: Interrogations: Understanding the Process," *Law and Order*, July 1998, p. 87.

Index

About the Author

ROBERT L. SNOW has been a police officer with the Indianapolis Police for thirty-four years and is currently a captain and commander of the Homicide Branch. He is the author of *The Militia Threat* (1999), *Looking for Carol Beckwith* (1999), and *Deadly Cults: The Crimes of True Believers* (Praeger, 2003).